Making of Modern India

Making of Modern India

Sociological Explorations into Postcolonial Indian Modernity

Paramjit S. Judge

RAWAT PUBLICATIONS

Jaipur • New Delhi • Bangalore • Guwahati • Kolkata

ISBN 978-81-316-1008-4

Published by
Prem Rawat for **Rawat Publications**
Satyam Apts, Sector 3, Jawahar Nagar, Jaipur 302 004 (India)
Phone: 0141 265 1748 / 7006 Fax: 0141 265 1748
E-mail: info@rawatbooks.com
Website: www.rawatbooks.com

New Delhi Office
4858/24, Ansari Road, Daryaganj, New Delhi 110 002
Phone: 011 23263290

Also at *Bangalore, Guwahati* and *Kolkata*

Typeset by Rawat Computers, Jaipur
Printed at Nice Printing Press, New Delhi

Contents

	Preface	vii
	Introduction	1
1	Constituent Assembly and Agenda for Modern India	21
2	Competing Modernities: Ambedkar and Gandhians	47
3	Minorities and Political Reservations	71
4	Discoursing the Partitioned Voices: Punjab and Kashmir	95
5	Property Acquisition: In the Name of Community	117
6	Fifteen Years that Never Ended: The Language Debate	143
7	Elusive Consensus: The Sikh Issue	171
8	Unrevised Perspectives: Third Reading	193
	Conclusions	215
	References	223
	Index	227

Preface

Despite being considered a general and much discussed theme of making of modern India, there is always something different to say and examine. Like all Indians, I also have a sense of imagining India in my own way—something which combines my sense of being Indian and a political sociologist. Located at the margin of India (border city of Amritsar), my sense of history reminds me of partition and riots which killed uncountable number of people and also that I am somebody whose family history has been lost on the other side of the border and what is left is memory inherited from those who left everything behind and moved to the other side to save their own lives and their children. Amidst unending massacres and suffering of the people in Punjab, the Constituent Assembly in Delhi kept on imagining India, apparently oblivious of the extent of tragedy the newly created frontier state of Punjab was facing. For the members, it was an event at one corner of the country which was celebrating the recently got freedom and 'tryst with destiny'. Occasionally, some members would raise the issue of riots and massacres in Punjab, but the business of making of modern India went on. What the members of the Constituent Assembly did in three years was a remarkable accomplishment in terms of laying the foundations of a democratic India, which, despite many predictions, remained firm on its foundations, but many institutional milestones began to crumble within a few decades after the Constitution was adopted in 1950. And this postcolonial modern

India imagined and then shaped by its founding fathers is what I plan to examine and how it could be modern and distinct from the colonial India is what makes an important theme for reflection and analysis.

I started reading the Constituent Assembly debates with the limited objective of examining and analysing certain issues with regard to caste, untouchability and reservations. However, I soon realised the tremendous sociological significance of the content of debates. It began to dawn on me that the debates and the finalisation of each article and adopting the same through voting constituted the essence of postcoloniality. As a result, I ended up reading the debates and selecting certain issues for understanding and analysis. Anybody who reads the debates cannot remain unaffected by the erudition and sagacity of many of the members. In the process of reading, I began to like some of the members who untiringly prepared notes and spoke in the Assembly. Some had an electrifying effect on the members. I should mention here some personalities like Nehru, Patel, Ambedkar and Munshi who can generally be singled out for their impact on the making of the Indian Constitution. However, Professor K.T. Shah and Maulana Hasrat Mohani would be remembered for many reasons. They remained ineffective, but vocal throughout the period of debates. I personally feel that Shah's comments on Kashmir issue should have been taken seriously by the Constituent Assembly.

I must acknowledge the honour given by the Indian Council of Social Science Research, New Delhi, for offering me Dr B.R. Ambedkar National Fellowship in 2013. My special thanks are due to the former Chairman of the ICSSR, Professor Sukhadeo Thorat. I must thank my dear friend Professor M. Rajivlochan for his critical comments on the draft. Also my special thanks to my wife Professor Gurpreet Bal for her encouragement and help. Professor Rattan Singh, my colleague from the Department of Law, lent me all the volumes of the Constituent Assembly debates in the initial stages. Dr (Mrs) Sanchita Dutta of ICSSR has always been helpful. My friends in the Department of Sociology, University of Mumbai, Professor P.G. Jogdand, Professor P.S. Vivek, Professor Balkrishna Bhosale and Dr Balaji Kendre extended their help in various ways during my visit to Mumbai. I am indebted to them.

Introduction

Venturing to write about the postcolonial Indian modernity invariably leads to the study of the Constitution, enactments and Five-Year Plans as its major sources. It is clear that all these efforts are rational and implicate the enlightenment philosophy that it is possible to bring about the desired change. The present work is an attempt to understand how the founding fathers of independent India envisaged and made an effort to formulate constitutive rules of Indian society based on the universal principles of equality, justice, freedom and socialism. All history of human societies has proved that with political will and commitment, it is possible to bring about transformation in the economy. However, the fate of bringing desired change in social and cultural affairs in society has remained an altogether different and highly challenging task. It is important to not only make an attempt to understand and interpret the efforts with ideological commitments to change the Indian society and give reasons for it, but also make an attempt to trace roots of how a particular viewpoint was thought to be relevant for India in contrast to the West. For the purpose, this work has been based on the debates of the Constituent Assembly in which the modern India was visualised. The theoretical position taken is that of Max Weber for whom rationality was the founding principle of modernity and this rationality included logico-meaningful basis of arguments and rational calculations by organically linking the means and ends. This introductory chapter has been divided into three parts. The first is a general statement about how modernity could be conceptualised, a Western concept originated with the renaissance and capitalism in Europe. The second part covers the background to the formation as well as certain salient features of the Constituent Assembly, whereas the third part is an introduction to various chapters of the book.

I. Modern and Modernity

The word 'modern' has been the subject of many conceptual and theoretical articulations in philosophy, literature, history, sociology and political science in particular. Various meanings of modern have been offered. Literally, the word carries a temporal sense as being something contemporaneous. There are two conceptual articulations which, I think, are important to make sense of how modern has been used. We know that somehow there is classification of the time as ancient, medieval, modern and postmodern. For example, in literature the temporal classification is as follows: ancient, dark ages, renaissance, classical, romantic and modern, but the arrival of the notion of the postmodern has shown the temporal nature of 'modern'. We may ask: Could we make sense of modern by understanding how the postmodern is understood? In this regard, Lyotard (1986) maybe of some help, as for him postmodern condition is characterised by 'the breakdown of the grand narratives'. It thus implies that the modern implied the existence of grand narratives and in a manner of speaking, it seems quite exotic and fascinating due to its playful engagement with the words and concepts, but underlying this grand narrative is the existence of not so grand a world. It is a world dominated by Western capitalism in the form of first colonialism and then imperialism in which the culture and civilisation of the colonised world is being treated as traditional and backward.

The construction of modern and traditional as a binary opposition is a politico-ideological conceptual tool to signify the subjugated and colonised natives. In the writings of some other enlightened social scientists, such as Fraser and Malinowski, the colonised could be called as savages. The best illustration in this context is Max Weber (1968) and his *The Protestant Ethic and the Spirit of Capitalism* in which he makes it clear that the Occident and the Orient are fundamentally different from each other. He identifies 'rationality' as the core element of the European/Western societies. He gives the instance of book-keeping and absence of magical practices as the core features of rationality. In his subsequent discussion, he brings out the idea of frugality as preached by some of the Protestant sects and it had a bearing on the emergence of the spirit of capitalism.[1] Rationality remained the core element in the Weberian paradigm so far as understanding the emergence of capitalism is concerned. His theory of social action and bureaucracy are all based on the principle of the centrality of the rational and thus modern world.

Venturing to examine and discuss the making of 'modern India' is a challenging task for anyone who wishes to make sense of 'modern' in terms of the operationalisation of the concept. In other words, if it is stated that there is something like modern India, then its beginning is to be identified in terms of certain key features of 'modern'. Invariably, such an effort would allude to the conceptual contestations with regard to what is modern. In this regard, the binary opposite of 'modern' and 'traditional' turns out to be a serious and contentious issue. Weber (Judge, 2012) in his discussion of both traditional action and traditional authority does not provide even a single clear-cut distinctive feature of the two, which could be treated as the exact opposite of rational action/legal authority. As a matter of fact, in the case of action he identifies a kind of rational action he calls 'wertrational action' in which the relationship between means and ends is established by the ultimate value. It becomes clear that instead of constructing tradition as the binary opposite of modern, Weber is essentially having a scale in mind in which there is also a possibility that traditional action could be rational. Weber's notions of affectual action and charismatic authority seem much closer to qualify as binary opposite of rational. The instance of Weber using the concept 'modern' is with regard to the identification of various features of modern state (Weber, 1978). Modern state, according to Weber (Judge, 2012: 177), could be distinguished in terms of certain features, which are:

> The monopoly of the state on power and administration is based on two systems: firstly, there is a central permanent structure for the collection of tax, and secondly, the central government has a control over a permanent army; (ii) the legitimate monopoly over enactment and exercise of force; and (iii) the organisation of such an administrative structure which is based on rationality.

Obviously, Weber is referring to bureaucracy. It is interesting to note that rationality remains the central element in Weber's construction of 'modern'. If that be so, then tradition could not be construed as the binary opposite of it.

It is thus possible to combine modern and traditional without any contradiction of terms but the underlying principle remains constant, that is rationality must remain as the basis of their correspondence. A difficulty emerges in creating a chronological ordering of the beginning and end of 'modern'. It may be noted that a considerable amount of literature on the issue of modernisation exists and most of it, particularly the one covering developing societies, takes stock of how the 'developing societies', in other words, 'postcolonial societies', modernise by adopting various models and strategies. In the post-Second World War period, a large number of colonised countries got their independence. In countries like India where independence was handed over by the imperialist governments to the local elites, who in most cases were Western educated. Such elites faced the challenge of transforming their society from the colonial to postcolonial in terms of political practice, economic reorganisation and above all nation-building to name a few. The greatest challenge was the language and in most of the cases the language known for communication was the language of the colonial masters. Thus, English, French, Spanish, Portuguese and Dutch were the languages known to the elite but were not spoken and understood by the most of the native populations. For them these were the languages of the colonial masters symbolising political and cultural hegemony, but at the same time, interestingly, these were the languages of the modern world.

English was not the only language brought to India by the colonial masters and historically, in general terms, it is not necessary that the rulers would rule through their own language. The significance of English in the Indian subcontinent was inseparably linked with the cultural package of the British. Science, industry, governance and administration of justice which reached India were symbols of the Western enlightenment whose underlying logic was capitalism. New institutions, practices and ideas had a language of their own as they tended to construct a new symbolic universe. Suddenly the Indian culture, institutions and practices were seen from a different light and the redundancy of some of them became obvious.[2]

Bayly (2004) makes a significant remark that despite the crusade of some enlightenment thinkers against God and religion in the 18th century, most people continued to go to churches and remained faithful to God. The modern world presented itself in Europe as a civilisation founded upon the new social and economic system, that is, capitalism, which revolutionised the way people thought and lived. The freedom of the worker to sell his labour power in the market, to use Marx's basic premise of capitalism, was the beginning of a new era of freedom of reason and work, which also gave rise to new kind of dehumanisation of labour. God and capitalism did not clash with each other in the making of the modern world despite Voltaire, Diderot, Marx and others, who had consistently questioned the existence and relevance of God.

Whereas modernity could be located in the context of state and market (capitalism), the same could not be clearly and unambiguously stated about social formations and cultural practices. Tradition could not be understood as the binary opposite of the modern by virtue of the simple fact that a tradition could possibly qualify as the modern practice.[3] The question of modernity is not an issue of good and evil. Each passing century has not been less violent than the earlier. The progress in science and technology has made people's life comfortable, but it has happened at the cost of environment. The technology has saved lives and the life expectancy in different countries of the world has gone up, but it is also a major reason for the destruction of human life. The consequences of technology have been paradoxical.

Combining God, religion, faith and belief into a single category as opposed to reason, science and critical inquiry, and the binary opposition of feudalism and capitalism may not necessarily offer us a coherent understanding of modernity. Attempts are made to locate modernity, historically, in the European Enlightenment of 17th and 18th centuries. European Enlightenment, as rightly pointed out by Israel (2006), was not singular, but could be differentiated into radical and conservative. Hamilton (1992: 36) identifies four major aspects of Enlightenment of 18th-century France generally known by the umbrella signifier *philosophes* as pursuit of modernity. These are 'Anti-clericalism, a belief in the pre-eminence of empirical and materialist knowledge, an enthusiasm for technological and medical progress and a desire for legal and constitutional reform'. The rise of reason over faith in the Enlightenment philosophy with tremendous commitment to knowledge and science could be singled out as the most important aspect of modernity. In a way, modernity, capitalism and sociology, to a great extent, could be treated as inseparably connected to each other. The emergence of sociology coincides with the dissolution of communities and the emergence of societies due to forces of industrialisation which forced the people to leave their age-old habitats to live in cities. Modernity in Europe was a package consisting of all aspects of life covering science, social sciences, technology, culture, morals, literature, art, political system, economic life and so on.

Economy, society and sciences interlinked to give rise to a new world in which the exploitation of nature intensified and the number and production of commodities increased and by radically transforming the entire social life. Obviously, language, culture and religion took longer than other aspects to adapt to the fast changing landscape of people's lives. The new world called capitalism subsumed under its myriad dimensions of people's collective living. Communities broke down (though new meaning of community emerged) and economic/instrumental rationality with legal framework took on the fundamental location to govern people's conduct in public life.

Instrumental rationality took on the dangerous dimensions during holocaust, as Horkheimer and Adorno (2002) would understand it. However, many things remained consistent with modernity, for example, industrialisation and urbanisation, technology and science, capitalism and liberal democracy, socialism and economic planning, constitutional rights and duties. Underlying all these was the principle of rationality.

European modernity remained exemplary for all the late starters, particularly for the Third World countries who attained freedom after 1945—the year Second World War ended. While the social scientists of the developed countries pondered over the issue whether democracy would succeed in the newly liberated countries, they were facing the challenge of backwardness, underdevelopment, illiteracy and poverty. For these countries a new expression coined by the social scientists was 'modernisation'. Huntington (1968) tried to connect the rise of political instability in the Third World countries with their effort at modernising their societies, ostensibly oblivious of the fact of the unprecedented interference of the superpowers (NATO vs Warsaw Pact countries) in the weak and developing nations. Luke (1990: 212) clinches the issue when he observes that modernity

> means gaining rational control of the physical and social environment, building a liberal democratic state, participating in the world culture, and joining the scientific revolution. The meaning assigned to the complex processes of modernization and development by this discourse similarly boils down to finding practical ways to engage certain states and societies in these macrosocial processes. Yet, in posing their discourses this way, and perhaps even contrary to their conscious intentions, these general social scientific theories actually serve as ideological legitimations for the 'modernized'—North America and Europe—to dominate the 'modernizing'—the so-called Third World of Asia, Africa, and Latin America—as the former developed 'underdevelopment' among the latter.

Following Luke, this is a study of postcolonial modernity as it was articulated through the rational construction of the goals of independent India in the form of the Constitution. Along with the socialist objective of the Republic of India, the Constitution provided for equality among the Indian citizens by abolishing all forms of discrimination based on caste, colour and creed. Social equality for citizens of the country was an objective of economic equality through the achievement of socialism, which could at least be interpreted as equality of opportunity and conditions of honourable living due to differing ideologies of socialism, provided for the postcolonial modernity. The separation of church and the state and rationalisation of economy and governance, which were the hallmark of Western modernity (as based on reason), provided the best platform by the imaginative and committed leaders of the independent India. We thus had planned development initiatives and democracy with universal adult suffrage.

Hobsbawm (1994) in his work, *Age of Extremes*, identifies two major revolutions in the post-Second World War Western world. These are social revolution and cultural revolution. By social revolution, he means the depeasantisation which occurred at a large-scale making most of these countries urban societies. The peasant population declined to less than 10 per cent in these countries. By cultural revolution, he means the enormous expansion of educational institutions and tremendous rise in literacy and educational levels. Within the framework of global portrait of the emergence, evolution and politics of modernity intertwined with capitalism and democracy, India was an important unit of the newly liberated nations.

When India achieved independence, it had numerous challenges to move forward on all fronts of a sovereign state's survival. India was partitioned in 1947 and it had happened due to the recognition accorded to religion as the basis of nationhood. On top of that the socio-cultural and linguistic diversity of the country posed a potential threat to its unity. Therefore, nation-building and national integration turned out to be the most significant challenge to the newly emerged state and they remain so till this date. The second major challenge was the overwhelming rural population which was illiterate and largely living in poverty under the zamindari system as well as the unequal distribution of land in non-zamindari areas. Besides poverty, illiteracy and backwardness of larger mass of Indian people, caste-based deprivation and discrimination of the most oppressed communities known by the nomenclature of untouchables or depressed classes existed with the overt sanctions from traditions and Hindu religion based on karma principle. Their problems were not confined to their being the poorest of the poor; rather they were kept at the lowest rungs of the Indian society facing everyday humiliations and discrimination at the hands of the upper castes. Brahmanism as ideology was partly blamed for the existence of the caste system. Such a kind of birth-based inequality was not acceptable in postcolonial India. The universal principles of equality and justice were upheld through the abolition of caste-based inequality and discrimination. The trajectory of the social development underscored these inequalities and sought to remove them through interventionist strategy. The objective of caste-free society and special treatment to the most oppressed went hand in hand. It was hoped that the two would not come in conflict with each other. Once the underprivileged castes get education and better economic opportunities, there would emerge caste equality. Whereas villages symbolised backwardness, illiteracy and marginality, cities were the symbols of colonial power. On top of all these challenges was the socio-cultural diversity of the country's population.

II. Constituent Assembly

The members of the Constituent Assembly dominated by the Congressmen who were mostly the freedom fighters under Gandhi took upon themselves to carry the daunting task of drafting the Constitution which would seek to resolve all contradictions and take the country on the path of not only development but also nation-building.

Imagining radiant future for India might seem quixotic during the late 1940s, but there were many such members who had the optimism of transforming India into a modern state combining both the ancient Indian traditions with the Western modernity, whereas some of them were of the convinced view that socialism was the only solution to a backward, illiterate, poor and rural India with some oases of prosperity, modernity, education and urbanism. The representatives of the zamindars and princely states defended the right to property while supporting the dream for new India. Surprisingly, treating private ownership of property as the guiding principle of postcolonial India was as much modern as abolishing private ownership, for both were the results of European modernity. Importantly, understanding the making of modern India begins with the perspective that there is no such thing as singular modernity. Rather multiple modernities may coexist or compete representing different schools of thought and the holders of diverse views may debate and participate in the politics. Therefore, modernities play important role in the making of totality, for in the intersubjective social and political world, continuous dialogue and debate keep taking place.

India attained freedom on 15 August 1947, but the process of making the Constitution had started in 1946 after the Cabinet Mission was formed by the British Government in the beginning of 1946. The formula it devised was that the Constitution would be prepared by an elected body through elected members of the Legislative Assemblies and the Sikhs and Muslims were to have their separate quota of representation in the Constituent Assembly (Chandra, et al. 1999). Thus, the Constituent Assembly became the platform for debating the nature and form of postcolonial India. This work is exclusively based on the interpretative analysis of the Constituent Assembly debates on certain sociological issues, such as village, minorities, caste, reservation, untouchability, property and language. All issues have been taken up chronologically, that is in the order in which these were discussed in the Constituent Assembly. There are four phases of the debates of the Constituent Assembly. The first phase started with the first session of the Constituent Assembly which was held on 9 December 1946 and concluded on 31 July 1947. During this period, the rational foundations of the making of Indian Constitution was laid through discussions and consensus and sometimes through the persuasive influences of a few top leaders. The second phase began on the evening of 14 August 1947 and continued till 27 January 1948 during which all formalities were made. It may be added that immediately after the completion of the second phase, the Constitution Drafting Committee chaired by Dr B.R. Ambedkar prepared the first draft and it was handed over to the members for the first reading. There was a gap of 10 months between the last meeting of the second phase and the first meeting of the third phase.

The third phase started on 4 November 1948 for the purpose of second reading of the Draft Constitution. It was the longest period in terms of the intensity and extensity of the debates on each article of the Draft Constitution. The second reading concluded on 16 November 1949. The fourth phase began on 17 November 1949 and ended on 25 January 1950 during which the third reading of the Draft Constitution took place and it was finalised and finally the final draft was signed by members. During the period of three years and a month, the form and content of the debates, which took place in the Constituent Assembly, indicated tremendous commitment and hard work of the members who gave equal attention to both governance and social issues. Sometimes the matters related to governance took little time to get settled, but most of the sociological issues such as religion, caste, secularism, untouchability, socialism and language evoked emotional and intellectual responses of the members delaying the final decision for days.

To gauge the magnitude of enormous work done in roughly three years' period, the best source is Ambedkar's last speech in the Constituent Assembly he delivered on 25 November 1949. Quantitative description of the overall work done is as follows: Duration of the Constituent Assembly was two years eleven months and seventeen days. Total number of sessions were eleven of which six were consumed in the passing of the objectives in which 51 days were spent and it took five sessions covering 114 days for the discussion on the Draft Constitution. The Drafting Committee was constituted on 29 August 1947, which held its first meeting on 30 August 1947 and it completed its work in 141 days. At the time of its presentation in the Constituent Assembly, it contained 243 Articles and 8 Schedules. In the final form, it consisted of 395 Articles and 8 Schedules. Total number of tabled amendments was 7,635 of which 2,473 were actually moved.

We may also look into the composition of the Constituent Assembly in terms of certain parameters identified along diverse axes by Chandra et al. (1999: 39). Out of the total 389 proposed members of the Assembly, 296 and 93 respectively were to be elected/nominated/chosen from British India and princely states. As per the results of the elections held in July–August 1946, the Congress won 199 out of 210 general seats, three out of four Sikh seats and all the three from Coorg, Ajmer-Merwara and Delhi. Total tally of seats that went to Congress was 208, whereas Muslim league won 73 out of 78 Muslim seats.

Rationality as the basis of modernity could be understood while debating each issue at length and then taking decision on the merit. Accommodating myriad voices in the Assembly required thorough discussion as well as concession on certain rational criteria. The best way to achieve such objective was to take decision by majority vote, seemingly a rational way of taking decision. However, with an overwhelming majority of the Congress, it was quite clear that what its leaders thought good for the country would be the outcome of the debate. However, the Congress was not composed of yes-men of particular leaders. Members were divided on the basis of ideology and there was no unanimity among them on various issues.

We have diverse views on the composition and functioning of the Constituent Assembly three of which may be given here. Guha (2008: 104) comments,

> Eighty-two per cent of Assembly members were also members of the Congress. However, since the party was itself a broad church they held a wide range of views. Some were atheists and secularists, others 'technically members of the Congress but spiritually members of the RSS and the Hindu Mahasabha'. Some were socialists in their economic philosophy, others defenders of the rights of landlords.

Khilnani's (2004: 34) following observation tends to suggest that the composition of the Constituent Assembly should be treated as illegitimate:

> The Constituent Assembly was remarkably unrepresentative body: around 300 men (more were added after the princely states

entered the Union), elected on the restricted franchise of provincial legislatures, and overwhelmingly dominated by the upper-caste and Brahminic elites within the Congress. There was no organized representation of India's Muslims, no presence of Hindu communal groups (although Congress itself harboured many Hindu conservatives) and, after 1948, no socialist voice. To Gandhi, for instance, it was quite clearly not a sovereign body. Within the Assembly itself, the drafting of the Constitution rested in the hands of only about two dozen lawyers.

What was unrepresentative at the time of the establishment of the Constituent Assembly could be understood by examining the circumstances which led to its Constitution. Is it possible to argue that certain alternatives were available for the colonial masters to make the Constituent Assembly representative? But, what should have been the axis along which the people could be divided into different groups/categories? It is quite obvious that religion, besides the princely states, was considered to be the one criterion along which the population could be represented. In the absence of the Muslim League members of the Constituent Assembly, due to reasons best known to the students of history, the Congress was left to itself to decide the destiny of the country.

Chandra et al. (1999: 39) are in agreement with Khilnani so far as the unrepresentative character of the Constituent Assembly is concerned:

> Especially since the Constituent Assembly was not elected on the basis of universal adult franchise and was thus not truly representative in character as the Congress had wished and demanded, and also because only Muslims and Sikhs were recognized as 'minorities' deserving special representation, a special effort was made to see that the Assembly did indeed reflect the diversity of perspectives present in the country.

As a result, the Congress made efforts to include 'Scheduled Castes, Parsis, Indian Christians, Anglo-Indians, tribals and women'. Chandra et al. have argued that attempt was also made to achieve intellectual balance in the Constituent Assembly.

Whatever could be the weaknesses in the composition of the Constituent Assembly, it should be emphasised that such conclusion as has been drawn by Khilnani could be justified through the level, magnitude and quality of the debates. In this regard, there is a reasonable basis to argue that all issues were settled after extensive debates. At the same time, overwhelming influence of some of the leaders, particularly Jawaharlal Nehru, tilted the outcome along certain lines. Nehru's role in the Constituent Assembly leads us to ambivalent conclusions. In most of the debates, Nehru's absence was quite conspicuous, whereas his presence in the matters such as Kashmir, property and India's decision to join the Commonwealth to mention a few was for the purpose of putting his weight behind the resolutions. In this regard, Guha (2008: 106) has aptly described the overwhelming influence of Nehru and Patel:

> The speeches of symbolic importance were naturally made by Nehru. Just as naturally, the bulk of the back-room work was done by Vallabhbhai Patel. A consummate committee man, he played a key role in drafting of the various reports. It was Patel, rather than the less-patient Nehru, who worked at mediating between warring groups, taking recalcitrant members with him on his morning walks and making them see the larger point of view. It was also Patel who moved one of the more contentious resolutions: that pertaining to minority rights.

During the period of drafting of the Constitution certain personalities/leaders were visible and their views, thoughts and interventions played important role in not only raising the level of discussion but also offering alternative windows to understand reality in myriad ways. It is important that some of them should be mentioned. Among the major personalities Nehru, Patel, Rajendra Prasad and Ambedkar do not need any introduction. Guha (2008) adds two more names in the list, that is, K.M. Munshi—a novelist, lawyer and freedom fighter from Gujarat—and Alladi Krishnaswami Iyer—the advocate general of Madras Presidency for one and half decades. Austin (1972: 13) has described K.M. Munshi as estranged Congressman. One leader who was prominent was Maulana Azad, but he did not participate in debates in a big way; the exception being his participation in language debate.

The two interesting and prominent figures in the Constituent Assembly were Professor K.T. Shah and Maulana

Hasrat Mohani. Professor Shah was professor of economics at Bombay University. Like K.M. Munshi, he was also a Gujarati writer. He was the candidate for the first ever elections held for the President of India against Rajendra Prasad. On 14 March 1953, *Economic and Political Weekly* (p. 1990) published an obituary to him. He was a staunch socialist and argued for socialist state. Most of his arguments were rejected in the Constituent Assembly. Born as Syed Fazl-ul-Hasan, Maulana Hasrat Mohani was the penname he chose as a poet. He is allegedly considered to be one of the founders of the Communist Party of India, but he also had affiliations with the Muslim League[4]. At the time of partition of the country, he chose to live in India. Both Shah and Mohani remained the objects of criticism and sometimes pun. However, both of them in their own ways remained committed to what they were saying. Still another personality which requires special mention is Raghu Vira. No-note known for his contribution to the coining of administrative and parliamentary terms, he succeeded Syama Prasad Mookerjee as the President of the Jan Sangh. He spoke on the occasion of the debate on language in the Constituent Assembly. Picking up a few names for small introductory remarks does not undermine the importance of many other prominent personalities. When some of them would prominently figure in various debates and require some introduction the needful shall be done. We may now outline the plan of this book.

III. Outline of the Book

The present book is divided into eight chapters and each chapter does not only cover the nature of debate but also the time when the discussion took place. In other words, it is also the history of the trajectories of the debates as these unfolded on specific issues in the Constituent Assembly. While going through the debates one is struck by various unique features of the content of debates. The foremost feature is the commitment of the speaker to the cause. All members were aware of the fact that they were participating in the epoch making exercise and they seemed to be clear that they should make positive contribution in making the country modern. Issues dealing with language and property tended to threaten the integrity and prioritise regional and class interests. However, each and every member did not speak in the Assembly and interestingly many of the silent participants became powerful political leaders and ministers afterwards, as if they were rewarded for their silence.

The first chapter outlines various aspects of the debates and discussions which took place from the time when the Constituent Assembly met for the first time on 9 December 1946 and till it worked out and completed various modalities of forming committees and setting up agenda and finalising definitions of certain terms by 27 January 1948 when all formalities were completed. Nehru and Patel played a significant role in working out the objectives and identification of key issues for discussions. Before the Drafting Committee was constituted on 29 August 1947, various issues were discussed and settled. This chapter takes cognisance of all sociological issues, which remained important for the members as well as India.

The second chapter covers the debate on village which was not the core issue in the Constituent Assembly debates, but Ambedkar made a special mention of it in his speech on 4 November 1948 while moving the resolution in the Constituent Assembly for the adoption of the Draft Constitution. One of the issues he emphasised was that in the Draft Constitution individual is the unit of citizenship and then he created binary opposition of individual vs village instead of individual vs society which had been the usual Western social science practice. However, his condemnation of the Indian village was exemplary. Ambedkar faced opposition from the Gandhians who reminded him of the views of the great man. Interestingly, Nehru had already expressed his views on village life in response to Gandhi's letter, but in the Constituent Assembly he never supported Ambedkar's viewpoint. Ambedkar remained unaffected by the reaction of Gandhians. For him, the more important issue was the unit of citizenship. When the amendment was proposed to introduce the village panchayat as democratically elected body, he accepted it. However, commentary on village raised issues of concern in the making of modern India.

Chapter 3 takes cognisance of the debate on the issue of reservation which was reopened when Sardar Patel moved an amendment that the provision of reservation of seats for minorities except the scheduled castes as well as four castes among the Sikhs should be abolished. Various religious minorities identified were Muslims, Christians, Sikhs, Anglo-Indians and Parsis. In terms of their population size, only the Muslims had significant percentage of population in India even after the partition. As a matter of fact, the religious minorities did not press for reservation, though some of the Muslim members demanded that the provision of joint electorates should be introduced. The Sikhs were the only religious minority which demanded for special treatment. Since the decision had been taken that there would be reservation on caste basis only, certain castes among the Sikhs were recognised as scheduled castes and thus eligible for the provision of reservations. It may be pointed out that the Sikhs remained dissatisfied that they had not been given the fair share.

In the fourth chapter, the debates on Punjab, Bengal and Jammu and Kashmir, the states which were partitioned between India and Pakistan, have been covered. These states drew the special attention of the Constituent Assembly, first due to the issue of their representation and then the challenges these were posing to the idea of nation-building. Bengal and Punjab were the two states which were partitioned and the major territory and majority population of these states went over to Pakistan for obvious reasons. Jammu and Kashmir joined these two states after India and Pakistan fought war in 1947 when the Pakistani soldiers disguised as tribal militia invaded Kashmir. Soon after the King of Kashmir signed the instrument of accession, the Indian army intervened and recovered the area presently falling in the Indian Territory. The partitioned Punjab had numerically a large population of the Sikhs and there was a need to decide the representation of these states in the Constituent Assembly. Owing to riots and violence, the exact size of population of the Sikhs was not known.

Property as an issue, discussed in Chapter 5, figured predominantly in the debates of the Constituent Assembly, largely dealing with the issue of its acquisition. Ownership was assumed to be a natural corollary to the existence of society. India had a class of zamindars/big landowners controlling the rural mass of people with great degree of force and they formed a pressure group to make sure that their interests were watched. The most important aspect of the debates, though the Constituent Assembly decided to treat zamindars as their fellow Indian brethren and not the support base of the British colonialism, was that members also debated the concept of property. The conceptualisation of property varied from property as theft to property as a changing concept with the passage of time.

The debate on language issue covered in Chapter 6 has been questioning the nation-building since independence. Language and linguistic identity articulations do not get influenced by ideologies. Thus, nothing divided the Constituent Assembly as strongly as the language issue. Language issue entailed numerous aspects. First of all it was to be decided which language would be the national language. Then the issues of script, numerals, administrative language and the language to be used in courts were to be decided. No Indian language could quickly replace the already established English from its high pedestal. Moreover, the Indian elite were used to English and English was regarded as the language symbolising knowledge, education and culture. The nationalist position was obvious, that is, English could not be the national language and a language belonging to and spoken in the country could be the national language. It was thought that the language spoken by the majority of the people of the country should be the national language. Hindi was identified as the only language which fulfilled all these conditions. However, Hindi was the language of north India and the south India was opposed to it. We thus find that despite some members raising the issue of national language, the matter was postponed almost till the end and was taken up on 19 September 1949.

In the seventh chapter, the Sikh issue has been covered largely due to its prominence in the debates that occurred in 1949 in particular. Interestingly, the Sikh issue has now retrospectively become important due to one and half decades of militancy and separatism among the Sikhs. The need to relook into the Sikh perception during the making of modern India has acquired a paramount importance. The final and eighth chapter underlines the unrevised perspectives of the members, which the Constituent Assembly failed to achieve. The third and final reading of the Constitution began on 17 November 1949. By that time all the Articles of the Draft Constitution had been discussed, debated and finally adopted through either voting or consensus. It seemed that everything was fine with the Constitution, particularly the areas dealing with social issues, such as minorities, scheduled castes, tribals, property and language. The main feature of the third reading of the Constitution was that members voiced their opinions and views on the amended Draft Constitution, as no work on further amending it occurred in the last phase of the making of the Constitution. As the members began to speak, it became clear that considerable number of members were not satisfied with the outcome of earlier debates.

In spite all these reservations, the Constitution was passed by the Constituent Assembly and it turned out to be one of the major social documents for the transformation of the Indian society. The contemporary situation is the one referring to the Constitution as one of the most important foundations of the modern India. Challenges, however, continue to haunt the Indian state. English has not been displaced from its privileged place and any attempt at enforcing Hindi meets with tremendous resistance from the South. In the process, the vernacular languages have become more important which have begun to articulate into the linguistic and ethnic identities.[5] Ambedkar's faith in the role of city in ending caste identities has not been empirically established, for the caste association and caste identity politics have dominated the Indian urban scene. However, Indian modernity has begun to envelope the society in a visible way giving hope that social transformation should be seen from the perspective of long duration.

Notes

1. As an Indian what come to my mind are the Indian business communities. None could be more frugal than the Marwaris of Rajasthan and the Baniyas of North India, who also maintained their accounts.
2. Heaven and paradise could not be the promise for a woman who would commit Sati. Sati became an archaic practice. Interestingly, heaven has remained a cherished dream even in the West, and bullfight is still a sport in Spain.
3. There seems to be a subconscious opinion that modern is good and tradition is outdated. Such a normative perception is linked with many practices and institutions.
4. Inputs from Prof. Bhagwan Josh are gratefully acknowledged.
5. Considerable amount of social science literature has come up on identity issues during the last two decades.

1

Constituent Assembly and Agenda for Modern India

The first chapter is a prelude to the subsequent discussions on certain issues of sociological nature. Despite its importance as describing the background of the issues which became subjects of discussion and analysis in the subsequent chapters, it also helps us to foresee how social and political issues are intertwined in the Constituent Assembly debates. It covers largely the time between the formation of the Constituent Assembly and the completion of various formalities required for the drafting of the Constitution. In the process, it took up various issues concerning the minorities, communities and partitioned states. Accordingly the five parts of this chapter cover the formation of the Constituent Assembly, discussion on the rights of communities interrupted by the eve of independence, minority rights and partitioned states of Bengal and Punjab.

I. Constituent Assembly

The formation of Constituent Assembly marked the beginning of the process of imagining postcolonial modern India. Accompanied by independence was partition of the country prior to which the Congress and the Muslim League seemed to be the two major political parties on whose shoulders the future of the country had fallen. They parted ways on the issue of two-nation theory and partition of the country became a reality in 1947. Nehru and Patel were the two principal actors in the Constituent Assembly and their contribution to the drafting of the Constitution was central due to their political influence in the Congress. However, the contributions of a large number of members of the Constituent Assembly have been equally important. Ambedkar's emergence as an important player during the drafting of the Constitution is an interesting aspect of how the major leaders conducted themselves. Ambedkar was not the only lawyer in the Constituent Assembly, though he might have been the most educated member eclipsing all others in terms of degrees he had in his kitty. He was not a member of the Congress; rather he had a background of conflict with Gandhi over the issue of separate electorate for the untouchables which culminated into the Poona Pact in 1932. However, his role in the drafting of the Indian Constitution is part of history.

The making of the Indian Constitution was also the making of modern India, for it handled and touched upon various social issues on the principles of rationality, equality and justice. At the same time, it recognised diversity as the defining principle of the Indian society and in the process recognised communities and their rightful existence, after making the individual as citizen and the unit of the state policy. The primary objective of this chapter is to take stock of the content of various debates which occurred in the Constituent Assembly with regard to certain social issues before the country was partitioned. Social diversity, untouchability, minorities, tribals, customs and tradition entailing marriage, family and inheritance of property were some of the issues which were keenly debated in the Constituent Assembly meetings. This chapter contains five parts. The first part is a general introduction to the Constituent Assembly largely covering its formation and outlining of broader framework for framing of the Constitution. The second part covers the initial discussion on the issue of rights of minorities, whereas the third includes the narration of the proceedings of the Constituent Assembly on the eve of independence which began on the night of 14 August 1947 and concluded in the early morning of 15 August. In view of the fact that minority rights posed a major challenge for India as well as the partition of India on religious basis, the debate immediately after independence was expected to change. This change has been covered in the fourth part. The final part takes stock of the initial discussion on the partitioned states, namely Bengal and Punjab, mainly on the issue of their representation in the Constituent Assembly.

The first meeting of the Constituent Assembly was held on 9 December 1946 at 11 am. It was a Monday morning and Acharya J.B. Kripalani chaired the first meeting. Its first task was to elect the permanent chairman, which it completed in four days and Dr Rajendra Prasad was elected unanimously. Subsequently, the Chairman was rechristened as President. The first task at hand was to start the process of drafting of the Constitution and it began when he called upon Pandit Jawaharlal Nehru to move the resolution. On 13 December 1946, Nehru moved the resolution by first giving a lecture in Hindustani. He said,

> You all know that this Constituent Assembly is not what many of us wished it to be. It has come into being under particular conditions and the British Government has a hand in its birth. They have attached to it certain conditions. We accepted the State Paper, which may be called the foundation of this Assembly, after serious deliberations and we shall endeavour to work within limits. But you must not ignore the source from which this Assembly derives its strength. Governments do not come into being from State Papers. Governments are, in fact, the expression of the will of the people. We have met here today because of the strength of the people behind us and we shall go as far as the people not of any party or group but the people as a whole—shall wish us to go. We should, therefore, always keep in mind the passions that lie in the hearts of the masses of the Indian people and try to fulfil them.

Nehru's words about the composition of the Constituent Assembly do not clarify which particular set of people should have been there. However, it becomes clear that the representatives of the princely states and the members of the Muslim League were absent when he proposed the resolution. It was not only the freedom which was round the corner, but also the partition. There are two things about which Nehru's words before moving the resolution suggest. First, there seems to be continuity between the colonial India and the imminent postcolonial India. Second, Nehru articulates a sense of autonomy in determining the destiny of the country and this autonomy is vested with the people of India. It may be concluded that Nehru was trying to convince the members of the Constituent Assembly that independence was not simply a transfer of power. His emphasis on people of India showed his commitment to democratic India. Let us now move to the resolution he presented to the Constituent Assembly and he expected, as he observed little later, that the resolution would be accepted without any discussion, but it did not happen the way he thought. Some crucial and relevant portions of the resolution are quoted as follows:

> (1) This constituent Assembly declares its firm and solemn resolve to proclaim India as an Independent Sovereign Republic and to draw up for her future governance a Constitution;
>
> (4) wherein all power and authority of the Sovereign Independent India, its constituent parts and organs of government, are derived from the people; and
>
> (5) wherein shall be guaranteed and secured to all people of India justice, social, economic and political; equality of status, of opportunity, and before the law; freedom of thought, expression, belief, worship, vocation, association and action, subject to law and public morality; and
>
> (6) wherein adequate safeguard shall be provided for minorities, backward and tribal areas, depressed and other backward classes.

The resolution moved by Nehru in the Constituent Assembly, part of which is outlined above, formed the foundation on which Indian Constitution was finally drafted. After moving the resolution, Nehru reminded the Assembly of some absent members and wished them to be present at that historic moment. Subsequently, it became clear that those absent members belonged to the Muslim League some of whom were destined to return to participate in debates after they chose to stay in India. Nehru also reminded that the Father of Nation, Mahatma Gandhi, was also not present and paid him a tribute. At this moment Nehru showed his awareness of the task ahead, but did not fail to emphasise the great civilisational past of India dating back to 5,000 years. In a nutshell, when Nehru moved the resolution, it was a great historic moment in various ways. The continuity in terms of transfer of power, freedom of the country, drafting of Constitution of a sovereign nation and rational foundations of the new state and nation in the making, all these impressions one gets while reading Nehru's speech.

Ambedkar spoke on the resolution on 17 December 1946, that is, four days after Nehru moved it. After Dr Syama Prasad Mookerjee, who was to form Bharatiya Jana Sangh in 1951, pointed out the absence of the members of the Muslim League and problems, thereby emerging from the legality of the Constituent Assembly, Ambedkar was invited to speak on the resolution. Ambedkar expressed his disappointment with the resolution moved by Nehru. It is important to note that he was not a member of the Congress and he seemed to share apprehension with Dr Syama Prasad Mookerjee that the drafting of the Constitution was going to be the Congress show, as is evident from his following comments:

> I should have thought that in order to make us willing friends, in order to induce every party, every section in this country to take on to the road it would be an act of greatest statesmanship for the majority party even to make concession to the prejudices of people who are not prepared to march together and it is that, that I propose to make this appeal. Let us leave aside slogans, let us leave aside words which frighten people. Let us even make concessions to prejudices of our opponents, bring them in, so that they may willingly join us on marching upon that road, which I said, if we walk long enough, must necessarily lead us to unity.

Reference, obviously, was made to the absence of the members of the Muslim league, as the creation of Pakistan was approaching fast. Ambedkar's sentiments, well-articulated, situate him on the issue of secularism and national unity in a nationalist perspective, and he also emphasised that the 'Hindu–Muslim' problem would not be solved by violence. Ambedkar suggested wisdom and prudence over power on the issue of Muslims. He did not raise the issue of the untouchable castes in his first major speech in the Constituent Assembly.

The untouchables prominently figured in P.R. Thakur's speech which he delivered on 19 December 1946 on the resolution when he said,

> Sir, in this big august House of the Constituent Assembly, we belonging to the Depressed Classes, are very few in number, but in the country as a whole our population is 60 million. We are no doubt a part and parcel of the great Hindu community. But our social status in the country is so very low that we do feel that we require adequate safeguards to be provided for us. Firstly, we should be considered as a minority—minority, not in the sense in which a community is a minority on religious or racial grounds, but a minority which is a separate political entity. It is needless however to, point out that we are a separate political entity. I think those who have got themselves interested in the uplift of the Depressed Classes will admit, as Mahatma Gandhi himself has admitted by his words and deeds, that adequate safeguards are necessary for these classes for their political salvation. The Poona Pact is Mahatma Gandhi's creation, and his writings in the 'Harijan' amply prove that the interests of the Depressed Classes must be carefully looked after.

P.R. Thakur represented Bengal and had been elected from general constituency, though later on, he contested the Lok Sabha elections from Nabadwip reserved constituency as the candidate of Bangla Congress in 1967.

There were two issues which weighed heavily on the members of the Constituent Assembly, namely, Muslims and Pakistan, and the princely states. Whereas the issue of Muslims as a religious minority had turned complex due to the two-nation theory and the certainty of formation of Pakistan through the partition of the country, the status of the princely states within the Indian Union presented a serious challenge for the democratic norms in operational terms. It seemed clear to the Congress-dominated assembly that the status of the Muslims after the partition was going to seriously change both in terms of the communal relations and the perception of safeguards to be provided for minorities in the Constitution. Muslims were one of the minorities among Anglo-Indians, Parsis, Sikhs and Christians, but they were numerically the largest among them. Thakur had raised the important issue of untouchables which even Ambedkar had not touched in his comments on the resolution. Despite the fact that Thakur reiterated Gandhian model and the promise of ameliorating the conditions of the depressed classes, he was essentially seeking a constitutional remedy, unaware of the fact that many other social groups would follow suit. The same day Damber Singh Gurung from Bengal raised the issue of Gurkhas who had been the loyal soldiers of the Raj. He claimed that there were 3 million Gurkhas in India—the population equivalent to that of the Sikhs—and might have to serve the nation in future the same way they had served the British.

In a way, most of the elements of the postcolonial modernity had been discussed in 1946 and the issue of communities existing either on religious or caste-based criterion was weighing heavily on the minds of the members who had been projecting India as highly complex entity facilitating the idea that religion could not be the sole basis of the construction of nation. Gurung's comment added ethnicity to the already existing criteria. Nehru responded on 21 December 1946 to the issue of constituting various committees and the inclusion of various members in them. He said,

> I submit that the question of any particular group—communal, provincial or state—coming into this Committee will not arise. We should take, of course, competent men who are here, but in this particular matter you cannot enter into group representations, because if we do there is no particular reason why we should deny that representation to the many separate interests that exist there.

The Assembly adjourned on December 1946 till 21 January 1947.

The discussion on the resolution continued on 21 January 1947. Next day, Nehru rose to speak on whatever had been said on the resolution and, reiterating his position on its adequacy, he tried to feel the pulse of the members and articulated the same in the following manner:

> The first task of this assembly is to free India through new Constitution, to feed the starving people and cloth the naked masses and to give every Indian fullest opportunity to develop himself according to his capacity. This is certainly a great task.

Afterwards he shifted from Hindi to English and said, 'May I confess that I was a little disappointed because I was impatient that we should go forward'. After Nehru's long speech, the President of the Constituent Assembly put the resolution on vote and it was passed amidst cheers. It is interesting to note what the president (Dr Rajendra Prasad) said, 'I will request Members now to stand in their places and vote in favour of this Resolution'. Nehru's speech showed his concern for the individual—the future of the citizen of the Democratic Republic of India—the significance of which was not realised in its fullest extent till Ambedkar presented the Draft Constitution in 1948.

Before we proceed to discuss the reports of various committees with regard to certain social issues concerning India, it is important to mention that the Constituent Assembly meetings were held in full public view. People could sit, watch and listen to the proceedings of the meeting while sitting in galleries. Obviously, journalists and other interested people could sit in galleries and hear what was going on.

II. Rights of Communities

After the resolution was passed, the Assembly proceeded on to form various committees to do the business of drafting the Constitution. When Pandit Govind Ballabh Pant made the motion to the election of the Advisory Committee on 24 January 1947, he made certain interesting comments on the issue of communities in India. He said,

> It is not for me to attempt any dissertation on the various aspects of minorities or fundamental rights. I cannot refrain from referring to a morbid tendency which has ripped this country for the last many years. The individual citizen who is really the backbone of the State, the pivot, the cardinal centre of all social activity, and whose happiness and satisfaction should be the goal of every social mechanism, has been lost here in that indiscriminate body known as the community … . We find that in our own country we have to take particular care of the Depressed Classes, the Scheduled Castes and the Backward Classes. We have to atone for our omissions—I won't use the word commissions.

The statement of Pant symbolised what was haunting the members of the Constituent Assembly, namely, the fundamental opposition between the rights of the community and the rights of the individual. On top of that the defining principles of community had not been standardised. It could be religion, caste or language. In the beginning of 1947, the spectre of partition of India was haunting the nationalists to the extent that even Maulana Hasrat Mohani, who was one of the founders of the Communist Party of India, was accused of being hand in glove with Muslim League despite his emphatic claim of being a nationalist and an Indian. There is a reasonable basis to reflect that in the absence of two-nation theory and the partition, the members of the Assembly, particularly those belonging to the majority community, would not have been as intolerant towards the question of minorities as was suggested by many speeches. Since the individual vs community as an issue was inseparably linked with the rights of the communities, the most important concern for the Assembly was to frame fundamental rights. For the purpose, the Assembly remained busy in constituting various committees, but the important one was the Advisory Committee which was formed on 24 January 1947 consisting of 50 members. Among these fifty members eight were from Punjab of which six belonged to the Sikh community.[1] However, after partition all this was destined to change.

On 29 April 1947, Sardar Vallabhbhai Patel presented the interim report on the fundamental rights in the Constituent Assembly. The Assembly indulged in an earnest debate when Patel moved the Fourth Article of the fundamental rights.[2] Articles 4 to 7 were covered under the title 'Rights of Equality', which tended to cover the issues of discrimination and untouchability. Srijut Rohini Kumar Chaudhury from Assam insisted that there should be an unambiguous definition of 'untouchability' and he moved the amendment: 'Untouchability' means any act committed in exercise of discrimination on grounds of religion, caste or lawful vocation of life mentioned in Clause 4'. He was supported by Dr S.C. Banerjee from Bengal, but K.M. Munshi was of the view that Clause 4 did not concern with untouchability, as it was regarding discrimination and subsumed untouchability too. It may be informed that Chaudhury who had initiated a serious conceptual debate about one of the most dehumanising practice in the history of India withdrew the amendment he moved to Clause 4.

In the backdrop of impending partition of the country on the religious basis, the fundamental rights concerning religious conversion became a serious issue of reflection. Patel moved Clause 17 on 1 May 1947, which stated 'Conversion from one religion to another brought about by coercion or undue influence, shall not be recognised by law'. K.M. Munshi moved the amendment which stated that all conversions of persons who were less than 18 years of age would not be recognised by law. In response to both the clause and the proposed amendment, the Christian members of the Assembly reacted sharply. F.R. Anthony from Bengal stated that 'My community does not propagate. We do not convert, nor are we converted. But I do appreciate how deeply, how passionately millions of Christians feel on this right to propagate religion'. Rev. J.J.M. Nichols-Roy[3] argued that the clause should not be amended at all, but at the same time he added,

> The amendment seeks to prevent a minor, who is twelve years of age, or thirteen years of age, up to eighteen years of age from exercising his own conscience. To think that a youth under the age of eighteen does not have conscience before God, and, therefore, he cannot express his belief is wrong.

Ambedkar, who was the member of the committee, also opposed the amendment. Finally, Clause 17 was referred back to the Advisory Committee. It was interesting to note that issue of religious conversion generated heated discussion between the Christian and some Hindu members and the same Hindu members were also the Congressmen. However, the real differences were destined to emerge on the issue of rights to minorities.

Intellectuals, politicians and social scientists have given us various interpretations of the word 'minority'. In the literal sense of the term, minority means less in number than some reference group. However, the notion of power is also linked with the number because along class lines the rich are always less in number than others, but they are not identified as minority, though minority is understood along axes which do not subsume class issue. Therefore, religion, ethnicity, language and sometimes caste and so on could be the axes along which minorities in India are defined. It is also important to know how the members of the Constituent Assembly articulated the concept of minority and what they thought about it. Clause 18 of the fundamental rights was entitled 'Cultural and Educational Rights' and it was moved by Patel on 1 May 1947,

> (1) Minorities in every Unit shall be protected in respect of their languages, script and culture, and no laws or regulations may be enacted that may operate oppressively or prejudicially in this respect.
>
> (2) No minority whether based on religion, community or language shall be discriminated against in regard to the admission into State educational institutions, nor shall any religious instruction be compulsory imposed on them.
>
> (3) (a) All minorities whether based on religion, community or language shall be free in any Unit to establish and administer educational institutions of their choice.
>
> (b) The state shall not, while providing State aid to schools, discriminate against schools under the management of minorities whether based on religion, community or language.

It is interesting to note that the word 'community' is used in the clause without essentially referring to the indicator, whereas religion and language are specifically mentioned. K.M. Munshi moved the amendment that Sub-clause 2 should be withdrawn for reconsideration and Patel accepted his amendment. Ambedkar saw no reason why the amendment should have been accepted. Some other members mentioned complexities involved in the issue of language and scripts. The discussion on fundamental rights concluded on 2 May 1947, but the issues concerning minorities remained inconclusive. By this time the reality of Pakistan had been accepted by the members and frequent references were made to Pakistan Assembly. After this, various issues of governance and government structure were earnestly debated by members.

III. On the Eve of Independence

The historic meeting of the Constituent Assembly was held on 14 August 1947 at 11 in the night and it began with the singing of the first verse of *Vande matram* by Sucheta Kriplani which was followed by the President's address, and he mentioned minorities among the challenges he thought were confronting India:

> To all minorities in India we give the assurance that they will receive fair and just treatment and there will be no discrimination in any form against them. Their religion, their culture and their language are safe and they will enjoy all rights and privileges of citizenship, and will be expected in their turn to render loyalty to the country in which they live and to its Constitution. To all we give the assurance that it will be our endeavour to end poverty and squalor and its companions, hunger and disease; to abolish distinction and exploitation and to ensure decent conditions of living.

Dr Rajendra Prasad delivered his address in Hindustani and it seems that he started by saying, '*Hum Bharat ke alap sankhiyan ko ashvasan dete hai*'. Was he saying all this as a Hindu—a member of the majority community—or he was saying it as member of the Indian Government? Is it that only minorities had to be loyal to the state and the Constitution? Why did he not say that all citizens would be equal partners in the making of the destiny of the country? It is interesting as well as ironic that the President of the Constituent Assembly, who was destined to be the first President of the Republic of India, spoke in the language which reminds of Ramananda Chatterjee (Israel, 1983) and the only difference was that Rajendra Prasad did not put it as a condition (that is 'If they want to live in this country ...'). However, the going-to-be the President of India belonged to the secular party and there should have been no reason why he should have the company of the Hindu fundamentalists. There is a reasonable possibility that the two-nation theory and the formation of Pakistan loomed large on the minds and ideas of the political leaders. A sense of insecurity in which suspicion rules the roost develops under such circumstances. We can only offer reasoning, but from the standpoint of what he said with regard to religious minorities was quite close to making minorities a suspect population in the project of nation-building.

We may now come to the most famous speech of Nehru, 'Long years ago we made a tryst with destiny, and now the time comes when we shall redeem our pledge, not wholly or in full measure, but very substantially'. After this short speech about which most of the intelligentsia is aware, Nehru moved the resolution that 'after the stroke of midnight all members of the Constituent Assembly take the pledge to serve the country and its people'. Nehru had properly worded the pledge for all and also suggested that those members who were absent should do so in the next session. Following the taking of pledge, the President proposed and the motion was adopted that the 'Constituent Assembly has taken over the power of governance' in the country and appointed Lord Mountbatten as the Governor-General of India. After the motion was adopted by the Assembly, Shrimati Hansa Mehta[4] presented the National Flag 'on behalf of women of India', following which she read out the names of 74 women who were members of the Flag Presentation Committee and she emphasised that these women wanted to be present on the occasion but could not be accommodated.[5] With the singing of few lines of *sare jahan se achha* and the first verse of *Jana gana mana* the Assembly adjourned till next day.

It was a momentous occasion for both the leaders and the people of India. Amidst joy and celebratory mood, the speech of Rajendra Prasad remained un-interpreted and ignored. The pain and pang of partition of the country and communal riots were momentarily forgotten on that occasion. What was presented was the project of nation-building in which all communities and women shall equally participate as, what Nehru meant to say, people of India.

IV. Minority Rights

Minority rights remained one of the main issues occupying the minds of the members and it seemed that the partition of the country was the major reason followed by the horrifying killing of Muslims in North India and Hindus and Sikhs in West Pakistan which turned into nightmares for many of them. After the Governor General's speech on 15 August, the report of the Union Powers Committee was taken up for discussion and the matter was concluded by 26 August 1947. Patel presented the Report on Minority Rights on 27 August and in his speech, he said,

> An attempt has been made in this report to enumerate those safeguards which are matters of common knowledge, such as representation in legislatures, that is, joint versus separate electorates. This is the question which has raised controversy for almost a decade and we have suffered and paid heavily for it. But fortunately we have been able to deal with this question in such a manner that there has been unanimity on the points that there should be no more separate electorates and we should have joint electorates hereafter.

After stating that there would not be any separate electorates for minorities, Patel submitted that there should be representation and reservation according to their population. Then he went on to identify two minority communities, namely the Anglo-Indians and the scheduled castes, who deserved special treatment which would also include the public sector jobs. Patel further informed the House that the committee categorised the minorities on the basis of their population size. The first minority community referred to was that of the Anglo-Indians for whom it was recommended that various privileges they had been enjoying in services and education should continue. However, their representation in legislature posed a difficulty due to their small size, which was one lakh and they were widely spread all over India. Provision to nominate them was made.

The second minority community was that of Parsis, and Patel informed the Assembly that 'they have themselves voluntarily abandoned any concessions that may be given to them and wisely they have done so'. Why did Patel add 'wisely so'? He stated that 'They (Parsis) know that any concession that they may get would perhaps do more harm to them than any good' because Parsis were prosperous and their standard of living was higher than the 'general standard of nation'. The third community Patel mentioned was that of Christians who, according to him, were populous in two or three provinces where they could have direct representation. However, Christians had agreed not to demand for separate electorate, but wished to have reservation. They did not claim any other safeguard, Patel informed the Assembly. Patel did not mention Muslims, Sikhs, Jains and Buddhists among minorities in terms of any safeguards, but while identifying Muslims and scheduled castes he informed the assembly that the issue was 'thrown out by a large majority' in the Advisory Committee.[6]

After the wholehearted support from Dr P.S. Deshmukh[7] from CP and Berar, V.I. Munuswamy Pillai from Madras delivered a long speech and supported Patel. However, Pillai touched upon various aspects of the issue of minorities by putting only the Dalits in the centre of his arguments, thereby showing the issues lurking in the minds of the members. He said,

> I do admit that, but, Sir, it was given to Mahatma Gandhi as a great *Avathar* to find the disabilities of a section of the Hindus, namely, depressed classes known by various names, to come to their rescue and to take that great epoch-making fast which evoked all the Caste Hindus in the whole realm of India to think what is 'Untouchables', what is 'Depressed Classes', what is 'Scheduled Castes' and what should be done for them. It was that Poona Pact to which you yourself have been a signatory along with me and Dr Ambedkar, that produced a great awakening in this country. Then, Sir, one question was in the mind of everybody, whether Poona pact will show signs of change of heart by caste Hindus in this country. Today I may assure you, Sir, that that change has come, though not 100 per cent, at least more than 50 per cent ... . The very inclusion of Dr Ambedkar in the present Dominion Cabinet is a change of heart of the Caste Hindus that the Harijans are no more to be neglected.

Pillai further averred that he was in favour of the representation of minorities in the government and the part of his speech cited above is important in many ways. First of all, he informed the House that along with Dr Rajendra Prasad, the President of Constituent Assembly and Dr B.R. Ambedkar he was the signatory of the Poona Pact on 24 September 1932. The Poona Pact was a result of the conflict between Gandhi and Ambedkar when the latter demanded the separate electorate for the untouchables to which the British had agreed. Finally, when Gandhi went on fast, Ambedkar was coerced into withdrawing his demand for the separate electorate. The schism between the Congress and Ambedkar was complete and in the subsequent period the Ambedkarites remained hostile to Gandhi. In such a situation, Nehru appointed Ambedkar as the first Law Minister of India. Pillai's speech metaphorically underlined both the change which the Congress leadership had initiated and the possibility of ending caste-based inequalities through political representation. Importantly, Pillai's view represented the typical Congressmen's views on the separate electorate. Since he was Dalit, it amply demonstrated that all Dalits did not support Ambedkar on the issue of separate electorate.

More serious than the issue of Dalits with regard to separate electorate was the communal issue. The discussion that took place on 27 August 1947 was entirely devoted to it, when communal riots and violence was in full swing in Punjab. The partition and communal violence combined to create an unconscious opposition to any idea of separate electorate with regard to minorities. It was seen as a ticket to another Pakistan. Chaudhuri Khaliquzzaman from UP articulated the conditions of Muslims in India:

> Today there is no third party to whom we can appeal ... Rightly or wrongly the Muslims did realise electorates were the cause of dividing communities. But today those arguments do not hold good. If you concede separate electorates, the Muslim community feels that they will help in returning their true representatives, representatives who will lay before you—not to any other power, not to any other government, not even to Pakistan—our grievances and our claims, therefore I beg of you and beg of this house to consider the new situation in which the question is being discussed.

Pandit G.B. Pant attacked the idea of the separate electorate which was originally the demand of the Muslim members of the Assembly. However, it is likely that the members of other minorities were also waiting for the response of the Congress big-wigs. After partition, the Muslims continued to be numerically the largest religious minority in India, whereas the scheduled castes/depressed classes, who had demanded separate electorate long time back, constituted minority on a different scale and were internally caste divided. Thus, Sikhs and Christians could have supported the Muslim members, particularly the Sikhs if we keep in mind the subsequent developments in Punjab. Before the issue of the separate electorate for the minorities was put to vote in the Assembly, Patel responded to all the issues raised with regard to minorities. He made it clear that he did not expect that much discussion on the issue of one man one vote. His ideas seemed to be representing the dominant opinion on the issue of that time. Whatever he said had the history of previous few decades with it. Let us quote his speech at length:

> My friends in the Muslim League here who moved this amendment and supported it took for granted that they had a duty to perform in a sense. They had been pressing for separate electorate and enjoying it for a long time and felt that they should not leave it all of a sudden, but just move the motion and have the vote of the House... there are many eminent Muslims who have recorded their views that the greatest evil in this country which has been brought to pass is the communal electorate. The introduction of the system of communal electorates is a poison which has entered into the body politic of our country ... Well, when Pakistan was conceded, at least it was assumed that there would be one nation in the rest of India—the 80 per cent India—and there would be no attempt to talk of two nations here also ... in the rest of India, in the 80 per cent India, do you agree that there shall be one nation? Or do you still want the two-nation talk to be brought here also?

Patel concluded his speech amidst cheers and the proposed amendment regarding the separate electorates for minorities was rejected after voting. Patel's speech is important in the sense that it ended the politics of difference and representation along a particular trajectory the reasons for which was the two-nation theory and the subsequent partition of the country. There was a degree of hostility towards the members of the Muslim League in the Assembly due to partition and violence which was still going on. Patel represented that feeling and causally connected separate electorate and two-nation theory with the subsequent partition of the country. In a way, Patel created an episteme which rejected the partition and made Muslims responsible for it as if the Hindu political and communal politics had no contribution to make it plausible. When he mentioned 80 per cent, he was essentially talking about the Indian Territory and population after the partition, but it may be imagined that he could have very well conveyed that what he actually meant was 'Hindus'.

The rejection of the proposed amendment for separate electorate also implied the existence of an alternative means of political reservation for minorities in the opinions of the leaders. Patel proposed different ways of giving representation to different minorities. In the case of the Anglo-Indians, the proposal was that there would be no reservation of seats for them, but the President would nominate one or two members. No provision for any reservation for the Parsis was made, but in the case of Christians reservation of certain seats in the centre and the 'provinces' was recommended in Madras and Bombay. Since the situation in Punjab was not yet clear, it was decided to postpone the issue of minorities in that state. Provision for political reservation was recommended for the Muslims and the scheduled castes. All these provisions were adopted by the Constituent Assembly.

The discussion of the Report on Minority Rights continued on 28 August 1947 and one of the important issues raised by Debi Prasad Khaitan, one of the leading lawyers of the country from Calcutta, was that combined together the Muslims and the scheduled castes constituted half of the population of the country added to which would be the population of Indian Christians and Buddhists. There would be few seats left for the general category if the provision for reservation were made. However, K.M. Munshi pointed out that the figures were applicable to the newly formed West Bengal about which valid and reliable data was not available. Interestingly, none of the Punjabi members of the Assembly mentioned Sikhs. Khaitan saw India through the glasses of Bengal. However, the Assembly passed the clause empowering any member of the minority communities to contest elections from even the non-reserved constituency, but due to partition and unclear picture of Punjab and Bengal, the matter was kept pending.

What was the nature of imagining India and its communities? The best illustration of the answer to this question came when Patel moved Clause 6 of the minority report, which states,

> No condition for a minimum number of votes of one's own community. 'There shall be no stipulation that a minority candidate standing for election for a reserved seat shall poll a minimum number of votes of his own community before he is declared'.

There was a long discussion on this matter including both the Hindu and the Muslim members. However, Kazi Syed Karimuddin's[8] proposal to V amend the clause seemed to sum up the feelings of the most of the Muslim members of the Assembly. He said,

> Mr. Ibrahim[9] has moved an amendment, Sir, that there should be joint electorates with reservation of seats and that a member of a particular community should secure 33 per cent of the votes of the community. We cannot forget that there are misgivings. There is mistrust and we have to move on very carefully and very calmly. This House has already decided on the abolition of separate electorates and we have to find out a formula that would satisfy the minorities. We must have the progress of the country in view also. The formula or amendment moved by Mr. Ibrahim lays down that there should be joint electorates. A candidate from a minority community will have to go with his cap in hand to beg the votes from other communities. Communalism will be gradually killed.

Karimuddin made it quite clear that the logic of reservation of seats is that the community should be represented.

It should be of interest to refer to Ambedkar in this context because of the obvious and well-known fact of his demand for separate electorate in the First Round Table Conference which led to the Poona Pact in 1932. Ambedkar was one of the members who wrote to the President the amendment he wanted to move in the Assembly. But he did not move the amendment on 28 August 1947. It seemed that he was absent on that day. H.J. Khandekar[10] made an interesting speech which referred to Ambedkar. He said,

> For the last 15 years, I have listened with interest to the speeches of Dr Ambedkar and read them in newspapers too, but there was no argument in them in support of the demand for separate electorates. In this way, as the demand did not stand to reason, he did not press it but withdrew it. It is a great victory for us.

When Nazirudin Ahmad spoke after Shrimati Renuka Ray, the President put to vote the motion that whether further discussion should be stopped because it was turning out to be the division between Hindu and Muslim members of the Assembly, particularly after Ambedkar withdrew his proposed amendment. By majority decision further debate on the issue was stopped and then the President asked Patel to respond to the proposed amendment moved by S. Nagappa.[11]

Patel's speech, whether out of exasperation or conviction, was an indicator of what the state of mind of the main leadership of India was. The best way to inform what he said is to quote him little more than usual:

> When I agreed to reservation on the population basis, I thought that our friends of the Muslim League will see the reasonableness of our attitude and allow themselves to accommodate themselves to the changed conditions after the separation of the country. But Now I find them adopting the same methods which were adopted when separate electorates were first introduced in this country, and in spite of ample sweetness in the language used here there is a full dose of poison in the method adopted.
>
> Since the introduction of separate electorates in this land, there were two parties amongst the Muslims. One was the nationalist Muslims or the Congress Muslims and the other Muslim League members, or the representatives of the Muslim League … . If the process that was adopted, which resulted in the separation of country, is to be repeated, then I say: those who want that kind of thing have place in Pakistan, not here … . Here, we are building a nation and we are laying the foundations of One Nation, and those who choose to divide again and sow the seeds of disruption will have no place, no quarter, here, and I must say that plainly enough … . Let us face the realities. Ask yourself whether you really want to stand here and cooperate with us or you want again to play disruptive politics … . You have got a separate state and remember, you are the people who were responsible for it, and not those who remain in Pakistan.

Was it a Patel's outburst in reaction to what the Muslim members of the Assembly were demanding? Or was it cool and reasonable response to the demands for joint electorates? It is very difficult to say, but one thing was clear that after his speech was over the matter was concluded and the Assembly adopted the Clause 6 as it was moved by Patel. If the words of Patel are quoted out of context, he resembled the typical Hindutva leader. In the present day politics, Prime Minister Narendra Modi's liking for Patel despite political opposition makes lot of sense. However, Patel could have used different language and got Clause 6 through, but he did not do that. The members of the Congress were in majority and anything could be cleared only if Nehru and Patel had supported any resolution. Long debates occurred only when they wanted them to happen, but it also seems that most of the time they were busier in the affairs of the government than debates in the Assembly unless something crucial came up, for example, the Amendment to 1935 Act or the issue of joining the British Commonwealth. What establishes Patel's secular credentials and indicates that he said it due to impatience are two important things. One, there were Muslims in the Congress Party—some of them were prominent leaders. Secondly, he did not have any kind words for the scheduled castes either. He said,

> To the scheduled caste friends, I also appeal: 'Let us forget what Dr Ambedkar or his group have done. Let us forget what you did. You have very nearly escaped partition of the country again on your lines. You have seen the result of separate electorates in Bombay, that when the greatest benefactor of our community came to Bombay to stay in bhangi quarters it was your people who tried to stone his quarters.

One way of gauging the impact of Patel's speech is that S. Nagappa withdrew his amendment and the President of the Assembly allowed him to do so.

The same day, when the debate on minority committee report was over, Ambedkar presented before the Assembly the Report of the Constituent Assembly Functions Committee. On 30 August 1947, Patel moved the Supplementary Report on Fundamental Rights in which the issue of discrimination in public-funded educational institutions on the basis of religion was debated.

V. Two-States

The Constituent Assembly re-assembled on 27 January 1948, which began with the issue of additional representation to West Bengal and East Punjab. Whereas M. Ananthasayanam Ayyangar[12] moved the resolution on West Bengal which was adopted after minor amendment, Giani Gurmukh Singh Musafir[13] moved the resolution on East Punjab in which he submitted that four Sikh members and eight general members were entitled to return in the Constituent Assembly. Jaipal Singh[14] from Bihar opposed the motion characterising it as 'dangerous, mischievous and sectarian'. One of the major reasons for raising the doubts about Musafir's motion was the probable inaccuracy of the population figures. The President referred the matter to a smaller committee comprising Ambedkar, Diwan Chaman Lal, Gurmukh Singh Musafir, Rafi Ahmed Kidwai and Ananthasayanam Ayyangar. However, the observations of Jaipal Singh had provoked Musafir, who got the chance to speak towards the end. It will be of interest to know what he said:

> I thought it to be simple matter, and therefore the speech I made, while moving the motion, was also simple. Even now I regard it as simple. One of our Honourable members objected to it as being sectarian. If you regard it as sectarian simply because of my beard then it is a different thing; otherwise there is nothing as such in it ... . At present, Punjab's case is a special one. I am obliged to say that only those, who have suffered can realise and not others.

The proposal of two more seats for the Sikhs, in addition to the two already in place, was adopted in the Assembly at the end. It is interesting that Musafir saying something about his distinct appearance to argue his point indicates how Sikhs had constructed their identity in the twentieth century. It may be informed that one of the two members who were nominated to the Constituent Assembly from Punjab owing to the creation of additional seats for the Sikhs was Hukam Singh. Nobody had anticipated that his inclusion would change the discourse on the Sikh issue, as we shall see in the seventh chapter, in a fundamental manner. In the meeting of the Constituent Assembly held on 27 January 1948, the President informed that the Assembly had 'come to the end of the agenda'. Now, the Assembly meet after the Drafting Committee chaired by Ambedkar[15] would complete the draft of the Constitution of independent sovereign India.

The first chapter in the imaging of modern India had come to the close with all discussions about the desired nature and character of the independent country. The next meeting would be held after a gap of 10 months. In a way, the first phase was characterised by the domination of Nehru and Patel as political leaders, but the second phase was destined to make Ambedkar the most prominent personality who responded to each and every criticism and amendment moved and showed a rare ability of comprehending and articulating all issues—social, religious and administrative.

Notes

1. They were Dr Gopi Chand Bhargava, Prithvi Singh Azad, Sardar Jogendra Singh, Sardar Partap Singh, Sardar Baldev Singh, Sardar Harnam Singh, Sardar Ujjal Singh, Gyani Kartar Singh and Raj Kumari Amrit Kaur.
2. Article 4 under the Justiciable Fundamental Rights reads as follows: '4 (1) the State shall make no discrimination against any citizen on grounds of religion, race, caste or sex. (2) There shall be no discrimination against any citizen on any ground of religion, race, caste or sex in regard to—(a) access to trading establishments including public restaurants and hotels, (b) the use of well, tanks, roads and places of public resort maintained wholly or partly out of public funds or dedicated to the use of the general public: Provided that nothing contained in this clause shall prevent separate provision being made for women and children'.
3. 'The architect of the Autonomous District Councils, J.J.M. Nichols Roy, was born on June 12 1883. He was a pastor and politician par excellence. His political life spanned nearly forty years (1920–1959) during which, he was a prominent member of the legislative council and Assembly, and was a minister of undivided Assam.

   As India moved towards independence, Rev Nichols Roy keenly observed the developments. He knew what the ultimate sociopolitical landscape of such a scenario would be especially when self-rule would begin a new Constitution would be adopted. Along with a few other contemporaries in Khasi Hills, he was instrumental in the formation of the Khasi National Dorbar in 1923 which deliberated the fate of the smaller principalities and communities in India, especially the indigenous tribals of the Northeast'. http://meghalayatimes.info/index.php/front-page/3948-khadc-unveils-statue-of-rev-jjm-nichols-roy-on-50th-death-anniversary (Accessed on 15 April 2016).

4. Hansa Mehta was well-known social reformer, educationist and writer from Gujarat. She was also the president of the All India Women's Conference, 1945–1946. She remained the Vice Chancellor of SNDT University, Bombay, and M.S. University, Baroda, after independence.
5. One of the members of the Flag Presentation Committee was the famous sociologist, Iravati Karve.
6. However, Patel's speech was prelude to the Report and the first paragraph of the report presented by him reads as follows:

   Groups

   A: Population less than ½ per cent in the Indian Dominion omitting States.

   Anglo-Indians, Parsees, Plains' tribesmen in Assam (other than Tea Garden's tribesmen).

   B: Population not more than 1½ per cent.

   Indian Christians, Sikhs

   C: Population exceeding 1½ per cent.

   Muslims Scheduled Castes
7. Panjabrao Shamrao Deshmukh famously known as Bhausaheb Deshmukh was a social activist and a farmers' leader in India. He was the Minister of Agriculture in the first cabinet of Pandit Jawaharlal Nehru in 1952.
8. Kazi Syed Karimuddin, born in Maharashtra (Yavatmal) and studied at the Aligarh Muslim University, was a member of the Congress Party.
9. Refers to T.M. Ahmed Ibrahim Sahib Bahadur from Madras.
10. H.J. Khandekar, a Mahar born in Nagpur, began his political career as Dalit activist but later on joined the Congress and got elected to Constituent Assembly from CP and Berar.
11. S. Nagappa, it seems from the debates, was not a Muslim representative. As it turned out later, he belonged to the Dalit community from Madras.
12. Lawyer by profession M. Ananthasayanam Ayyangar (1891–1978) was a Congressman from Madras Presidency. He hailed from Tiruchanur (Tirupati). After independence, he was the first Deputy Speaker of the Lok Sabha and then he became Speaker in 1956.
13. Gurmukh Singh Musafir was a Punjabi writer and freedom fighter. He became the first chief minister of Punjabi Suba in 1966.

14. Guha (2008: 115) informs that 'Jaipal was a Munda from Chotanagpur, the forested plateau of South Bihar peopled by numerous tribes all more-or-less distinct from caste Hindu society. Sent by missionaries to study in Oxford, he made a name there as a superb hockey player. He obtained Blue, and went on to captain Indian team that won the gold medal in the 1928 Olympic Games'. He was the founder of the Jharkhand movement.
15. The Drafting Committee was constituted on 14 August 1947 and following were the members: Dr B.R. Ambedkar (Chairman), Pandit Govind Ballabh Pant, Kanaiyalal Maneklal Munshi (K.M. Munshi, Ex-Home Minister, Bombay), Alladi Krishnaswamy Iyer (Ex-Advocate General, Madras State), N. Gopalaswami Ayyangar (Ex-Prime Minister, J&K and later member of Nehru Cabinet), B.L. Mitter (Ex-Advocate General, India), Md. Saadullah (Ex-Chief Minister of Assam, Muslim League member) and D.P. Khaitan (Scion of Khaitan Business family and a renowned lawyer). Sir Benegal Narsing Rau was the Constitutional Advisor. Later B.L. Mitter resigned and was replaced by Madhav Rao (Legal Advisor of Maharaja of Vadodara). After the death of D.P. Khaitan, T.T. Krishnamachari was inducted as the member.

2

Competing Modernities

Ambedkar and Gandhians

Village occupies the central place in any imagination of India. It creates ambivalent feeling among the Indian scholars; from the perspective of the Western modernity, Indian village is the symbol of backwardness and ignorance. However, village as an epistemic category divides modernists in terms of whether its extinction is indispensable in the project of the creation of modern society. Or modernity is predicated upon the process of modernisation in which what defines tradition and backwardness could be eroded. This chapter underlines two competing models of the postcolonial modernity with a special focus on the status of village, which were perceived, articulated and voiced at the time of India's freedom. The roots of these competing models lie in the way India was imagined as civilisation, nation or state. The articulators of the models were largely Western educated and they got the best opportunity to express them during the debates of the Constituent Assembly. The members of the Assembly were committed to modernise independent India, but they were guided by their perspectives and ideologies. The British rule in India had already established the foundation of Western modernity in areas, such as education, law, bureaucracy, transport and communication networks and rudimentary democracy. However, the British rule was not founded on the principle of welfare state. Some of the steps undertaken by the British government were later on recognised as harmful to the Indian society, for example, the permanent settlement and provision of separate electorate. Notwithstanding the fact that the members of the Constituent Assembly could be divided along multiple axes, thereby indicating that there were many models of modernity, the issue of village drew two points of view in the domain of discussion: one representing Gandhian perspective and the other liberal Western perspective. However, the issue was much more complex due to the intertwining of various forces, interests and ideologies.

The concepts of modern and modernity have been subjects of serious theoretical discourses and some aspects of them have been precisely outlined in the introductory chapter, but I have two points to make by way of reemphasising my viewpoint. First, the concept of 'modern' is connected with some degree of temporality and ambiguity, in the sense that in common parlance contemporary times are used as coterminous with modern times. At the same time, modern world is interpreted as the period which began at the time of the breakdown of the Dark Ages and ushering in of the renaissance in Europe through the rediscovery of Greek philosophy and the beginning of capitalism. The best way to describe modernity is to identify it with the age of reason and science. The arrival of postmodernity has turned it into a sandwiched stage between pre-modern and postmodern.

Second, following Chandra (1992: 2–3), I strongly hold the view that the binary opposition between modernity and tradition is normative and ideological. It is important to quote him at length:

> The dichotomy is projected back to explain and categorize even those actions, attitudes, beliefs and values that did not rest on, or stem from, such a polarity. After all, people can—as often happened in nineteenth-century India—view the phenomena designated 'modernity' and 'tradition' without opposing them to each other. In such perceptions there may even be reversing of the way in which these two constituent units figure in the explanatory framework of modernization.

Therefore, it is important that imagining postcolonial modernity could not be treated as either dichotomy or in the singular. There is a need to use modernity in plural to pave the way for accommodating and arguing in a historical situation in which the future of the country is at stake. In the case of India, extensive debates on the future of India took place in the meetings of Constituent Assembly between 9 December 1946 and 26 November 1949. The contents of these debates clearly show that there were multiple imaginings of modern India and on each issue the members were divided not necessarily along party lines, but on the bases of perspectives and ideologies. One of the issues debated was the conceptualisation of the Indian village as site of tradition. Four parts of this chapter take cognisance of the two competing modernities by centring the discussion on village in the independent India. The first part outlines Ambedkar's views on Indian village, while the second part takes stock of the reaction of the Gandhians to the views of Ambedkar. In the third part, the mode of inclusion of village in the Constitution in a modified way has been outlined. The final part deals with how the village became a metaphor of Indian nation.

I. Ambedkar and Village

On 27 January 1948, the Constituent Assembly completed all formalities required to facilitate the drafting of the Draft Constitution. The President of the Constituent Assembly told the members, 'I expect the drafting Committee to give me the final draft about the middle of February and as soon as the final draft is received, it will be printed and it will be sent to the press and it will also be published in the Gazette'. He informed that he would fix a suitable date for the next session of the Constituent Assembly. The next session was held on 4 November and interestingly, it began on a note of condoling the death of Quaide-e-Azam Muhammad Ali Jinnah. The President of the Assembly said Jinnah 'by his grim determination and steadfast devotion was able to carve out and found Pakistan and whose passing away at this moment is an irreparable loss to all'. It also mourned the loss of two of its members, namely Dabi Prasad Khaitan and Damber Singh Gurung. Despite the fact that the meeting was scheduled after the Draft Constitution was finalised, the issue which caught the attention of some members was that of language. The President made it clear that

> Whatever our sentiments may dictate, we have to recognise the fact that most of those who have been concerned with the Drafting of the Constitution can express themselves better in English than they can in Hindi; it is not only a question of expressing in English or Hindi, but the ideas have also been taken from Constitutions of the West.

The members were further informed that there would be discussion on the Draft Constitution starting next day, which would be divided into two parts, that is, general discussion and article by article discussion.

It was a historical occasion when Ambedkar began his speech on 4 November 1948. In a way, the most educated man in the Constituent Assembly was appointed as the Chairman of the Drafting Committee and he was a Dalit—belonging to an untouchable caste. Two things were unprecedented in this. One was that a Dalit could get higher education which showed that the colonial India had provided certain enabling environment for the lower castes to get education, which also included the changing minds of some princes in India. Secondly, nationalism enabled a Dalit to be the chairman of the Drafting Committee, particularly in the backdrop of the fact that Ambedkar–Gandhi relationship remained sour throughout after the Poona Pact in 1932. It is important to quote his preliminary remarks before taking up his views on village:

> The Draft Constitution as it has emerged from the Drafting Committee is a formidable document. It contains 315 Articles and 8 schedules. It must be admitted that the Constitution of country could be found to be so bulky as the Draft Constitution. It would be difficult for those who have not been through it to realize its salient features.
>
> The Draft Constitution has been before the public for eight months. During this long-time friends, critics and adversaries have had more than sufficient time to express their reactions to the provisions contained in it. I dare say some of them are based on misunderstanding and inadequate understanding of the Articles. But there the criticisms are and they have to be answered.

Was this bulky Draft Constitution a result of the hard labour of the Drafting Committee? It seemed so, but T.T. Krishnamachari[1] from Madras, who was inducted in the

Drafting Committee against one of the two seats said in the Assembly on 5 November 1948 that

> I am one of those in the House who have listened to Dr Ambedkar very carefully. I am aware of the amount of work and enthusiasm that he has brought to bear on the work of drafting this Constitution. At the same time, I do realise that that amount of attention that was necessary for the purpose of drafting a Constitution so important to us at this moment has not been given to it by the Drafting Committee. The House is perhaps aware that of the seven members nominated by you, one had resigned from the House and was replaced. One died and was not replaced. One was away in America and his place was not filled up and another person was engaged in State affairs, and there was a void to the extent. One or two people were far away from Delhi and perhaps reasons of health did not permit them to attend. So it happened ultimately that the burden of drafting this Constitution fell on Dr Ambedkar and I have no doubt that we are grateful to him for having achieved this task in a manner which is undoubtedly commendable.

It thus becomes clear that in certain ways Ambedkar was the spirit behind the drafting of the Constitution of India and his role should not be seen as merely the chairman of the Drafting Committee. After introducing the Draft Constitution, he moved the motion in the Assembly for consideration. He spoke on salient features of the Constitution in the beginning and in the process also responded to some of the criticisms which had already been made in the public domain. It is interesting to note that Ambedkar gave considerable space to the question of village in his speech. He reacted to criticism wherein it was stated that the Constitution did not provide the central space to the village panchayats; it should have been drafted on the basis of ancient Hindu model of political system. He said,

> The love of the intellectual Indians for the village community is of course infinite if not pathetic. It is largely due to the fulsome praise bestowed upon it by Metcalfe who described this as little republics having nearly everything they want within themselves, and almost independent of any foreign relations. The existence of these village communities each one forming a separate little state in itself has according to Metcalfe contributed more than any other cause to the preservation of the people of India, through all

> the revolutions and changes which they have suffered, and is in a high degree conducive to their happiness and to the enjoyment of great portion of the freedom and independence. No doubt the village communities have lasted where nothing else lasts.

He concluded his comment by stating, 'What is a village but a sink of localism, a den of ignorance, narrow-mindedness and communalism? I am glad that the Draft Constitution has discarded the village and adopted the individual as its unit'. 4 November 1949 is a moment in the history of India when liberal democracy was founded on the individual as the unit. And the individual overrode the village—the most chastised unit of Indian social life. In this way, Ambedkar's part of speech which critiqued Indian village has twofold significance in the construction of postcolonial modernity. Ambedkar broke the imaginary construction of the village as the ideal social space. Simplicity, tradition, closeness with nature and a great sense of community were attached with the meaning of the village. He provided an opposite picture of the village which was that of a social space of human degradation. Secondly, his comment on village confronted and contested Gandhi's idea of Hind Swaraj. However, Ambedkar was not alone in his condemnation of the Indian village life. Even Nehru did not share Gandhi's views on village. At the end of the Second World War in 1945 when independence was imminent and it was also the time. as Chandra (1994) informs, Gandhi wrote a letter to Nehru, which reiterated his position with regard to his conception of independent India. Gandhi believed that in order to attain true freedom we would have to live in villages. He wrote to Nehru, 'You will not understand me if you think that I am talking about the villages of today … . My villages today exist in my imagination … . After all, every person lives in the world of his own imagination'. He then outlined the village of his imagination,

> The villager in this imagined village will not be apathetic—he will embody pure consciousness. He will not lead his life like an animal in a squalid dark room. Men and women will live freely and be prepared to face the whole world. The village will not know cholera, plague or smallpox. No one will live indolently, nor luxuriously. (cf. Chandra, 1994: 45–46)

It is clear from the above that Gandhi was building a utopia, but in the process, he was also constructing the Indian nation and showing the way for nation-building. Chandra (1994: 45–46) informs us that Nehru received the letter and 'sent off a provisional answer on October 9'. His answer envisaged an altogether different notion of India—a notion representing European modernity. He wrote,

> Briefly put, my view is that the question before us is not one of truth versus untruth or non-violence versus violence ... I do not understand why a village should necessarily embody truth and non-violence. A village, normally speaking, is backward intellectually and culturally and no progress can be made from a backward environment. Narrow-minded people are much likely to be untruthful and violent. (cf. Chandra, 1994: 46)

In the light of the knowledge about Nehru's views on village, it was expected that he might support Ambedkar in the Constituent Assembly.

II. Gandhians and the Indian Village

Reminding oneself that Gandhi and his ideology had permeated into the Congress cadres, it is also possible to look back at the reaction of some of the members of the Constituent Assembly. It began immediately after Ambedkar had moved the Draft Constitution for discussion, which began on 5 November 1948. After the preliminary discussion on modalities, expressions and legalities, the first to make comment on Ambedkar's views on village was H.V. Kamath who said,

> One thing I join issue with Dr Ambedkar. He was pleased to refer to the villages ... as 'sinks of localism and dens of ignorance, narrow-mindedness and communalism' and he also laid at the door of certain Metcalfe our 'pathetic faith' in village communities. Sir, I may say that it is not owing to Metcalfe but owing to far greater man who liberated us in recent times, our master and the Father of our nation, that this love of ours for the villages has grown, our faith in the village republics and our rural communities has grown and we have cherished it with all our heart. It is due to Mahatma Gandhi, it is due to you, Sir, and it is due to Sardar Patel and Pandit Nehru and Netaji Bose that we have come to love our village folk.

He contended that Ambedkar's attitude towards the village was that of an 'urban highbrow' and was not acceptable. He then went on to identify the problem in terms of the urban background of the members of the Drafting Committee and pointed out that with the exception of Sriyut Munshi, none of them had participated in the freedom struggle. He then went on to underline that India's ancient polity was organised around village communities 'which were autonomous and self-contained'. Obvious implication of such an emphasis was that the villages were indispensable for the political life of the country. He further added,

> I believe the day is not distant when not merely India but the whole world, if it wants peace and security and happiness, will have to decentralise and establish village republics and town republics, and on the basis of this they will have to build their State; otherwise the world is in for hard times.

Kamath was interrupted by the President that his time had exhausted. After requesting the President for another couple of minutes, he went on commenting on Ambedkar's speech and argued for panchayati raj.

It is essential to inform that the discussion on Ambedkar's speech and the Draft Constitution was of general nature, as the debate on each of the articles of the Constitution had not yet started. Village did not occupy the importance among members if compared with the question of minorities, parliamentary system vs presidential system, or federal structure vs unitary structure. Despite all this, some members could give the issue importance simply because Ambedkar had drawn a negative picture of the Indian village. Various comments in reaction to Ambedkar's speech showed the way village was imagined under the leadership of Gandhi. On 6 November 1948, Arjun Chandra Guha from Bengal made it a point to digress from his main arguments to give special attention to what Ambedkar had said about village. He said,

> Dr Ambedkar has passed some remarks about the village units. We have been in the Congress for years. We have been taught to think of the village panchayats as the future basis of administrative machinery. The Gandhian and the Congress outlook has been that the future Constitution of India would be a pyramidal

> structure and its basis would be the village panchayats. According to Dr Ambedkar, the villages have been the ruination of India, the villages have been the den of ignorance. If that has been the case now, that is due to us who have been living in towns, who have been shining under the foreign bureaucracy and foreign rule. Our villages have been starved; our villages have been strangled deliberately by the foreign government; and towns—people have played the willing tool in this ignoble task. Resuscitating of the villages, I think, should be the first task of the future free India.

Guha made a politically correct speech, but his comments were sociologically inappropriate. It seems reasonable to argue that Gandhi–Ambedkar conflict worked in the background when such comments were made. Immediately after Guha, T. Prakasam from Madras[2] was asked to speak after the Vice President cautioned the members not to exceed time limit while speaking. He was blunt enough to say, 'With all due respect to the Honourable Dr Ambedkar, I must say that he has not been able to put himself in the position of those who had been fighting for the freedom of this country for thirty long Years'. It was quite clear that the man of the moment was resented by many Congressmen for his anti-Gandhi stance as well as his non-participation in the freedom movement. Prakasam went on to add,

> It is not a matter which should have been treated by Dr Ambedkar in that manner. That was a condition to which we had been reduced, after the village panchayats had been exhausted on account of the oppression of the various foreign rulers who had come over to this country. Still in spite of all that had been done for their suppression, they had survived. That is what Metcalfe wanted to explain to the world and to us who have been ignoring it. Therefore village panchayats are not to be condemned on this basis. I do not advocate for one moment today that village panchayats should be such as described by Metcalfe under those circumstances. Village panchayats should be one which is up-to-date, which gives real power to rule and to get money and expend it, in the hands of the villagers.

One may be reminded of the 73rd Amendment of the Constitution, which has been considered a landmark act in empowering the Dalits and women. Prakasam's comment offers us a new window to peep into the village to understand the drudgery of village life in the light of what history has done to it. However, little is realised in such a way of empowering the excluded in the village. If we keep in mind Ambedkar's views, it would simply imply that the desired outcome is likely to happen. It may be stated that though Prakasam's statement makes it clear that in the absence of his participation in the nationalist movement, that is Gandhi-led movement, Ambedkar was the least qualified to draft the Constitution of India; or at least make judgement on Indian villages. He did not understand that drafting of the Constitution was an act for which he was supremely qualified.

On the same day in the afternoon, that is, 6 November 1948, K. Santhanam,[3] while referring to Ambedkar's comments on village, said, 'I do not agree with his condemnation of the village panchayats and his statement that they are responsible for all the national disasters'. As a matter of fact, he opined, that despite all changes, the villages have preserved the Indian culture and saved society from anarchy. An attempt should be made to set autonomous village panchayats for which there is a need for such provision in the Constitution because 'in the long run local autonomy for each village must constitute the basic framework for the future freedom of this country'. The same day, Pandit Thakur Dass Bhargava from East Punjab, after a long speech touching on various aspects of the Draft Constitution, spoke on what and how the Indian village should exist. He said,

> The urban people and the rural people are so much apart from each other in their modes of living and outlook on life. To go near the villages is very difficult. The urban people do not go to the villages. I know the Congress has gone to the villages all honour to the Congress. But, there are a good many in the Congress also who do not wish to go to the villages; they cannot go because their mode of living is different. You will have to evolve such constituencies in which the cities and villages come in without any distinction; if there is a constituency for a lakh of the population, the cities and villages should be included in one constituency.

Bhargava seemed in agreement with Ambedkar on the characterisation of the Indian village, though he argued that something could be done instead of damning the villages. He misunderstood Ambedkar, for Ambedkar constructed binary opposition between individual and village/collective. In the process of elimination and with the knowledge that Gandhi had extolled villages, Ambedkar argued that village could not be the unit of citizenship. However, the matter was clearly discerned by some of the members among whom many chose to ignore the issue of village, but some of them took it up quite seriously. One of them was Professor Shibban Lal Saxena[4] from United Provinces who spoke in the afternoon of 6 November 1948. He spoke as a Gandhian activist with a sense of history about what happened in 1932 between Gandhi and Ambedkar. He said,

> Sir, Dr Ambedkar has criticised the system of village panchayats which prevailed in India and which was envisaged by our elders to be an ideal basis for our Constitution. I was just now reading Mahatma Gandhi's speech in the 1931 Round Table Conference in London. He was speaking about the method of election to the Federal Legislature. There he recommended that villages should be the electoral units. He in fact gave fundamental importance to the village republics. He said that it was in villages that the real soul of India lived. I was really sorry that Dr Ambedkar should express such views about the village panchayats. I am certain that his views are not the views of any other members of the House.

Then Saxena quoted the statement of Ambedkar on Indian village verbatim what Ambedkar had stated about village. He reiterated his position by referring to the successful running of Congress village panchayats for two and half decades and hoped that 'village republics, like the Russian village Soviets, can become models for good self-government'. Saxena was followed by Sarangadhar Das[5] from Orissa who expressed his shock that Ambedkar could characterise Indian village as 'a sink of localism' and asserted that 'there is more wisdom and more knowledge in the villages than in our modern cities'.

When the House met on 8 November 1948 on Monday, Ambedkar found one supporter in Begum Aizaz Rasul from United Provinces who took note of lot of criticism of Ambedkar on account of his remarks on village. The next speaker, Dr Mono Mohan Das from West Bengal, pointed out that the Drafting Committee had forgotten to include the village panchayat system and had 'wilfully left it to the provincial legislatures to frame whatever they like about this Village Panchayat System'.

Das cautioned members who were enthusiastically supporting the village panchayats by pointing out that so long as the villagers were not educated and politically conscious, the panchayat system would do more harm to them than good. In the absence of education and awareness,

> the local influential classes will absorb to themselves all the powers and privileges that will be given to the Panchayat system and they will utilise it for their selfish motives. This system will enable the village zamindars, the village talukdars, the Mahajans and the money-lending classes to rob, to exploit the less cultured, the less educated, poorer classes of the village.

Das made prophetic observation on the future of village. The present scenario is more or less similar to what he told in the House.

On the same day, another speaker expressed his feelings on Ambedkar's views on village as 'sink of localism and den of ignorance' was Gokulbhai Daulatram Bhatt[6] from Bombay. He stated,

> I was grieved to find that our great Pandit with all his knowledge of Sanskrit and politics, has opposed the system of village Panchayats in this way. If the village is to be discarded, someone can also boldly demand that this Constitution be discarded. But I am a humble person and do not have much experience either.

Bhatt was aware of the fact that Ambedkar had the knowledge of Sanskrit and we may assume that he also knew that he learnt Sanskrit from outside his country. Could he learn Sanskrit in an Indian village? It seemed that Ambedkar by intent did not attend the general discussion on the Draft Constitution. Bhatt was followed by Nehru who gave a long speech, but nowhere did he mention village and its virtues.

The general discussion on the Draft Constitution, as had been decided by the Vice President, Dr H.C. Mookherjee who was chasing the proceedings of the Assembly in the absence of the President, was to be concluded on 8 November 1948. When the Vice President asked Alladi Krishnaswami Ayyar from Madras, to speak still 40 members had not spoken their views. Ayyar started his speech by saying that 'I do not share the views of my honourable Friend in his condemnation of village communities in India'. He then went on to summarise the debate that so far had taken place. His stirred the issue of village in the following manner:

> The Constitution does not give sufficient importance to village communities which are an essential feature of India's social and political life. With the large powers vested in the provincial or state legislatures in regard to local self-government and other matters, there is nothing to prevent the provincial legislatures, from constituting the villages as administrative units for discharge of various functions vested in the state government.

It should be recalled that Ayyar was member of the Drafting Committee, which means that he largely agreed with Ambedkar on the question of individual as unit, but he felt that villages could be the administrative units in certain ways. Ayyar came from a village in Madras and had excelled in education and become the advocate general of Madras. He was not an active Congress nationalist, but he felt that perhaps Ambedkar had exceeded limits by manifesting his views about village. Ayyar's summing up should have concluded the general discussion, but it was extended by one day, as more members wanted to speak on the Draft Constitution. On 9 November 1948, the first person to take into consideration the issue of village was Professor N.G. Ranga[7] from Madras. He said, 'I am most unhappy that Dr Ambedkar should have said what he has said about village panchayats'. He asserted that Ambedkar had no knowledge of the village panchayats in Southern India. Rather than reading the history of other countries, he should have read Indian history, he said. He also argued that instead of centralisation, India needed decentralised administration in which the village as a unit would play the most important role. For Professor Ranga, village symbolised decentralisation. It will be important to quote some of his lines to have a taste of his language of ideas,

> The necessity for providing as many political institutions as possible in order to enable our villagers to gain as much experience in democratic institutions as possible in order to be able to discharge their responsibilities through adult suffrage in the new democracy that we are going to establish. Without this foundation stone of village panchayats in our country, how would it be possible for our masses to play their rightful part in

> our democracy? Sir, do we want centralisation of administration or decentralisation? Mahatma Gandhi has pleaded over a period of thirty years for decentralization.

Thus, village then became a symbol of decentralisation and realisation of Gandhi's ideas and philosophy. It should also be noted that most of the comments did not take cognisance of Gandhi's *Hind Swaraj* and, as his letter to Nehru mentioned earlier shows Gandhi's village as an ideal existed in his mind. It is possible to interpret the importance of village in Gandhi's philosophy. Kishorimohan Tripathi from CP and Berar states spoke on 9 November 1948 and took up the matter of villages in his speech, which seemingly clinched the issue:

> There has been very sharp criticism of the view expressed by Dr Ambedkar when he said that 'the villages are den of ignorance'. There has been ruthless criticism. I know this criticism is because of a genuine feeling on the part of the House. The House desires that the villages should come forward and play their full part in the national reconstruction. Since the desire is very genuine, I would request the House to detail out the election procedure in the Constitution itself. While giving adult franchise to every citizen of India, the eligibility for election to legislatures should be restricted to such persons as neither pay income-tax nor hold land in excess of 100 acres. That, I am sure, would bring in most of the villagers to the legislatures and they will be able to play their best role.

In the afternoon of 9 November 1948, Moturi Satyanarayana[8] from Madras brought up the issue of Swaraj with regard to village without criticising Ambedkar. He said, 'The people know what swaraj means ... But only the international view-point, and not the national nor the swaraj, nor even the villagers' view-point, is being given weight in the framing of this Constitution'. It is interesting to note that most of the speakers including Satyanarayana placed their discourse in the centre of the 30 years of struggle. It seems that the period they had been identifying as a phase in national struggle was the one during which Gandhi became the main political and ideological force. When N. Madhava Rau[9] from Orissa state spoke, he seemed to be critical of Gandhians in the Assembly and made a comment that 'It is very unfortunate that a good deal of controversy arose in regard to village panchayats. Ambedkar's strong remarks on the subject were apparently based on his own experience'. However, he reverted back to Gandhi on the question of village after narrating the positive experience of development of village communities in Mysore and then he quoted Gandhi, 'If the majority of congressmen were derived from our villages, they should be able to make villages models of cleanliness in every sense'. Then Rau pointed out that there was nothing in the Draft Constitution which would prevent the state governments from developing the panchayat institutions.

After five days of discussion on the motion and the response of Syed Muhammad Saadulla (a member of the Drafting Committee) to the motion, 'That Constituent Assembly do proceed to take into consideration the Draft Constitution of India settled by the Drafting Committee appointed in pursuance of the resolution of the Assembly dated 29th day of August, 1947'. On 9 November 1949, the Assembly proceeded to take up the proposed document article by article.

III. Village Included

On 22 November 1948, after the Article 31 was added to the Constitution after discussion and amendments, a new Article 31A as an amendment was moved in the Assembly. It was Amendment No. 927 which stood by the name of M. Ananthasayanam Ayyangar who requested the Vice President that K. Santhanam's amendment was better worded than his and should be taken for discussion. The Vice President accepted his request and asked K. Santhanam to move the amendment who did so:

> That after Article 31, the following new article be added:
>
> '31-A. The State shall take steps to organise village panchayats and endow them with such powers and authority as may be necessary to enable them to function as units of self-government'.

Santhanam went on to elaborate that many other members had proposed similar amendments. He emphasised that how much power was to be given to the village panchayats was a matter which would vary from state to state. He added, 'What is attempted to do here is to give a definite and unequivocal direction that the state shall take steps to organise panchayats and shall endow them with necessary powers and authority to enable them to function as units of self-government'. Immediately after Santhanam completed his speech, Ambedkar was on his feet and said, 'Sir, I accept the amendment'.

It might have been assumed that once Ambedkar accepted the amendment the matter would be finally laid to rest, but it did not happen. Some members still felt the need to remind Ambedkar how erroneous his views about Indian villages were. The first to speak at length was T. Prakasam, the future chief minister of Andhra Pradesh and destined to be remembered as Andhra Kesri. He was the first to create ripples in the minds of the modernists who might be sharing with Ambedkar the view about Indian villages. He said,

> Sir, a very serious situation was created by not making the village republic or the village unit as the real basis of the Constitution. It must be acknowledged on all hands that this is a construction which is begun at the top and which is going down to the bottom. What is suggested in this direction by Dr Rajendra Prasad himself was that the structure must begin from the foundations and it must go up. That, Sir is the Constitution which the departed Mahatma Gandhi indicated and tried to work up for nearly thirty years.
>
> One of the distinguished friends of this House was remarking the other day to me, 'why are you thinking of these village republics and all these things? The bullock cart days have gone; they will never come back?' This was his observation ... . [But] these village republics would convert the work of these bullock carts to work of carrying paddy and other produce which they produce in the village for their own benefit and for the benefit of the public.

The speech of Prakasam did not have any such content which had not been said earlier. For example, 30 years of Gandhi's political life and his emphasis on village remained the core of such speeches of most of the members. However, Prakasam was able to pinpoint one issue which he thought was connected with villages. The year 1948 was the year of communist movements in India and the Communist Party of India (CPI) had been engaged in various mass struggles most of which involved peasantry. Even in Punjab, a strong peasant movement called the Red Communist Party movement was essentially the culmination of tenant movement which came under the control of breakaway group of the communist party. The Telangana movement was still going on. The CPI was experimenting with different tactics and Ranadive's mass upsurge line was just a couple of weeks away. After treading the usual path, Prakasam added the following comment:

> Communism can be checked immediately if the villages are organised in this manner and if they are made to function properly. There would be no temptation for our own people to become communists and to go about killing our own people as they have been doing.

Surendra Mohan Ghosh from West Bengal expressed his views that the importance or relevance of the Constitution could only be ascertained if it had taken under its umbrella the 'crores and crores of the people of India' and by amending the Draft Constitution the right action had been undertaken. However, Seth Govind Das from CP and Berar, who figured prominently later on in the discussion of national language, were intent upon beating the old bush but also added some fresh elements into it. He said,

> Ours is an ancient, a very ancient country and the village has had always an important position here. This has not been so with every ancient country. In Greece, for instance, towns had greater importance than villages. The Republics of Athens and Sparta occupy a very important place in the world history today. But no importance was attached by them to the villages. But in our country the village occupied such an important position that even in the legends contained in most ancient books—Upanishads—if there are descriptions of the forest retreats, of the sages, there are also descriptions of villages ... . Modern historians have also admitted this fact.

Seth Govind Das mentioned Henry Maine,[10] Baden-Powell[11] and B.C. Pal and concluded his comments on village by mentioning Gandhi, but with a little difference. He informed that Gandhi was clear that if anyone wanted to know the real India, then he or she should go to villages. Das lamented in the end that despite the fact 80 per cent of the population in India lived in villages, there was no mention of villages in the Constitution. Das was followed by V.I. Munuswamy Pillai from Madras, who reiterated his commitment to village and Gandhi and welcomed the decision that finally village had found a mention in the Constitution and also added that villages were also the source of revenue from which towns had been created, but the same villages were not provided amenities. V. Subramaniam from Madras went to the extent of expressing that 'If there is any living cell in the Constitution, it will be this village panchayats amendment which has been brought forward'.

The speech of L. Krishnaswami Bharathi from Madras makes an interesting reading in two ways. First, it suggests that members of the Assembly had taken the task as seriously as the nature of the work demanded. Second, it seems to be the culmination of all discussion that had taken place by rooting the argument in the exact thoughts of Gandhi. It also implicates the idea of empowerment as reflected in the thoughts of Gandhi. Bharathi pointed out that Gandhi emphasised that political and economic decentralisation was indispensable for the functioning of democracy. At this moment, K. Santhanam interrupted Bharathi and pointed out that self-government might be as much economic and spiritual as it was political. Bharathi responded by saying that he was aware of these dimensions of decentralisation, but wished to enlighten the members by making it clearer. He pointed out that for Gandhi self-sufficiency was central to the concept of self-government and quoted Gandhi: 'My idea of village Swaraj is that it is complete republic, independent of its neighbours for its vital wants and yet interdependent for many others in which dependence is necessary'. After quoting Gandhi's notion of village Swaraj, Bharathi elaborated and interpreted Gandhi's ideas:

> Gandhiji was emphatic in saying that he was not at all suggesting that the village should be independent of all these things, but in certain matters you must have self-reliance, the basic idea being, '*no work, no food*'. Now the villagers think that as it is a Swaraj Government, *khadi* and food will flow from heavens as *manna*. Gandhi's idea in this self-sufficiency is, 'Don't expect anything from the Government. You have got your hands and feet; work; without work you will have no food. You can produce your own cloth, you can produce your own food. But if you do not work, you shall have no food, no cloth'. That is the basic idea of decentralisation and economic democracy.

After saying all this Bharathi quoted Gandhi at length elaborating the idea of village Swaraj. He completed his speech by quoting from Gandhi the following views on village panchayats:

> There will be a compulsory service of village guards who will be selected by rotation from the register maintained by the village. The government of the village will be conducted by the Panchayat of five persons annually elected by the adult villagers, male and female possessing minimum prescribed qualifications.

He concluded his speech by saying that for Gandhi 'India could live only if the villages live'. Immediately after that Ambedkar said, 'Sir, as I accept the amendment, I have nothing more to add'. The Vice President commented that all these speeches were nothing except praising the amendment and then he moved the amendment which was passed and Article 31A was added to the Constitution on 22 November 1948.

IV. Village as Metaphor of Unfinished Project

The day Ambedkar delivered the historic speech to move the Draft Constitution in the Constituent Assembly was the day of the paradigmatic shift in the way India was imagined, understood and defined as civilisation, nation and society. Village, the foundation of Gandhian thought, crumbled under the weight of a new modernity to which the Gandhians reacted sharply. Ambedkar could have avoided mentioning village, but he chose to do so because he created a dichotomy/binary opposition of village and individual.[12] What did it mean? It meant the breakdown of the archaic and oppressive system of living in communities founded on the village settlement where all kinds of discriminations perpetuated. By making the individual as the unit of citizenship, the so-called unbreakable shell of village community was broken.

Ambedkar was not the only one to treat village as the den of darkness and oppression and the only remedy to come out of it was to break it. Marx (1975) pinpointed village as the foundation of unchanging character of Indian villages. The causal relationship established by the 19th-century sociologists between population increase and social change mediated through the change of division of labour constituted an exception in India. Marx (1975) argued that the population increase of the Indian village did not lead to the emergence of new division of labour. On the other hand, the surplus population moved out of the village and established a new settlement which was the replica of the original village without changing property relations. Marx thought that the British colonialism would be good for Indian society, for it would break the unchanging character of the village.

Ambedkar's comments on Indian village in his speech were a part of his writing on the village. He dealt with the notion of Indian village in contradistinction to its colonial construction. He (Rodrigues, 2002: 325–326) argued that 'the Indian village is not a single social unit. It consists of castes'. He made a binary opposition of touchables and untouchables who differ in terms of their location with regard to social status, residential locations, political status and economic conditions. Ambedkar (Rodrigues, 2002: 325–326) identified 15 offences which an untouchable must not commit in his conduct with the touchable castes. He concluded his essay with the following: 'In this republic, there is no place for democracy. There is no room for equality. There is no room for liberty and there is no room for fraternity. The Indian village is the very negation of a republic' (Rodrigues, 2002: 330).

Dumont (2002: 50) rejected Maine's characterisation of Indian village as little republics and almost agreed with Ambedkar's characterisation:

> The truth is that Maine carried on the approach inaugurated in *Ancient Law*, arbitrarily abstracting his 'Community' from the data and reducing it to those features which, he assumed, were characteristic of the pristine Indo-European community. He did away with caste and kinship with a leger de main, just as he did not feel the need for any detailed and localized description.

Dumont's remark is obviously implicating caste and kinship as antinomy of community in which homogeneity rather than heterogeneity is the principle. In this regard, the Indian village resembled what Ambedkar said it was. Gandhians, on the other hand, failed to apprehend the deep philosophical construction which Gandhi made of village as the ideal site. When he told Nehru, as discussed in the beginning of this chapter, that the village he was referring to was residing in his imagination, he was essentially looking at future where the contradictions and darkness of the present would be absent.

To what extent Ambedkar's unintended appreciation for the city could be regarded as justified is a matter of empirical investigation and some attempt in this direction would be made here. However, it is clear that Ambedkar's vision of modernity was linked with the end of communities and emergence of society where anonymity of the individual's birth-based status would be the dominant feature of social life. Sociological studies show that the urban localities are caste-centric in considerable cases as well as class-centric. Judge and Bal (2005), Bhosale (2003) and Sharma (2003) have shown how the Dalit localities exist in cities. Virtually all over India, the caste associations are active in cities. Mumbai, being the major metropolitan city with its distinct urban character, has all kinds of indicators of the existence of caste, regional and religious associations. Certain localities have emerged purely on the criterion of caste, religion or region where all others are not allowed to reside.[13] Thus, the issue of modernity in the case of India decentres the notion of village as a symbol of Indian backwardness in terms of its practice of discrimination and exclusion in certain respects.

Therefore, village is a metaphor in the writings of Gandhi and Ambedkar where the two are opposite to each other. Metaphor, it may be reminded, by definition is vague and ambiguous. Gandhi's ambiguity has resulted from his imagination, whereas Ambedkar's ambiguity is existential and also based on his experience of living in the Western countries as well as in Mumbai. For Gandhi, the village of his imagination was the ideal locality without dirt and hatred. Gandhi's views had great appeal and his village of imagination was thought to be the village in reality by his staunch followers. The imaginary village of Gandhi became the ideal site—a metaphor of what signified ideal Indian village. Ambedkar sought to end community and make individual as the unit of citizenship and the first community that he touched upon was 'village'. When he delivered his speech in the Constituent Assembly, the decisions to discontinue separate electorate and any reservations on religious basis had left for Ambedkar only the Indian village—the metaphor of darkness.

Notes

1. Not too many details are known about the early life of Tiruvellore Thattai Krishnamachari but, from what is known, it is easy to establish that he was born into a Tamil Brahmin family. After his initial years of schooling, T.T. Krishnamachari went on to study and graduate from the Madras Christian College. He was Union Finance Minister of India twice. As a member of the Constituent Assembly, he was nominated in the drafting committee. http://www.iloveindia.com/indian-heroes/t-t-krishnamachari.html#OJSEDro6PwC1Zr5b.99 (Accessed on 18 April 2016).
2. Rao (1995: 165), in his biography of T. Prakasam—a lawyer and regarded as founder of Andhra Pradesh, is of the view that he was largely responsible for the inclusion of Article 31A in the Constitution, 'With his background and orientation, he took keen interest in the debates of the Constituent Assembly. As discussions went on, he found that panchayati Raj and democratic decentralisation was not on the agenda. He was pained that the subject was not given the importance it deserved keeping the ideals of the freedom movement and the teachings of Gandhiji in view'.
3. K. Santhanam belonged to Tanjore district of present Tamil Nadu. He left his practice as an Advocate at the Madras High Court and joined the freedom movement. He served as railway minister in Nehru's cabinet. He was staunch Gandhian and devoted his life to spreading Gandhian thoughts after independence (Narasimham, 1974: 38–40).
4. Shibban Lal Saxena was born in Agra. He was the Professor of mathematics and philosophy at St. Andrews College, Gorakhpur. He was a member of the Lok Sabha for two terms from 1954 to 1962. He was a socialist (Lohiaite) in his ideological orientation (Srivastava, 1974: 95–96).
5. Sarangadhar Das was a graduate of Ravenshaw College, Cuttack, after which he went to Japan on a scholarship where he studied chemistry. He got a higher degree in chemistry and agriculture from California University and after returning to India he established a sugar factory in his village (Harekrushnapur in the state

of Dhenkanal). He ran the factory along socialist lines which made the ruler suspicious of his intentions and confiscated his factory. He remained in Congress till 1952, and he joined the Socialist Party of India and became its president (Sahu, 1972: 360–362).

6. Gokulbhai Bhatt was from a village in Sirohi district in Rajasthan. He studied till intermediate class and then joined the noncooperation movement. He was a freedom fighter and a part of the Congress movement. After independence, he joined the Bhoodan movement (Guru, 1972: 179–181). However, when Emergency was imposed in 1975 he was arrested and he remained in prison during the period.
7. Professor N.G. Ranga belonged to Guntur district of Andhra Pradesh. He got his BLitt from Oxford and came under the spell of socialist ideology while he was studying at Oxford. He taught history at Pachaiyappa's College, Madras. He left Congress in 1952 and founded the Krishikar Lok Party and later he joined the Swatantra Party in 1959 and was its President (Masani, 1974: 485–487).
8. Moturi Satyanarayana (1902–1995), a freedom fighter and member of the Congress, is known for his activities in promoting Hindi in South India. He belonged to a village in Krishna district of Andhra Pradesh.
9. N. Madhava Rau is listed as representing Orissa state, though he was the Diwan of Mysore state. It is obvious that he refers to his experience of Mysore, but it is quite possible that he might have been inducted from Orissa state. It may be clarified that by Orissa state it means the princely states in Orissa.
10. Interestingly, it is Henry Man instead of Henry Maine in the English text.
11. It may be of interest to sociologists in particular that Emile Durkheim reviewed Baden-Powell's book *The Village Communities in India* in 1897 and thought that its 'joint family is by far the more ancient form' (Dumont, 2002: 50).
12. In sociology, the dichotomy if village/city or rural/urban is quite popular in comparing forms of society and/or way of life.
13. Observation is based on author's field work in Mumbai.

3

Minorities and Political Reservations

The primary purpose of this chapter is to underline and examine certain moments of great historical importance with wider and unseen ramifications in the contemporary India. Within the framework of this broad, general and obviously ambiguous purpose is the specific objective of making a discourse analysis of the particular and specific moment of history. This moment came when the British decided to give independence to its colonies, particularly India, after the Second World War. Preparations for the great moment were combined with the great self-conscious responsibility of helping the local elite, who were largely trained in the Western educational institutions, to prepare the framework of governance of independent India. The arrival of Cabinet Mission and the subsequent formation of the Constituent Assembly in 1946 for the purpose of drafting the Constitution of sovereign India initiated the process of articulation of diverse views on the nature and character of postcolonial modernity. The leaders who were entrusted with this huge responsibility took the task seriously and what haunted them most was not just the backwardness, illiteracy and poverty, but also the management of diversity for nation-building. The spectre of partition loomed large on the minds of the leaders and the plausibility of such division could not be ignored. One element of diversity was the existence of minorities. Let us begin by understanding the concept of minority.

Literally speaking, minority means numerically less than some other group or entity. In a democracy, a minority may consist of people distinguished by a common feature having fewer shares of votes than other set of people. However, the writers on minority do not take cognisance of merely the size of the group or community; rather the power equation is treated as an important element (e.g. see Farley, 1982). However, ethnic communities across world, blacks and religious communities are regarded as minorities in plural societies. The minority group could be defined as having 'inferior status in society—that is, any group that has less than its proportionate share of wealth, power and/or social status. Frequently, minority group members are discriminated against by those in the majority' (Farley, 1982: 6–7). In other words, minority group is identified in terms of discrimination and lack of power. Any criterion, such as religion, caste or race could be used to identify a minority group. As we shall see, the Constituent Assembly did exactly the same, but certain paradoxes existed.

Ambedkar delivered the speech on 4 November 1948 to move the Draft Constitution for approval. He outlined salient features of the proposed Draft Constitution and responded to criticism it encountered between February and November 1948. One of the issues he touched upon was the provision for adequate safeguards for minorities in the Constitution.[1] While responding to the criticism of the Draft Constitution with regard to the issue of minorities, his argument reflected not only his sense of balance but also an advice to the members of the Constituent Assembly. He said,

> I have no doubt that the Constituent Assembly has done wisely in providing such safeguards for minorities as it has done. In this country both the minorities and majorities have followed a wrong path. It is wrong for the majority to deny the existence of minorities. It is equally wrong for the minorities to perpetuate themselves. A solution must be found which will serve a double purpose. It must recognize the existence of the minorities to start with. It must also be such that it will enable majorities and minorities to merge someday into one. The solution proposed by

> the Constituent Assembly is to be welcomed because it is a solution which serves this twofold purpose. To diehards who have developed a kind of fanaticism against minority protection I would like to say two things. One is that minorities are an explosive force which, if it erupts, can blow up the whole fabric of the State ... . The other is that the minorities in India have agreed to place their existence in the hands of the majority ... . The moment the majority loses the habit of discriminating against the minority, the minorities can have no ground to exist. They will vanish.

The interpretative analysis of Ambedkar's speech provides us certain interesting insights. One of the most important viewpoints offered by him was that a society without discrimination could also be a society without minorities. It seems that he wanted and believed in total fusion of all communities along certain axes which he did not identify. At the same time, he considered minority politics dangerous for the body politic. Despite the fact that his speech, in the beginning, seemed to suggest that reservations might not be the solution, he endorsed fully the decision of the Constituent Assembly to provide certain safeguards to the minorities. The major speaker on the same day was the veteran leader, Maulana Hasrat Mohani who moved the amendment that the discussion for consideration of the Draft Constitution be postponed and be taken only after the fresh elections of Constituent Assembly based on the joint electorate and 'formation of political rather than communal parties of India'. Maulana's speech was interrupted first by Pandit Balkrishna Sharma and later by Satyanarayan Sinha. The following are few lines from Maulana's speech:

> You have provided in the Constitution that 14 per cent of the seats should be reserved for Muslims. You still consider yourself 86 per cent and Muslims to be 14 per cent. So long as you have this communalism, nothing can be done. Why do you say that Muslims are in a Minority? So long as you depict them in communal colours Muslims shall remain a Minority.

Subsequently, Maulana was destined to become the laughing stock of certain diehard members of the Assembly who opposed the issue of any further benefits to Muslims. Maulana was about 73 years old and belonged to the respected political leaders' category. However, his speech was an indication enough that the issue of communal identities could not be set aside. Right from the beginning the fundamentals of the Constitution dwindled between the individual as citizen and communities from the perspective of rights. It was a strong point towards the epistemology of 'political', as it progressively became clear that in India social was political.

On 6 November 1948, two days after Ambedkar moved the Draft Constitution, Pandit Thakur Dass Bhargava reflected upon the rights of minorities with serious concern by pointing out that there should be 'perfect equality' between the members of the minority and majority communities with regard to the electoral rights. He further claimed that he had been working all throughout his life for the minority community people, but 'in regard to this aspect of reservation of seats, I must submit that I am dead opposed to it'. He further added,

> I maintain that in regard to Muhammadans and Sikhs and Christians no occasion for reservation arises at all and the entire population is almost homogeneous, so far as wealth, social influence and status and other things are concerned. In fact some of these communities are perhaps better off than the majority community. In regard to Harijans, members of the Scheduled Castes it may be said that in wealth, social influence and social status they are inferior, but all the same I want that their position may be levelled up in ways other than by reservation of seats ... There is no occasion for having reservations at all but if any are necessary this method of reservation is very humiliating to the majority community and will be very harmful to the minority community. Yesterday Mr Karimuddin gave very good reasons in the House.

Bhargava came out openly to oppose reservation for minorities. It may be reminded that the entire discussion was taking place on the issue of political reservation for minorities. In his opposition to the reservation for minorities, he gave reference to the speech of Kazi Syed Karimuddin, Congressman and well-known criminal lawyer from CP and Berar to assert his viewpoint. It thus becomes important for us to know what really Karimuddin did say on 5 November 1948. Though he asserted that the Muslims should be left to their own fate to determine their future, but his entire speech revealed something else. It is essential to quote him instead of paraphrasing it. He said,

> The Constituent Assembly last time considered the problem of separate and joint electorates with reservation of seats. In my opinion, it is neither here nor there. Joint electorate with reservation of seats is absolutely of no consequence to the minorities. It would do them positive disservice .... [T]his provision is detrimental to the interests of the minorities. If the two resolutions regarding the continuation of separate electorates or joint electorate with reservation of seats with fixed percentage of votes of the community to which the candidate belongs which were rejected last time are not acceptable to the House, the minorities should forego this reservation of seats under joint electorates.

Karimuddin's argument against reservation for minorities was not as simple as Bhargava interpreted them the next day in his speech. In fact, Karimuddin had taken cognisance of what had happened during the earlier debates in the Constituent Assembly, particularly the strong words Sardar Patel used on the issue of separate electorates.[2] In the absence of separate electorate, any other reservation for Karimuddin was likely to foster communal hatred, whereas most of the discussion earlier revolved around alleged reality that the major villain in causing partition of the country was separate electorate. Karimuddin was in fact not saying something novel but asserting that the only way minorities could be given justice was the award of separate electorate. Bhargava misunderstood his ideas. However, it is quite likely that he picked selectively from Karimuddin's speech to show that even the honourable Muslim member of the Assembly was not in favour of reservations for minorities.

On the same day (6 November 1948) when the general discussion on various aspects of the Draft Constitution was in full swing, Chaudhary Ranbir Singh from East Punjab took up the issue of minorities earnestly and strongly argued against the provision of reservation for minorities due to its non-secular character. He said,

> We have seen that by the power of their organisation and with the help of foreign power they [Muslims] brought about the partition of the country. The other minorities that have already been referred to are not less powerful. We cannot from any point of view call them backward communities. It is no doubt true that it may be said, if it can be said for any group at all, that Harijans

> constitute a backward class. Both from their educational and financial conditions they may be called backward class. But even in this respect we have to keep in view one other consideration. It is if we provide in this Constitution safeguards for Harijans, the word 'Harijans' would be perpetuated even though such is not our intention .... A classless society cannot be formed if we make a provision for reservation of seats.

Ranbir Singh's speech carried a view which might have been the widespread view of the times among the opponents of partition if not merely the Hindus. Making the Muslim unity and the foreign power responsible for partition had obvious and tremendous advantages for the Congress one of which was that its main leadership—Nehru and Patel—were absolved of any such historical responsibility. It also made the Indian Muslims guilty of dividing the country and compelled them to remain under the protection of the Congress. However, Ranbir Singh's argument that reservation could stigmatise the untouchables who, according to him, were the only minority deserving reservation seemed quite reasonable.

On 8 November 1948, the Vice President announced that he was finding it difficult to give opportunity to every member to speak and told the House that he would then allow the members of the minority communities to speak. Thus, Mahboob Ali Baig Sahib Bahadur from Madras was the first to speak. After touching upon various aspects of the Draft Constitution, he concluded his speech with a rejoinder to Karimuddin's statement that he did not want reservation for Muslims in the absence of the provision for separate electorates. He said,

> If in case of minorities a device is found, for instance, the election being based on what is called proportional representation by the system of single transferrable vote, if such a device is made by the party in power, by the persons responsible for the framing of the Constitution, I think that might go a long way.

V.I. Munuswamy Pillai, also from Madras, spoke on the Draft Constitution on the same day and argued for reservation for the minorities. Mohammed Ismail Sahib from Madras got his turn to speak after Rev. J.J.M. Nichols-Roy from Assam presented his views on the Draft Constitution without giving much importance to the idea of reservation for minorities.

Ismail Sahib emphasised, 'In my view there should not only be reservation of seats but these seats should be filled up through separate electorates'. After completing full circle, the issue had come back to square one.

As touched upon in the discussion on villages in the previous chapter, Nehru spoke at length but without touching the issue. Interestingly, he did not make any comprehensive comment on the issue of minorities. When Alladi Krishnaswami Ayyar summarised the entire debate on the Draft Constitution on the same day (8 November 1948), he made the following observation:

> The problem of minorities has been solved by common agreement in a manner satisfactory to the various parties concerned, and the draft Constitution merely seeks to give effect to the agreement reached. As has been pointed out in the spirited address of our Prime Minister this morning, while regimented unity will not do, nothing should be done which will tend to perpetuate the division of the nation into minorities and to prevent the consolidation of the nation.

Interestingly, Nehru took up the matter of language only in his speech wherein he touched upon the issue of imposition of a language on minority. It was emerging from various speeches of the members that there was a growing opposition to the provision of reservation for minorities. The Muslim members who took up the issue from a different perspective from others made the issue of minorities Muslim-centric, whereas there were other minority communities as defined by the Constituent Assembly. Despite the fact that the issue had been settled apparently unambiguously when the Minority Committee's report was discussed in the Constituent Assembly, the matter again caught the members with little less degree of emotion than earlier when partition had just occurred. Gurmukh Singh Musafir spoke after the lunch break when the morning session had concluded after Nehru's speech. Musafir pointed out that he had been the Congress worker and belonged to the minority community on the basis of religion. He averred that his community members had been proud of the fact that its members had sacrificed their lives for the country. He reiterated that

> From the point of view of the minorities, I venture to say that without weightage reservation is of no use. I think several provisions can be embodied which would help us in forging our nation. Governors and the President can be vested with the power of nomination in cases where minorities fail to secure their adequate place under election. If such method is devised whereby reservation is done away with, then it would be a test of the majority also, as well as a step forward towards forging one nation. We have seen how the reservation and separate electorates have worked under the British regime; instead of becoming one nation, the country had been torn to pieces. The treatment simply aggravated the malady. We should take a lesson from that; we should know what steps we ought to take for knitting the country into nation. Majority community ought to find out ways for filling up the shortage, if any, in the representation of the minorities.

Since Ismail Sahib was the last speaker among the minority communities and immediately after he completed his speech by insisting that the provision for the separate electorate should continue, Algu Rai Shastri from United Provinces pleaded before the Vice President that the members belonging to the majority community should be allowed to express their views on the issue. The Vice President agreed to give one more day to the general discussion on the Draft Constitution. The last speaker on 8 November was Pandit Govind Malaviya who said,

> The article in the Draft Constitution about reservation of seats should have one further clause added to it … . The clause as it stands today, says that the reservation shall automatically go after ten years unless otherwise decided upon. All I want, Sir, is that if the minorities themselves or any section of the minorities themselves desire, even before the lapse of those ten years, to do away with this reservation, then, that Article of the Constitution should not be allowed to come in the way.

It was an interesting day in terms of the quality of the debate and the passion and conviction of the honourable members of the Constituent Assembly in the making of modern India. The next day was no different, as the general discussion continued and a considerable number of members voiced their views and thoughts on various articles of the Draft Constitution and some of them took up the issue of political reservation for minorities. The issue, however, seemed politically dear to the

Muslim members of the Assembly, but they wanted more than what the provisions of the Draft Constitution had provided.

On 9 November 1948, Professor N.G. Ranga made his position against reservation clear and by directing his argument against Muslims, he said, 'They certainly cannot claim any longer to be such a helpless community as to be in need of these'. Renuka Ray from West Bengal was prophetic in her opposition to the reservation for minorities:

> It is psychologically wrong to lay down, as it has been laid down, that after ten years the right shall lapse unless extended by amendment. I am sure that if this privilege is conceded now there will be clamour for its extension.

We now know that there is no provision for the political reservation of the religious minorities, whereas it exists for the scheduled castes and scheduled tribes. After every 10 years, the provision is extended for another 10 years. In this churning of ideas and arguments, Mahavir Tyagi[3] from United Provinces claimed that the idea of minorities is a fiction and nothing more. He said,

> The fiction of minorities was a British creation. The Scheduled Castes are not a minority at all, simply because a few castes of the poorer classes have been enumerated together in a schedule, they have become a 'scheduled minority' … . It is being perpetuated now because some of the opportunist families among them want to reserve their seats in the legislatures.

Then he appealed to the scheduled castes, the Sikhs, the Muslims and other minorities not to ask for reservation.

L. Krishnaswami Bharathi from Madras, who had supported Ambedkar's views on Indian villages and was to support him again on Article 35 with regard to civil code, offered an interesting analysis of the issue of minorities. He said,

> In a secular State the right to representation is only the right to represent a territory in which all communities live and if a member is representing in the Assembly, he has the right to speak on behalf of all those living in the territory, of all communities and classes, men or women. That should be the idea with which we must function.

> One Honourable member wanted reservation in services. I should think though it is not undiluted nationalism, we must for some time to come give them reservation in services. But one thing you must have clearly in mind. There must be time limit for all these peace or compromise moves and you must make it clear that after the lapse of certain specified period all these special provisions must go.

Bharathi also supported Renuka Ray's suggestion about making it absolutely mandatory for these reservations to disappear after 10 years. He also praised and appreciated Christians and Parsis for not demanding any reservation.

General discussion on the Draft Constitution concluded on 9 November 1948, but issues relating to reservation kept on coming up during the discussion of certain articles of the Draft Constitution. Keeping in mind the identification of various minorities which was done during the debates held between 1946 and early 1948, it is clear that there was not a single definitional basis of identification. Religion, caste and tribe and then region in the special case of Assam were the indicators of minority status determined by the Constituent Assembly. However, the discussions on minorities revealed that the members were identifying minorities on the basis of exclusive identity and the numerical size of the communities which, it was thought, was leading to their marginality and oppression. The issue of political representation emerged in an important way and moreover, it was also a continuity of the colonial legacy. What the members of the Constituent Assembly were doing was the perpetuation of the world view created and acted upon by the British Raj by understanding India as a country of communities. The project of postcolonial modernity was implicated in the community rights instead of individual rights. Partition of the country was a strong reminder that communities as units could be dangerous and a disastrous way of nation-building. However, Ambedkar, in his speech, had said categorically that with regard to the communities the country was sitting on dynamite and there was an indispensable need for acknowledging their claims for special rights as privileges. However, the way communities were identified created a category which comprised communities based on different criteria and communities within communities.

It may be reminded that electoral democracy is also a game of numbers and all parties work out their strategy to garner majority votes on various issues facing society by appealing to voters. Appealing to communities adds to the difficult task of touching each voter's perception. The British India had a history of communal conflicts, but the politics of numbers began with the separate electorate. And other things followed. It seems difficult to accept the argument that separate electorate led to the partition of the country. Separate electorate could have given rise to political isolation of the minorities as well. The dialectical reverse of the argument is that the experience of separate electorates at least for two decades made the Muslim League realise that such a provision could not be effectively used in the interests of the Muslims in the face of the overwhelming presence of the members belonging to the majority community in the parliament. Conversely, it might have functioned very well in a multiparty system, the rights of communities could have been recognised, but the politics would always operate in terms of seats and votes. All arguments put forward in favour of and against political reservation for minorities, when general discussion took place on the Draft Constitution, moved to the background at the time of debates on each article of the Constitution till 25 May 1949—the day which turned out be of a great historical importance.

I. A Day of Historical Importance

It was Wednesday and Sardar Vallabhbhai Patel presented the Report of Advisory Committee on Minorities in the Constituent Assembly. It was not just in continuation with the earlier report he presented in August 1947, but the total break from it. Patel argued that the conditions after partition had undergone a radical change. At the time of partition, the picture was not clear, though in 1947 all members of the Advisory Committee on Minorities, Patel pointed out, were not in favour of political reservation for the minorities. Patel referred to Dr H.C. Mookherjee, the Vice President of the Constituent Assembly, and Rajkumari Amrit Kaur to underline that Christians were opposed to reservation by characterising them as having 'highly nationalistic tendencies'. He then mentioned the Muslim members of the House and their views. Patel said,

> The House will also recall that the representative of the Muslims in South India, Mr Pocker, the no-changer and confirmed Muslim Leaguer, then proposed an amendment in this House when the proposals were submitted to the House, for introducing or continuing the separate electorates, the effects of which have been fully known and felt all over the country and perhaps, known outside too.

Patel further argued that due to partition the picture was not clear in 1947 with regard to the Sikhs.[4] The conditions which changed almost two years after the first Minority Committee Report, Patel pointed out, were the reasons for the new report.

Since the report was accepted, though there was some discussion, it is important to present here certain excerpts from the report, which was submitted to the President of the Constituent Assembly under the signatures of Sardar Vallabhbhai Patel on 11 May 1949, in his capacity as the Chairman, Advisory Committee on Minorities, Fundamental Rights and so on. Following are the highlights of the report:

> (3) When the ... recommendations [Reference to August 1947] were being considered by the Assembly, events were taking place, following the partition of the country, which made it impossible to consider the question of minority rights in East Punjab, particularly in so far as the Sikhs were concerned. This question of East Punjab was accordingly postponed; and also the question whether the right to contest unreserved seats should be given to minorities in West Bengal.
>
> (5) ... . Although the abolition of separate electorates had removed much of the poison from the body politic, the reservation of seats for religious communities, it was felt, did lead to a certain degree of separatism and was to that extent contrary to the conception of secular democratic state ... . Accordingly the Advisory Committee, with one dissenting voice, passed the said resolution as amended by Shri Muniswami Pillai in the following form:
>
> 'That the system of reservation for minorities other than Scheduled Castes in Legislature be abolished'.

One of the notable recommendations of the committee was the recognition to certain castes among the Sikhs as eligible for political reservation. In other words, the Sikh religious community was considered to be at par with the Hindu community.

II. Debate on Minorities

The debate on the report was concluded on 26 May 1949, and it engaged considerable number of members again. The President of the Constituent Assembly, on 25 May 1949, made it very clear that it was

> not as part of the Draft Constitution that this motion has been brought before the House. The question of amendments to the Draft Constitution will be introduced at a later stage. At this stage we are only considering the Report of the Advisory Committee dated the 11th of this month.

Following the remarks of the President of the Constituent Assembly, the discussion on the resolution began in which the Muslim, Sikh and Christian members spoke at considerable length to present their views. It is interesting to note that despite considerable amount of debate on minorities earlier, the matter was discussed again in great detail. The Muslim members were not unanimous on the abolition of political reservation, as moved in the resolution, for religious minorities. Some of them proposed alternative methods to make the democracy representative in this regard. The most vocal member was Mohamed Ismail Sahib from Madras—a Muslim League member and who later became the first president of the Indian Muslim League. He tried to clear the air of suspicion with regard to the patriotism of the Muslims in India. He said,

> The Muslims have demonstrated that those suspicions were unjustified and unwarranted. They have proved that they are in forefront in the defence of the country and in upholding the honour of the motherland. So, Sir, this is the change that has taken place in the country, but this change is not in favour of abolishing even the niggardly safeguards that were given to the Muslims and other minorities. On the other hand the change is for giving them better and real safeguards.

Ismail Sahib insisted that the Muslims were not in favour of abandoning reservation. He compared Europe and India and pointed out that unlike Europe where language and race are important, religion is the basis of differentiation among people in India. 'What we want is harmony not physical oneness or regimented uniformity'. He told the House that there was a provision of separate electorate for minorities in Albania, and it was not afraid of partition of the country due to the provision. By making the comment, Ismail Sahib made an attempt to disconnect separate electorate from partition as causal factor. He said,

> There is nothing wrong if we ask for separate electorate in this country ... . It is only when people have separate electorate, the real representatives of the people having that system, can go and represent their views before the Government or in legislature or before the majority community.

Ismail Sahib, logically speaking, was on a sound footing and his interpolation of the justification of the provision of reservation for the scheduled castes is the culmination of the logical construction of his argument. He said,

> The Scheduled Castes have been given and rightly given the safeguard of the reservation of seats for them in the legislatures. They fully deserve it; they are a class of people who have been the victims of oppression, if I may say so, and so many difficulties for ages; and therefore, now when we are emerging into the world of freedom, it is only right that they should also be given the freedom of coming before the world and saying what they want to say ... . But when they according to the majority community form part of that latter community, they follow the same culture and same religion and when they are of the same race according to them, yet it was thought fit ... that they should be given separate safeguard of the reservation of seats. When it is justified for them ... is it not all the more justified in the case of other communities which are admittedly different from the majority community?

Ismail Sahib made a considerably long speech to the extent that many members felt irritated and interrupted his speech, but the President clarified that since only Ismail Sahib had the principle amendment to propose, he had been allowed to speak. Ismail Sahib was one of the leaders of the Muslim League from Madras. Reminding the Assembly that the separate electorate was still in force as he had been elected under that system, he pressed for the continuation of the provision. Despite the fact that the general view was that separate electorate system was responsible for partition of the country, he argued against such a viewpoint. He claimed that harmony in the country could be achieved only if minorities were given political space and making the separate electorate as the fundamental right.

However, Z.H. Lari, a Muslim League leader and major campaigner for Pakistan, was a lawyer by profession. Though he was disappointed with the way Pakistan came to exist, yet he later on migrated to Pakistan. He moved Ismail Sahib's amendment by starting with the comment that he supported the approach of the Advisory Committee on Minorities. Then he said,

> My amendment really means that there should be multi-member constituencies, of say two, three or four to be fixed by Parliament—resulting in allowing the minorities to group their votes. The solution—and I may say so with all respect, to disarm a section of the House, though it is a very meagre section—the solution that I have offered is not a Muslim League mixture, it is a solution which was made as far back as 1853 when it was advocated by Mr Marshell in open letter, 'Minorities and Majorities, their relative rights' addressed to John Russell.

Lari emphasised that the problem of minorities was not unique to India and then he went on to refer various authorities and the case of Ireland to make his point. His scholarly arguments raised many questions and comments from two members, namely Lakshmi Kanta Maitra and K. Santhanam. In response to their comments, he referred the case of Switzerland and then outlined three reasons for the requirement of proportional representation. First, while giving the illustration of Socialists in United Provinces, where they got 35 per cent of the votes in 11 constituencies, but did not get a single seat, he pointed out the drawbacks of the majority vote system. Secondly, if the proportional representation was accepted, there would be no conflict between majority and minority. Thirdly, as a result of proportional representation, there would be a sizeable opposition in the House.

Thinking that Lari was asking for what should have been tenable in the absence of partition of the country, H.V. Kamath intervened, 'Why did you demand Pakistan?' Lari told him that he had opposed the creation of Pakistan in the meeting of the Muslim League held at Delhi and then proceeded on to speak again at length after this interruption. He took up the issue of reservation as such in the last leg of his speech arguing that why there should be reservation for the scheduled castes. It was an interesting point because Lari told the House that the scheduled castes, as part of the Hindu community, were basically a section of majority community. After Lari completed his speech M. Thirumala Rao from Madras (originally from Andhra Pradesh) stood up and said, 'I have got here a copy of the article on the Republic of Ireland. I do not find in it a single word of the quotation made by Mr Lari'. However, Lari did not respond to his comment. Pandit Thakur Das Bhargava from East Punjab then moved the amendment:

> The provision for reservation of seats and nominations will last for a period of ten years from the commencement of the Constitution.

The notice of similar amendment had also been given by Nagappa and Khandekar, but only Nagappa got the time and, quite a time, to speak. Nagappa, as his speech indicated, was from the scheduled Castes. He began his speech by praising Gandhi who, according to him, gave the Harijans an honourable place in Indian society and political freedom. Nagappa claimed that the Harijans were the original inhabitants of the subcontinent. He concluded his first leg of speech by saying that

> I have been telling you that the economic problem is the most important problem so far as this country is concerned. It is very easy question that can be solved if you make up your minds. You have been abolishing the zamindari all over the country. You have got lakhs and lakhs of acres of land. If you can give us, every Harijan family that is not possessing land; all the landless Harijans, at the rate of ten acres of wet land and twenty acres of dry land and educate the children to the University course, I am prepared to forgo the reservation. Here it is.

Mohan Lal Gautam from United Provinces commented that to get that size of land even a Brahmin was prepared to become a Harijan. Nagappa argued that the Brahmins did not have the experience of tilling the land and land should belong to the tiller. He further added that to become Harijan one had to be a scavenger. At that moment Z.H. Lari took the comment of

Gautam further by saying that he was willing to become Harijan for 10 acres of wetland. Nagappa repeated the comment that Lari should become scavenger to be a Harijan. When the President told him to confine himself to the motion, Nagappa made another speech outlining various aspects of the reservation for the Harijans and finally came to the point:

> As regards my honourable Friend, Pandit Thakurdas Bhargava, who claims the amendment to be his, namely, that the provisions regarding reservation of seats and nomination will last for a period of ten years, I would say this. We, almost all the Harijan Members of this House, sat together and the Honourable Pandit Nehru was kind enough to explain to us that in our own interest this will be the best thing. According to his advice we come to a decision on this point. After all, this is question that has to be reopened by Parliament. If, after ten years, our position happens to be the same as it is today, then, it is open to the Parliament either to renew it or abolish it. This does not prevent you from coming forward within next five or ten years or even two years with an Act of Parliament saying 'Harijans have been granted their demands, they are now on a par with others and they need not have this reservation'.

Nagappa's speech forms an interesting part of discussion on 25 May 1949, largely due to the reaction shown by the members on the motion moved by Patel. One of the various points one gathers while reading the debates is either the occasional interventions of Nehru and Patel or their frequent absence from the meetings. The responsibility of running the government might be the reason for their absence. However, Nagappa informs that on the issue of political reservations Nehru called all the 'Harijan' members and explained to them why they should support the motion. Obviously, despite the intense and, sometimes, emotionally charged speeches, many moves in the House were well planned and any issue of importance drew the attention of the major leaders of the Congress.

The perception that with the support of the members of the minority communities there would be greater legitimacy to the resolution than if done without them seemed ingrained in the mind-set of the leaders. It also implied that the debates and decisions were not always and solely settled on the majority votes, but certain legitimacy was sought from the representatives of the affected parties. Nagappa also highlighted the need for economic empowerment of the Harijans and his idea of 10 acres of wetland was not wrong, though in the light of the material conditions of the country it was impractical.

On 25 May 1949, another Muslim speaker Naziruddin Ahmad from West Bengal spoke against reservation for Muslims. He said, 'Reservation is a kind of protection which always has a crippling effect upon the object protected. So for all these reasons, I should strongly oppose any reservation for Muslims'. All other arguments he offered were aimed at reaffirming the above argument. He concluded his speech by informing that the Muslim opinion against reservation was widespread in West Bengal. The first Christian to speak was Dr H.C. Mookherjee from West Bengal. His opposition to reservation for minorities was well known. He spoke with the tacit understanding that the members were aware of his views. He again raised the issue that it was important to introspect whether they were trying to create a secular state. He particularly focussed on the backward groups and again raised the issue whether the political reservation would help them in improving their conditions. The third issue he raised was with regard to the trust the minorities could have in the majority community. He said,

> Now the question is: Can the majority community be trusted? The majority community has been very generous to every one of the minority communities. That is my firm belief. I may tell the House, Sir, with your permission that when for about two months I had the honour to occupy Chair which you are occupying today, I deliberately tested it for myself, whether we could trust the majority community. My Muslim, my Sikh and my Scheduled Caste friends will agree with me when I say that every opportunity was given to them by me so that they might voice forth their feelings and this was done with permission, with the silent permission of the majority community.

Begum Aizaz Rasul from United Provinces followed Mookherjee and supported the resolution by telling the Muslim members that reservation would 'tantamount to an act of charity on the majority community'. Begum originally belonged to the princely family of Malerkotla in Punjab but married into the royal family of Oudh. She was member of the Muslim League, but chose to stay back. She had every reason to say that 'those Muslims who wanted to go to Pakistan have done so. Those who decided to stay here wish to be on friendly and amicable terms with the majority community and realize that they must develop their lives according to the environments and circumstances existing here'. At this moment Syed Muhammad Saadulla from Assam and member of the Drafting Committee told the House that the issue of political reservation had been discussed with Muslim members, but the matter could not be decided. He was interrupted by B. Pocker Sahib, who claimed that no such discussion had taken place. Saadulla then asserted that Pocker Sahib might not have been in Delhi when the matter had been discussed. He pointed out that the reservation for Muslims would have tremendous psychological effect and then said,

> You admit reservation for the Scheduled Castes whose number is twice that of the Muslim community in India. You admit at least in two provinces the right of the Indian Christians for political safeguards or reservation. You admit it for the Anglo-Indian community. The only part where the recent report and the present resolution differ from the previous decision of the House is as regards the Muslims. I appeal to the House that they should not deny this safeguard when it is wanted by the minority concerned. If it is said that many members have said that they do not want it, let us take the majority view of the Muslim Members present here.

Proceedings of the day were concluded after Rev. Jerome D'Souza from Madras supported the resolution followed by Jagat Narain Lal's short speech in favour of the resolution.

On 26 May 1949, the Constituent Assembly met and resumed discussion on the Minority Report. The first to speak was R.K. Sidhva from CP and Berar and argued in favour of the resolution. Sardar Hukam Singh represented the Sikh minority community and he supported the resolution showering all praise on Sardar Patel for his kind words for the Sikhs. When Suchet Singh from Patiala and East Punjab States Union spoke later on, he followed the usual scheme of things. However, he appreciated the resolution for providing the reservations for the lower castes among the Sikhs and regretted, 'It is a matter for regret that Sikh society could not altogether succeed in eradicating class and sectional distinctions which it meant to wipe out'. He did not lag behind Hukam Singh in praising the two leaders at helm of power,

> What the Sikhs wanted was social justice and proper understanding of their legitimate aspirations which happily they have received abundantly at the hands of the architects of India's destiny—I mean the Honourable Pandit Jawaharlal Nehru and the Honourable Sardar Vallabhbhai Patel.

However, Nehru had already spoken in favour of the resolution, but was his usual self in presenting the issue in vague and imaginary way, making him an intellectual who was also reflecting on the issue while speaking. It would be interesting to know how he argued in favour of the resolution about which he stated that the support was so overwhelming that he had thought that there was no need to put his weight behind it. He said,

> There has been such an abundance of goodwill shown towards this motion that is hardly necessary for me to intervene in support of it. But I have felt the urge to do so because I wish to associate myself with this historic turn in our destiny: for, indeed, it is historic motion that my colleague, the Deputy Prime Minister has put before this House. It is a motion which means not only discarding something that was evil, but turning back upon it and determining with all our strength that we shall pursue a path which we consider fundamentally good for every part of the nation.

The opening lines of Nehru's speech clearly betrayed his conviction that the separate electorate was responsible for the partition of India. It seems strange that the modified version of the separate electorate in the form of reservation of seats was also categorised as an evil. Obviously, the numerically significant religious minority was only the Muslims. The scheduled castes were categorised as minority along a distinct axis of social discrimination. The depressed classes among the Sikhs were also recognised and made eligible for reservation in politics. Nehru stressed that thinking in terms of religious minority and majority in a democracy was wrong way of understanding the process because in democracy the will of the majority should prevail. However, the question was why there should be political parties along the religious lines. The formation of political parties might occur

> on other planes which will be mixed planes, thus developing the habit of looking at things in mixed groups and not in separate groups. At any time that obviously a desirable thing to do. In a democracy it becomes an essential thing to do, because if you do not do it, then trouble follows—trouble both for the minority and for the majority, but far more for the minority.

He then emphasised that he would rather go for ending reservation, but in the case of the scheduled castes it was needed and he did not regard them as religious minority. In his long lecture, Nehru remained vague most of the time. The following is the example of his ambiguity when the situation required clarity:

> Now I would like you to think for a moment in a particular way just to realise how the present is different from the past. Think of, let us say, five years ago which is not a long time. Think of the problems that you and I and the country had to face then. Make a list of them and then make a list of various problems that this honourable House has to consider from day to day. If you do this you will see an enormous difference between the lists. The questions that are before us demanding answer, demanding solution show how we have changed for good or for evil.

Nehru made little obvious that there should be no such thing as political reservation for religious minorities.

Tajamul Hussain followed Nehru and made it clear that he was against reservation for Muslims. He then told the House, 'Actually today there are 15 members present. And of them, four are for reservation of seats, three for separate electorates and the rest eight are with me'. He also added that the Shias had been 'opposing reservation of seats'. Sochet Singh from Patiala and East Punjab States Union expressed his happiness over the inclusion of the backward Sikhs in the gambit of reservation. Maulana Hasrat Mohani supported the resolution and said, 'I opposed the principle of reservation of seats at a time when Congress party was in its favour'. The last member to speak was the mover of the resolution, Sardar Patel, who reiterated his position and expressed satisfaction with the decision that was arrived at in the Committee. He also cautioned those Muslim leaders who had been insisting on the provision for separate electorates on communal basis by saying that their exclusion from power would happen. After the speech was over, the resolution was put to voting and it was adopted as part of the Constitution with an amendment that the reservations in politics would continue for 10 years.

Subsequent developments have shown that the political reservation is still continuing and after every 10 years the Lok Sabha has been extending the provision. Instead of following the wisdom of the Assembly debates that reservations are divisive, the Indian state is engaged in a debate on extending the reservation to other sections. Somehow the Indian leaders got into the trap of 'perfect world' and continue to be so. It seems that equal society marked by absence of discrimination, oppression and deprivation and prevalence of justice and freedom requires that there should be no reservations. Such a society cannot come to exist if the Indian state also ensures that capitalism should be the preferred social system. The British introduced all kinds of political conveniences, because understanding Indian complexity was not their cup of tea. The Indian leaders also did not show any intention of making an attempt in this direction.

The second issue involved in the entire debate on the reservation for minorities is the recognition of the presence of the depressed classes among the Sikhs as eligible for the provision of political reservation. There was no debate on the existence of such classes among the Muslims and Christians. Did they become prisoners of their own thoughts? Like Islam and Christianity, Sikhism also claims to be an egalitarian religion. However, the empirical reality, as various sociological studies have shown, is that there are castes among the Muslims as well as Christians. The notion of Dalit Christians is now in vogue in sociology. The Sachar Committee Report has shown that there are serious problems of poverty and exclusion among certain sections of the Muslims. Neither the Congress leaders such as Nehru, Patel and Azad nor the Muslim and Christian leaders such as Mookherjee, Mohani and Lari took cognisance of the fact of the existence of depressed castes among them. We thus find the demand in recent years for the recognition of Dalit Christians as the scheduled castes. We find that despite the serious engagement of various members of the Constituent Assembly on the issue of political reservation for minorities, the decision was neither justified in accordance with the empirical reality of the country nor was it discontinued after 10 years of implementation. The contemporary political reality of India renders the issue of political reservation for religious minorities irrelevant. Empirical reality shows that most of the candidates selected by political parties belong to the religion of the majority population in a constituency. As a matter of fact, caste and religion are two major considerations for the selection of a candidate for a particular constituency. The politics of identities is endemic in the democratic process of the country.

Notes

1. Please see Chapter 1 where issues concerning minorities have been discussed.
2. Chapter 1 covers those issues.
3. Mahavir Tyagi (1899–1980) belonged to Moradabad district of Uttar Pradesh. Parsad (1974: 367–368) informs that he joined army and in the First World War he fought in Iran. Later on he joined Gandhi and was court-martialled. After independence, he became minister in the Indian Cabinet. After split in the Congress in 1969, he broke away from Indira Gandhi and remained in Congress (O). He was highly critical of Emergency imposed by Mrs Indira Gandhi in 1975.
4. Detailed discussion which took place on Sikhs and Punjab would be taken up in the next chapter.

4

Discoursing the Partitioned Voices

Punjab and Kashmir

Religion seemed to be haunting the Constituent Assembly during its entire period of existence. Whereas two states were partitioned due to religion, one state was divided as a result of conflict between India and Pakistan. This chapter takes cognisance of how the discourse of religious minorities changed in the debates of the Constituent Assembly. Two parts of the chapter focus on Punjab and Kashmir respectively. Since there was no religious issue in Bengal, it remained absent in the debates, but due to the presence of Sikhs in Punjab, the issues concerning them were debated.

When the Constituent Assembly was constituted in 1946, the spectre of partition loomed large on the anticipated independence of India. It is evident from the fact that on 9 December 1946, when the members signed the register and presented themselves, 25 members were from Bengal, including (surprisingly) Dr B.R. Ambedkar, and 12 members from Punjab but there was not a single Muslim among them. The Muslim League had boycotted or chose to be absent from the Constituent Assembly. Some prominent Muslim League members were destined to join the debates in the Constituent Assembly after the formation of Pakistan mainly due to their decision not to go to Pakistan.[1] There was also one category of people who were not present and their fate was not then clearly decided. These were the representatives from the princely states of the country—who were believed to be the loyal supporters of the British rule in India. Three states, which were discussed in the Constituent Assembly, shared certain features, one of which was a Muslim majority state. Punjab and Bengal were among the biggest states of the country and had decisive role in the affairs of the country. As it was destined to happen, these three states were partitioned resulting into some kind of trauma. The case of Kashmir was different, but when the matter came up for discussion in the Constituent Assembly in 1949, it was partitioned as a result of the 'war' between Indian armed forces and the Pakistani soldiers disguised as tribals.

Bengal and Punjab began to figure in the debates on the issue of representation in the Constituent Assembly. In view of the fact that both the states had been partitioned and major portions of their territories had gone to the newly formed sovereign state of Pakistan, it was important for the Assembly to work out the exact size of their representation. However, the number of members to be taken in the Assembly was to be ascertained on the basis of the population for which a reasonably exact estimate was required. Punjab was undergoing communal cleansing and the Hindus and Sikhs were crossing to Indian side of the border in large numbers and the Muslims, except those who were within the territory of the princely state of Malerkotla,[2] were moving to Pakistan. The number of people killed on both sides of the newly created border was considerable and the movement of people across border was unprecedented.

By the time the Constituent Assembly resumed its business of discussing the Draft Constitution on 16 May 1949, the perspective of the leaders towards the issue of minorities had undergone a decisive shift. Reservation as a means to assure the representation of all minorities, both religious and social, was seen as a logical corollary of the earlier provision of separate electorate in the case of religious minorities. In view of the fact that partition had been consistently and continuously interpreted as a consequence of the provision of separate electorate, the committee headed by Sardar Patel, as discussed in the previous chapter, had revised its earlier position with regard to the political representation of minorities. It is interesting to note that despite the Muslim representation, Saadulla being one of them, the committee resolved to recommend the quashing of the provision of political representation to the Muslims and other religious minorities.

West Bengal did not figure much in the debates after it was recognised that a particular number of members would represent the state in the Assembly, whereas Punjab presented an altogether different scenario. Earlier, there were two independent units, namely Punjab and princely states. Patiala and Eastern Punjab States Union (PEPSU) comprising princely states were formed in 1948 and merged with Punjab in 1956. PEPSU had its own representatives in the Constituent Assembly. Interestingly, Punjab was not a Sikh majority state, but the Sikhs constituted a large minority and could not be ignored. It was the third largest (after Muslims and Christians) religious minority in the country. Chaudhary Ranbir Singh[3] was the first to moot the idea of Haryana in the Assembly with the argument that the Haryana part of Punjab was not historically its part, but the British merged it with Punjab after 1857. Anything could have happened, but Chaudhary Ranbir Singh did not insist on the demand for Haryana without the nod from the Congress leadership. It was also the time when partition had caused certain reasons for grief, for it was a failure of the imagination of the secular India.

I. Punjab and the Sikh Issue

Patel presented the report by moving the motion on 25 May 1949 that political reservation for religious minorities stood abolished, but recognised the existence of depressed classes among the Sikhs. How did the committee arrive at the conclusion of recognising depressed classes among the Sikhs? Patel devoted considerable part of his speech on the issue of Sikhs and the following were his opening sentences on the Sikh community:

> At a later stage we had to meet again because our proposals were incomplete in so far as the East Punjab and West Bengal provinces were concerned, because when the House passed the proposals in the August Session of 1947, the effect of partition was not felt or known and the vast migrations that took place

> were at that time in a process of continuation and the position of the Sikhs was practically uncertain at that time.

Patel went on to elaborate the entire process and the formation of the subcommittee which took into consideration the views of the Sikh representatives and finally arrived at the conclusion.

Patel took time to explain why the Sikhs were treated differently from other religious minorities and he touched upon various sociological issues to justify the decision to recognise certain castes among the Sikhs as eligible for political representation. Mention of West Bengal without any suggestion or recommendation made it amply clear that there was no issue of religious minorities. Moreover, the Vice President, Dr Mookherjee, had already shown his opposition to reservation for religious minorities. The case of Punjab was thus different and the difference due to the presence of a religious minority required some attention. We do not know how many Hindus had been killed in Punjab and Bengal during partition riots, but singling out the Sikhs for victimhood seemed less than rational assessment of the partition events. Patel seemed clear about his understanding of the Sikh community as is evident from the following part of his speech:

> The Sikhs themselves have thought that certain classes of people amongst them, who have been recent converts, and who were originally Scheduled Caste Hindus, are suffering from the fault of the Hindu community. The Sikhs are suffering for the fault of the Sikh community and nobody else. Really, as a matter of fact, these converts are not Scheduled Castes or ought not to be Scheduled Castes; because in the Sikh religion, there is no such thing as untouchability or any classification or difference of classes … . The Sikhs, today it should be recognised, have suffered from various causes and we have to regard with considerable tenderness of feeling in taking into consideration their existing state of mind and provide as far as possible to meet with the situation.

The Sikhs were treated with 'tenderness', as Patel would say, but it was clear that on the issue of political reservation for religious minorities the Christian and Sikh members of the Assembly moved away from the Muslims. Why the Sikhs were regarded at par with the Hindus so far as the identification of the scheduled castes were concerned is a matter for probing and interpretation. Much more important was the process in which Punjab and Sikhs began to appear as coterminous. Furthermore, when debate began on the new recommendations of the Minority Committee, none of members raised the issue of the Sikhs and both Muslims and Christian members did not point out that there were depressed classes among them. Their silence on this matter would have brought them to a certain degree of ridicule, for it would have been the acceptance of the fact that their egalitarianism had failed in India. On this issue, the learned Muslim and Christian members could not even have cited the instance of slaves in the United States as Christians. Only Mohamed Ismail Sahib took up the matter and said,

> The Sub-Committee appointed to report on the minority problems affecting the East Punjab and West Bengal met on 23rd November last year and recommended that the arrangements already approved by this Assembly in August 1947 for other provinces should be applied to those provinces as well and that no deviation was necessary.

Then he added that since the present report had opened the matter for reconsideration, it had also opened the issue for debate.

What the Muslim and the Christian members of the Assembly did not say, Sardar Hukam Singh[4] stated clearly and unambiguously on 26 May 1949, though his argument was not taken up by others. He said,

> We were told [reference to Patel] that the Sikh religion does not acknowledge any discrimination on account of caste and that for securing certain political rights for the section, the Sikhs are sacrificing certain principles of their religion. I am afraid I think otherwise because, when we say that all safeguards for religious minorities should go, it would only be natural corollary to that. If we give concession and certain privileges, certain rights to the Scheduled Castes simply because they are backward socially, economically and politically and not because they are religious minority, then other classes, whatever their religion, whatever the professions of their religion, who are equally backward socially, economically and politically must also be included in the list.

What Hukam Singh said made a lot of sense and could be empirically verified. Later on, when the Indian sociologists began to take up the study of castes in right earnest, the evidence of castes among the Muslims and Christians was overwhelming. At present the expression 'Dalit Christians' is frequently used. It is interesting to note that the persons belonging to the depressed classes were not categorised as the scheduled castes if they were Muslims or Christians. Although presently, assertive voices are being heard regarding the recognition of the Muslim and Christian Dalits as the Scheduled castes. None of the Muslim and the Christian members of the Constituent Assembly rose to reaffirm Hukam Singh's comments. However, when Sochet Singh from PEPSU spoke, he did not say much on the issue except for showering praises on Nehru and Patel for being so considerate towards the Sikhs. Subsequent speakers, particularly those belonging to the Muslim community, did not show any interest in Hukam Singh's argument and lost an opportunity to underline the problem of social marginality in India across religions. The religious self-pride prevented both the Christian and Muslim members to take up the issue of untouchable castes among them. Sardar Patel spoke at the end as the mover of the motion before it was put before the Assembly for voting and he had more things to say about Sikhs. He said,

> I have always held the Sikh community with considerable respect. I have been their friend even though sometimes they disclaimed me. On this occasion also I did advise them that if they insisted I will give it to them and induce the Committee to agree. But I do feel that this is not in their interests. It is for them to decide. I leave it to them to ask for this concession for the Scheduled Caste Sikhs does not reflect credit on the Sikh community .... I do not grudge this concession to the Sikhs to take control of the country and rule. They may be able to rule because they have got capacity, they have got the resources and they have got the courage. In any field, either in agriculture, in engineering or in the army, in any walk of life you have proved your mettle. Why do you begin to think low of yourself? That is why I am asking the Scheduled Caste people also to forget that they are Scheduled Castes?

In the middle of his speech, he mentioned the conversion of Sikh Dalits to Christianity in Pakistan. The closing argument of Patel was devoid of substantial argument on the issue of the Sikhs, but it was clear that the Sikhs were singled out as religious minority which had suffered considerably during partition riots. The identification of four castes, namely Mazhabis, Ramdasis, Kabirpanthis and Sikligars, as the scheduled castes among the Sikhs to be eligible for political reservation was also an example of shoddy work done by the Minority Committee, for there were many other scheduled castes among the Sikhs. The issue of special privileges in the form of political reservation was understood as a necessary evil, though, at the same time, it was regarded as divisive in the light of the connection which the Indian leadership developed between separate electorate and partition. How far such an understanding was appropriate is an altogether different matter.

Perspective of the Subcommittee on Sikhs: Before closing the discussion on Punjab by starting an altogether different trajectory of discourse, which has drawn tremendous attention in the history of postcolonial India, it is important to remind that the present chapter began with the issue of representation in the Assembly from West Bengal and East Punjab. What had happened actually was that the entire discussion revolved around the Sikhs as religious minority. The reason for giving such an extensive space to the Sikhs in the discussion was obviously due to the twists and turns in the decisions made by the Minority Committee. In August 1947, the decision was taken to give reservation to minorities in legislature (both central and provincial) as well as services. However, the discussion remained confined to political reservation when the Minority Committee revised its recommendations and moved the motion to end all reservations for minorities except the scheduled castes and certain castes among the Sikhs. The special subcommittee which recommended the above consisted of Sardar Vallabhbhai Patel, Jawaharlal Nehru, Rajendra Prasad, Ambedkar and K.M. Munshi—among the most prominent personalities in the Constituent Assembly. It is essential to know how the subcommittee worked out its recommendation:

> These decisions were reached at a time when the effect of the Radcliffe Award on the population structure of the East and the West Bengal Provinces was not accurately known, and a tragic and immense migration of population was taking place across the frontiers of the East and West Punjab. The Assembly accordingly decided to postpone consideration of the whole question of minority rights in the political field to be provided in the Constitution for Sikhs and other minorities in the East Punjab. They also agreed, at the suggestion of the representatives of West Bengal, to postpone consideration of the question as to whether minorities in the Province should have the right to contest general seats in addition to having seats reserved for them according to population strength.[5]

The report further informed that the 'most important problem' which the subcommittee received was with regard to the Sikhs. Various representations were submitted for Constitutional safeguards to the Sikhs, which ranged from none to numerous safeguards. The Shiromani Akali Dal (henceforth SAD) put forward the following five demands:

1. that the Sikhs should have the right to elect representatives to the legislature through a purely communal electorate;
2. that in the Provincial Legislature of East Punjab, 50 per cent of the seats and in the Central Legislature 5 per cent should be reserved for the Sikhs;
3. that seats should be reserved for them in UP and Delhi;
4. that scheduled caste Sikhs should have the same privileges as other scheduled castes; and
5. that there should be a statutory reservation of a certain proportion of places in the army.

The report of the subcommittee covered in detail the demands of the SAD, which it considered 'forthright', but 'too much'. At the same time, the demands of the SAD were neither identified as outrageous nor unacceptable by the subcommittee. The members of the subcommittee looked into the Sikh issue in a sympathetic way. It was aware of the 'tragic sufferings which the Sikh community suffered both before and after the partition of Punjab'. It was also noted that the Sikhs had suffered not only the loss of life and wealth (which Hindus had suffered as well), but they had also been deprived of their major shrines. As it turned out, such observations contained elements of future controversies. The most pertinent would be whether a community deserved special treatment as a religious minority as distinct from other religious minorities simply because it had lost some of its major shrines. The important question to ask was: what was the socio-economic condition of the Sikhs? Or what were the grounds on which the Akalis demanded 50 per cent political reservation. It became important for the subcommittee to make an observation on the general conditions of the Sikh community. The idea of minority as a concept also posed a serious challenge to the Constituent Assembly and sometimes members tried to point it out. However, it seemed that there had been an understanding that the numerical strength was one of the criteria of defining a minority. Parsis, Anglo-Indians, Christians, Muslims, Sikhs, scheduled castes and scheduled tribes were defined as minorities in India. Subsequently, Buddhists and Jains would join the list of minorities. The following observations of the subcommittee could be taken as one of the contradictions in the definition of minority adopted by the Constituent Assembly:

> The Sikhs are a minority from the point of view of numbers, but they do not suffer from any of the other handicaps which affect the other communities dealt with by the Advisory Committee. They are a highly educated and virile community with great gifts not merely of soldiers but as farmers and artisans, and with a most remarkable spirit of enterprise. There is, in fact, no field of activity in which they need fear comparison with any other community in the country, and we have every confidence that, with the talents they possess, they will soon reach a level of prosperity which will be the envy of other communities. Moreover, while, in the undivided Punjab, they were only 14 per cent of the population, they form nearly 30 per cent of the population in the East Punjab, a strength which gives them, in the public life of the Province, a position of considerable authority.

What was true of Sikhs at the time of independence may still hold valid at present. However, the separatist movement in the 1980s raised serious questions on the contribution of the Sikhs to the nation-building process in India, though all the Sikhs did not participate in that movement. However, 25 May 1949 marks the beginning of a new discourse which was created by SAD and is known to everybody, that is, the Sikhs are discriminated against by the Congress. Later on, when SAD established complete control over the Shiromani Gurdwara Parbandhak Committee (SGPC), another addition was made, 'Panth is in danger'. As a logical corollary to the rejection of the demands of the SAD, it was possible to argue that the then Sikh members of the Constituent Assembly had *betrayed* the Sikhs. However, the report of the subcommittee clearly and unambiguously identified two elements in the demands of the SAD which could not be accepted. First, a community could never get higher percentage of reservation of seats than its population proportion. Secondly, the SAD had drafted its demand for the separate electorate along the lines of the demands of the Muslim League and it was the perception of the most of the members that the provision for separate electorate had brought unfortunate consequences for the country. There was still another issue which prevented the subcommittee from recommending some safeguards for the Sikhs. How could the Constituent Assembly accept safeguards for one religious minority without providing the same for others at the same time? As a result, the subcommittee concluded,

> We cannot conceive of any valid argument which would justify the inclusion in the Constitution of safeguards for the Sikhs which are not available to the Scheduled Castes ... . We are convinced that to accede to the demands of the Shiromani Akali Dal will lead, by an inevitable extension off similar privileges to other communities, to a disrupting of the whole conception of the Secular State which is to be the basis of our new Constitution.

One may say that the Constituent Assembly after accepting the recommendations of the Minority Committee maintained the consistency of its approach to the religious minorities and upheld the concept of secular state which it alleged as the most cherished goal. The notable issue in the proceedings of the Constituent Assembly on 25 May and 26 May 1949 was that the Sikh members did not support the Muslims on the issue of reservation for minorities, whereas the Christian members opposed any reservation. The paradox in the case of the Sikhs emerged strongly when we find that the SAD, which was part of the Congress movement till 1948, put demands similar to those of the Muslim members later on. It is important to mention, as the subsequent developments in Punjab showed, that the issue has remained simmering and comes up as and when the SAD has to say something against the Congress Party.

In 1956, PEPSU was merged with Punjab and in 1966 the Punjabi Suba was formed. Owing to the linguistic census as well as the Hindi agitation, the issue of language had become highly communal within a decade of independence. The Punjabi Suba—the state of Punjabi-speaking people—turned out to be the Sikh majority state largely due to the recording of Hindi as the mother tongue by many non-Sikhs Punjabis, particularly a major section of the Hindus. Had the language issue been not communalised, East Punjab even after the merging of PEPSU might have never become the Sikh majority state.

Before we take up the Kashmir issue as debated in the Constituent Assembly, it is important to see what the subcommittee had to write about West Bengal, which was covered in the last paragraph of the report:

> The only reason why the Assembly postponed consideration of the question of giving to minorities in West Bengal the right to contest unreserved seats was that it was pointed out by the West Bengal representatives that the population structure of that Province was not known at that time. Although, on account of the recent exodus from East Bengal, any accurate estimate of the number of different communities in West Bengal is a matter of some conjecture, the broad picture is known clearly enough and we do not think there are any reasons why the arrangements already approved by the assembly for other Provinces should not be applied to West Bengal.

Thus, the curtain had fallen on the partitioned voices and the issue was settled. The partition, treated emotionally in the beginning, turned into a subject of rational and logical consideration. The provision of separate electorate on communal basis was identified as the culprit as a flea hidden behind the elephant. In the annals of the Constituent Assembly debates, the Muslim League, if not Muslims and the legal provision of the separate electorate created by the British became the responsible actors for partition. A perception inherited by the next generation created an environment in which not only the Muslims but also the other religious minorities were put in a state of insecurity where they had to constantly prove their patriotism and nationalist spirit. From here began the tragedy of postcolonial India.

II. Kashmir and the Referendum

The partition of Kashmir was not a part of the partition of India as such, but it was the result of the way the princely states were handled by both Pakistan and India immediately after they became two separate sovereign nation-states and the two fought proxy war within few months. The story of Kashmir is well-known largely due to the on-going contestation between Pakistan and India. The Kashmir issue in each country keeps the people united against the other. It may continue *ad infinitum*, but anybody who raises the issue of referendum to know what the people of Kashmir want could be attacked and insulted. However, the discussion in this chapter is limited to the debate which took place in the Constituent Assembly. It all began with the issue of the representation of Kashmir in the Constituent Assembly.

Kashmir drew the attention of the Assembly on 27 May 1949[6] on a trivial matter of representation when N. Gopalaswami Ayyangar[7] from Madras moved the resolution that addition should be made to 'paragraph 4 of the schedule of the Constituent Assembly':

> 4-A. Notwithstanding anything contained in paragraph 4, all seats in the Assembly allotted to the State of Kashmir may be filled by nomination and the representatives of the State to be chosen to fill such seats may be nominated by the Ruler of Kashmir on the advice of his Prime Minister.

The step to add representatives from Kashmir to the Constituent Assembly was taken after more than one and half years. The ruler of Kashmir had signed accession in October 1947 and since then no step had been taken to nominate the representatives, whereas in the case of all other princely states the matter had been successfully concluded. It indicated the special circumstances in which Kashmir was made part of the Indian Union. Ayyangar took time to explain the addition of Paragraph 4A and his explanation could be regarded as his as well as other leaders' apprehensions of the diverse reaction of the members. Ayyangar explained,

> Before I go to the Rules, I must point out that all states which have acceded to the Indian dominion have been included in the Schedule to the Constituent Assembly Rules. One of these States is Kashmir. Again, in the Draft Constitution that has been placed before the House, in Part III of Schedule I, Honourable Members will find Kashmir as one of the States which would be put into that Schedule. But, so far as representation goes, the procedure has undergone changes from time to time on account of the difficulties that cropped up in respect of implementing the rules that were originally framed for the return of State's representatives to this House. The list of such rules is contained in Rule 4 of the Constituent Assembly rules that are now in force. In this rule, the seats allotted to the States have to be filled up, not less than half by elected members of the legislatures of the States concerned, and the remainder to be nominated by the Ruler himself.

From the above statement of Ayyangar, the matter seemed relevant only in the technical sense of the membership in the Assembly of Kashmir, which was governed by certain rules. He then went on to narrate salient features of events that had unfolded in Kashmir.[8] At the end of his speech, he informed the members that there was a suggestion that Kashmir should be rechristened as Jammu and Kashmir. In response to a query made by Pandit Lakshmi Kanta Maitra from West Bengal, he replied that Kashmir meant 'the whole of Jammu and Kashmir'.

Maulana Hasrat Mohani stood up and told the President that he opposed the motion, but was interrupted by the latter informing him that he could do so after all amendments had been discussed. The first to move the amendment was Professor K.T. Shah who suggested addition or deletion of certain words in the original motion. Pandit Balkrishna Sharma requested Shah that he should 'read out to the House how the motion would read'. Shah read out the proposed amendment:

> Notwithstanding anything contained in para 4, the seats in the Assembly allotted to the State of Jammu and Kashmir may, pending the holding of plebiscite under the auspices of the United Nations Organisation, and without prejudice to the results of the plebiscite, be filled by election by the Praja Sabha of Jammu and Kashmir and the representatives of the State to be chosen to fill such seats may be elected.

There was no commotion in the Assembly on what Shah had proposed and interestingly, after framing the paragraph as an amendment he went on to explain his position. He was aware that his amendment could create emotional reaction and he made it clear that the issue of Kashmir was 'coloured very deeply by long-standing prejudice' and 'there would be deep feeling on the matter'. After claiming that he was personally acquainted with Kashmir, Shah proceeded on to explain his amendment. His first argument was why he had suggested that instead of Kashmir it should be the 'State of Jammu and Kashmir'. He said,

> It is a fact denied by the honourable Mover of this resolution, that that is the correct name of the State. And those at any rate who remember the campaign of the present Prime Minister of the State in connection with 'Quit Kashmir' will realise that in the sequence of events that had occurred, it is liable ... to be gravely misunderstood whatever nomenclature is allowed to be used.

Interestingly, when Shah started explaining the issue of plebiscite decided by the United Nations, B. Pattabhi Sitaramayya[9] from Madras interrupted him. He said that there was no connection between the issue of plebiscite and giving representation to Kashmir in the Assembly. The President asked Shah to explain the issue.

Shah responded,

> It has been the declaration of the highest authority in India also that the accession of the State made by the Maharaja, who was complete constitutional head on the day that accession was agreed to, was subject to confirmation by the result of the plebiscite.

Nehru reacted strongly to Shah's clarification by saying that what he said was absolutely incorrect. 'I am amazed, surprised and astounded that such a statement is made by Professor Shah', Nehru was perturbed by the motion of Shah. Shah responded by saying that he was amenable to correction if his statement was established to be wrong. However, it was obvious that most of the members were hostile to his motion. The President of the Assembly, despite his role as a neutral player in conducting the debates, seemed equally hostile when he said to Shah,

> The point is whether the accession was conditional. The accession, so far as I understand from the Prime Minister was unconditional and complete. The result of that accession maybe altered as a result of the plebiscite, but the accession as such was complete and final. Therefore the question of the accession does not arise.

Shah insisted that he was not against the induction of the representatives of Jammu and Kashmir in the Constituent Assembly, but Pandit Balkrishna Sharma made it clear to the House that the point of order raised by Sitaramayya was important and inclusion of representatives from Jammu and Kashmir must not be mixed with the issue of plebiscite. Ghanshayam Singh Gupta supported Sharma after which the President told the House that the point of order raised by Sitaramayya was valid and the House was only concerned with the issue of representation. Shah accepted the ruling of the President and started second part of his amendment in which he had proposed that the representatives should be taken by election of the Praja Sabha. He said,

> Now in the original motion, the whole of the representatives of Kashmir are required to be nominated and that too nominated on the advice of the Prime Minister. We have taken it for granted that the Government or that authority represents the majority of the Kashmir population. That would have been evident had any new elections taken place. But circumstances have changed and the nationalist party has come to power. The facts must be remembered by the House that the population of Jammu and Kashmir, put together, is something like 76 per cent Muslims and 24 per cent Hindus, including Dogras and other non-Muslims. It is for the House in its wisdom to decide whether, given this composition of population given this course of events that have happened in meanwhile, whether it is possible that the election could take place on a fair basis even while the frontier itself is in danger; and even while, though the 'cease-fire' has been declared, truce has not yet been signed and peace has not yet returned to the State. The danger to Kashmir, or rather danger to India from any untoward happening in Kashmir is left to the imagination of the House than any words of mine can describe.

Shah continued to speak by clearly showing his apprehension that most of the members would not like his wise counsel on the existing situations and possible future scenario of Kashmir issue by taking the events that had unfolded immediately after independence as the basis of his arguments. He insisted that elections should be held in Kashmir to elect the representatives in the Constituent Assembly. He made the issue complicated by arguing that Praja Sabha should elect representatives and the President cross-examined him on the issue with curt queries. After he was snubbed by the President, Shah became the target of verbal attacks from other members. Following exchange of dialogues on the Praja Sabha which Shah claimed was the only elected body which would sufficiently indicate what was happening:

> Pandit Balkrishna Sharma: May I know from the honourable mover of the amendment when the elections to the Sabha took place?
>
> Prof. K.T. Shah: In November or December 1946.
>
> Pandit Balkrishna Sharma: Was there snowfall in Kashmir at that time?
>
> Prof. K.T. Shah: I do not know that. The elections were held in winter.
>
> Pandit Balkrishna Sharma: The present Prime Minister was then in prison.
>
> Prof. K.T. Shah: He was not the Prime Minister then. He was in prison.

Only when Shah was reasonably ridiculed by Sharma that President intervened which meant that Shah should conclude his speech. Shah raised a pertinent issue by pointing out that lot of money (100 crore) had been spent and lot of lives had been lost, but there had been no gain. At this moment, Nehru protested what Shah had said by saying that the House was not debating on the future of Kashmir. Shah's voice was lost among the powerful voices which followed Nehru's protest. Kamath pointed out that Kashmir should be regarded at par with other states, whereas Sidhva wondered why a simple matter had been made complex and 'why extraneous matter is brought in by the Honourable Member'. It obviously referred to Shah. Nehru expressed his uttermost dislike when he said, 'The Honourable Member is a master of irrelevancy. He does not quite understand what has happened'. Interestingly, Kamath pointed out that the Prime Minister was becoming impatient on the matter to which Nehru said, 'Depressed'.

Despite being aware of Nehru's displeasure over seemingly simple matter of nominating representatives from Kashmir, as had been done in the case of other states, Kamath raised another issue. He told the House that he had read in the newspaper that the 'Maharaja of Kashmir' was going out of the country for some time. He also suggested the change in the nomenclature of 'Prime Minister of Kashmir', as it was causing confusion. Maulana Hasrat Mohani was the next speaker and he sought clarification on various matters with regard to the accession of Kashmir and the nomination of representatives, but only after making it clear that he did not care how the representatives were nominated. In view of the alleged fact that Kashmir had acceded to India, it had every right to send its representatives to the Constituent Assembly. He said,

> I accept this contention of the Prime Minister that this accession has been complete although I am doubtful whether he is absolutely right in this. Because, he himself not once or twice, but many times, has said that this accession depends on the final decision of the plebiscite, of the votes of the Kashmir people. Of course, now, he has made up his mind; he has created difficulties and his move is that this plebiscite will never take place and therefore he says that this accession is complete and there is no doubt about it ... . Unless and until you decide the status of Kashmir Government and the status of the Maharaja, it is hopelessly absurd to set down any proposal of this kind. It is on this ground that I totally object to this motion.

Maulana Hasrat Mohani's speech further provoked Nehru to intervene, for most of the times Nehru did not effectively participate in the debates and he intervened only in those situation where he could decisively shift the decision in a particular way. In other words, he always spoke to influence the decision. Nehru's speech is a combination of making subjective judgements on empirical situations with an air of idealism. At the same time, despite being irritated/depressed on the proposed amendment of Shah, he seemed polite but desperate. He began by commenting that there was the Kashmir problem and as an issue it was 'difficult and intricate' and should be separated from the simple matter of representation. He then began commenting on the amendment proposed by Shah. He said,

> I say that I have a vast admiration for the erudition and learning of Prof Shah. Nevertheless, I have followed with some surprise not only what he said today, but what he has said and done in regard to Kashmir for a number of years. I have also been connected with Kashmir in many ways and, in a sense, I belong to Kashmir.

He then responded to the amendment of Shah. He pointed out that Praja Sabha was bogus because the elections to it were held under questionable circumstances. Interestingly, Nehru pointed out that the elections to the Praja Sabha were boycotted by the 'decent' people. Nehru further informed that the elections of the Praja Sabha were held in winter when people could not vote. Above all, Sheikh Abdulla was in prison and even when he put up candidates they were arrested. All such people had gone to Pakistan. Nehru reaffirmed that Professor Shah was not aware of the conditions of Kashmir and his proposal was 'monstrous'. After that he requested Maulana Hasrat Mohani to accept minor changes in the 'wording of the motion'.

In view of the fact that N. Gopalswami Ayyangar was the mover of the motion, he finally rose to respond to various issues and he took up the issue of plebiscite with a degree of openness. He said,

> The accession is complete. No doubt, we have offered to have plebiscite taken when the conditions are created for the holding of a proper, fair and impartial plebiscite. But the plebiscite is merely for the purpose of giving the people of the State the opportunity of expressing their will, and the expression of their will, will be only in the direction of whether they would ratify the accession that has already taken place—not ratify in the sense that that act of ratification is necessary for the completion of the accession, but if the plebiscite produces a verdict which is against the continuance of accession to India of the Kashmir State, then that we are committed to is simply this, that we shall not stand in the way of Kashmir separating herself away from India.

Ayyangar's speech did not carry the conviction of a political leader who was capable of enforcing his will. Nehru had not even mentioned the issue of plebiscite. Except for drubbing the Praja Sabha as bogus, Nehru did not take any significant issue related with Kashmir. The members of the Constituent Assembly delved into the technical matters of representation and it seemed that even the Legislative Assembly did not take up the matter of plebiscite seriously. Why did it happen? It seemed that on the issue of Kashmir, Nehru's will and charisma had prevailed. If we go by the existing literature, we come across an interesting fact about the partition of Punjab. It is alleged that earlier Lahore was to go to India, whereas Gurdaspur district was awarded to Pakistan due to its Muslim majority status. Nehru traded Gurdaspur with Lahore. The reason was that Gurdaspur district was the only link with Kashmir through plains (Lapierre and Collins, 2011). Obviously, Kashmir was in the scheme of the Indian leaders. Nehru admitted that he was personally interested in Kashmir, for in a way he was Kashmiri.

Shah seemed a sensible voice with an element of pragmatism. He talked about war without any returns to India. Knowing quite well that his views would fall on deaf ears, he articulated the issue of plebiscite in Kashmir from the perspective of the United Nations. On top of that it was clear that India had approached the UN and then it rejected the plebiscite. Considering that accession of Kashmir was complete was an indication enough that there would not be any plebiscite. India should not have approached the UN, but it did and made Kashmir the issue of contention between India and Pakistan, which has turned out to be the apple of discord between the two.

In the end, we may take up the issue of Kashmir for discussion because the discussion that took place in the Constituent Assembly was incomplete. There were obvious signs of irritation on the part of some Congress leaders when Shah raised the issue of plebiscite. The hostility of otherwise rational Nehru was transparent and seemed out of character. The paradox of Kashmir issue is located in the way the UN recommendation of plebiscite was ignored and accession treaty between the Indian government and Maharaja Hari Singh was upheld. Kuldip Nayar (2012: 61), the veteran journalist, has made the following comments on the issue:

> Mountbatten later told me that Patel agreed to let Kashmir go to Pakistan if the state so wished. 'By sending its irregular troops into the state, Pakistan spoiled the whole thing', added Mountbatten. He was, however, worried that Nehru's Kashmiri ancestry would lead him to unwise decisions.

Nayar (2012: 63) also tends to respond to another enigma of why Indian army had not taken over the whole of Kashmir. He informs that he asked Lt. Gen. Kulwant Singh this question whose response was: 'He said the prime minister had instructed him to go up to the area where population spoke Kashmiri. Nehru did not want the army to go into the Punjabi-speaking territory'.[10]

Once accession had taken place the issue of plebiscite seemed irrelevant, but the UN resolution stands in the way of legitimacy to the accession. Shah was not out of context, but the way he was snubbed might never be justified by any supporter of Nehru and other Congress leaders.

Notes

1. Migration to Pakistan from India predominantly started from particular areas. In the case of the Muslims from the southern parts of India, it did not occur. Therefore, many Muslim League members such as Pocker Sahib remained in India influenced by both their choice and the absence of migration from their constituencies.
2. The Muslims of Malerkotla in Punjab were protected by the Sikhs owing to the close relationship between the Sikhs and the nawab. It is alleged that the nawab of Malerkotla opposed the execution of the two sons of the tenth Guru of the Sikhs in the early 18th century.
3. His son, Bhupinder Singh Hooda became the Chief Minister of Haryana from 2004 to 2014.
4. Hukam Singh emerged as the most vocal representative of the Sikh community during the Constituent Assembly debates. He is remembered as the speaker of Lok Sabha till 1967. According to Major Gurmukh Singh (1996: 292–294), Hukam Singh was born at Montgomery in 1895 and had his preliminary education at his birth place. He did his LLB from Law College, Lahore. After

partition, he migrated to the Indian Punjab. 'On a motion from Giani Gurmukh Singh Musafir, the Assembly, on 27 January 1948, approved to elect two Sikh and two Hindu members from the East Punjab. By a stroke of luck and again with the help of Giani Kartar Singh, Hukam Singh was elected a member'. Rest is history.

5. The report of the subcommittee was submitted under the signatures of Patel.
6. The entire debate on the issue of representation took place on 27 May 1949.
7. N. Gopalaswami Ayyangar (1882–1953) hailed from Tanjore district of Madras Presidency and was a graduate of Law College, Madras. He was a bureaucrat and was uniquely qualified to speak on Kashmir because he was appointed Dewan of Kashmir in 1937. He was also a minister in the Union Government after 1947 (Subrahmanian, 1973).
8. Considerable literature is available on the circumstances of the accession of Jammu and Kashmir to the Indian Union.
9. B. Pattabhi Sitaramayya was from Krishna district of Andhra Pradesh and was a doctor by profession. He was appointed governor of Madhya Pradesh in 1952.
10. There seems to be no refutation of the facts narrated by Kuldip Nayar.

5

Property Acquisition

In the Name of Community

One of the primary concerns of sociology is to examine how an inegalitarian society maintains consensus of values and sustains equilibrium. Inequality of wealth and property has historically remained significant factors in not only building the critique of such a society but also a reason for change and revolution. In the context of this crucial importance of property, it was important to see how the issue of ownership of property was taken up in the Constituent Assembly. The fact that the idea of socialism dominated in the minds of many members, it was pertinent to know whether private property would be treated as sacrosanct or crime. Keeping in mind these objectives, the discussion has been divided into two parts. The first deals with the issues of right to property, whereas the second part takes stock of how the relationship between property and community was sought to be established by the members of the Constituent Assembly, particularly Jawaharlal Nehru. But first some general comments on property.

Property, in the recent times, has become a much wider concept including even ideas, inventions and resources. The mention of property conjures up multiple images of good, evil and respectability. There is a fundamental difference between two major views, namely belonging and ownership, to understand the external world in relation to human kind. Belonging subsumes not only the mankind but also all the living creatures, whereas ownership is linked with the idea of wealth and property as an exclusive human reality. Scepticism demands that we should not ignore the intense struggle in the animal world over the territory, but the emergence of the world marked by the domination of the humans transforms this imperative into nation-state and collective will. Within the given society, property as an institution as well as structural principle has evolved over a period of time. However, the modern state has kept and sustained its power and right to acquire any property in the name of the interest of the community and society. There are two aspects of property ownership which have remained in practice and therefore part of the custom/tradition: ownership of property and inheritance of property. Leasing out property varied across time, but rentier class constituted an important category in our identification of social groups. Arrival of ideologies of anarchism and communism (and earlier, certain religious sects) began to question the private ownership of property particularly in the 19th century.

Ideologies against private ownership of property were largely an outcome of reaction against capitalism which simplified social stratification by destroying birth-based privileges. In a way, Europe experienced secularisation as a result of destruction of communities and emergence of societies. The birth of sociology was recognition to the fact that the overlapping of physical and social spaces did not correspond to village communities. The birth of cities assured the death of communities and the idea of social without any communitarian basis began to define how society was different from community. In this social world, property became the main criterion of recognition, status and wealth, by giving rise to distinct life styles, which even marginalised religious charity and emphasis on simple and frugal living. The opposition to private ownership of property began in a crystallised form in the 19th century through the emergence of anarchist and communist ideologies and this opposition was independent of the religious discourse in support of the poor. The communist ideology, after Marxism became its theoretical foundation, did not have any religious-spiritual basis. The materialist philosophy of Marx recognised capitalism as a powerful and revolutionary system, but not the absolute and final social and economic system. The critique of property divorced from religious ideology was the major change that took place in the 19th century.

The members of the Constituent Assembly predominantly belonged to the Congress and unlike the present times, the Congress was a movement comprising members having different and sometimes opposing ideologies. Hindu right wings, socialists of all varieties and liberals were all there in the Congress. Predictably the issue of property seriously engaged the members and the debate reflected their diverse ideologies. The debate on property was going to decide whether India would be adopting the socialist path or would be going the capitalist way, though all varieties of socialism was not synonymous with the idea of social ownership of property so far as the Indian socialists were concerned. There were shades and diversity of views on the idea of socialist India with regard to private ownership. In addition to ideologies, the class background of the members was an important basis of the views they held. Combination of ideology and class background created multiplicity of views turning the simple issue of compensation to the acquired property into the ideological contestation and clash of classes.

I. Right to Property

It is important to remind that one of the most exploitative socio-economic systems in India as introduced by the British in 1793 (by Lord Cornwallis to be exact) was the zamindari system. Essentially the zamindari system was a system of revenue collection. There were two other systems of revenue collection and these were Ryotwari system and Mahalwari system. Whereas under Ryotwari system the owner of the land was responsible for the payment of revenue, the entire village was liable to pay the revenue under the Mahalwari system. The introduction of Permanent Settlement created a new system of revenue collection under which a class of intermediaries was created which was accountable to pay revenue to the government by collecting it from the cultivators. The system was such that it virtually took away the ownership rights from everybody and brought the control over land under the zamindars. One of the biggest zamindars was Raja of Darbhanga and interestingly, he was the member of the Constituent Assembly. Under Ryotwari system of revenue collection, there existed a large number of big landowners who had created a class of non-hereditary tenants to get their land cultivated. The abolition of zamindari system never meant the end of big landlordism. Even the issue of ownership under the zamindari system was a contestable subject.

The discussion on property-related rights began with the presentation of the interim report on the fundamental rights in the Constituent Assembly[1] on 29 April 1947. There were two interesting rights included in the interim report covered under 'Rights of freedom' and 'Miscellaneous Rights'. Under the former, it was proposed that the citizen of the country could live, settle and acquire property anywhere in the country, whereas under the latter it was proposed that no personal property could be acquired without adequate compensation as prescribed by the law. The latter was going to be the major subject of debate after two years, but the discussion on fundamental rights hinged on culture, minorities and untouchability. On 30 April 1947, Rao Bahadur Chaudhary Suraj Mal from Punjab made two interesting points and proposed amendments to the interim report. He argued that on the issue of freedom to follow any trade and occupation, there was a need to do something with regard to agriculture. He then spoke in support of biswedars/zamindars arguing that they should be protected, for they were the major sources of soldiers of the Indian army in Punjab. Prithvi Singh Azad[2] from Punjab voiced his strong opposition to Suraj Mal's defence of biswedars. Azad said,

> There is a black law in the Punjab, which is, known as Land Alienation Act. The purpose of this amendment [moved by Suraj Mal] is to preserve this law. It is highly detrimental to our depressed and other non-agricultural classes. It has allowed those who go under the name of Zamindars or label themselves as peasants to permanently enslave a large section of people in the Punjab.

Azad's argument was well placed. The major provision of the Land Alienation Act, 1901, was that the traditional non-peasant castes could not own land by purchasing or mortgaging it. It is a general perception that the act was passed because the Punjab peasant was progressively losing land to the moneylenders due to indebtedness. The British had passed the act in order to stop the negative consequences of the introduction of colonial capitalism which reflected in the high level of indebtedness among the Punjab peasantry. True to the colonial spirit, the law never prevented the alienation of land because traditional peasant castes could always buy and mortgage land. The ghost of usurer entered the body of the peasant castes. However, Punjab was an exception in this matter.

On 2 May 1947, Sardar Vallabhbhai Patel moved Clause 19 (Miscellaneous Rights) which dealt with acquisition of property:

> No property, moveable or immoveable, of any person or corporation including any interest in any commercial or industrial undertaking, shall be taken or acquired for public use unless the law provides for the payment of compensation for the property taken or acquired and specified the principles on which and the manner in which the compensation is to be determined.

Patel made it clear that he did not expect any amendment, but discussion followed and amendments were moved. 2 May 1947 was the last day of the debate on interim report on the fundamental rights. Discussion followed after the motion was moved and members presented their views on different matters concerning acquisition and compensation and property. The most important element which occasionally emerged was the philosophy and history of property in India. S. Nagappa from Madras argued that compensation given to the owner of property should be reasonable and by reasonable he meant it should be according to class variations in the society. He said,

> Once you acquire land, you must see that the tiller of the soil is made the owner of the soil. Then alone we will be able to give a kind of encouragement to the toilers and make them increase the produce and the national wealth for the maintenance of the country. I hope this clause will not stand in the way of the provinces pushing forward land legislation which they have in some cases already undertaken ... . Once the zamindaris are

> abolished and the Government acquire their properties, it must be their endeavour to make the best use of such properties. The Government must see to it that collective farms are formed and that, through them, the maximum is produced and the tiller is given sufficient for what he does.

Subsequent speakers continued to attack the zamindari system and argued that the matter of compensation should not be considered to be universally applicable and zamindars did not deserve to get compensation at par with other cases. The debate did not go further as the President asked Patel to respond to the issues raised by the members. Patel said that the entire discussion had been misplaced. The proposed clause was not meant for the zamindars. It intended to cover that property which could be acquired by the government for public purposes. When put to vote after Patel's comments, the clause was passed. The matter regarding property was settled for the time being. It was destined to come up again for discussion largely due to the vital nature of the property matters.

II. Property and Community

The debate on Article 24 was taken up on 24 September 1949—more than two years after the earlier debate in 1947 when independence was not far away. It began with Amendment No. 369 which was moved by no less than the then Prime Minister, Jawaharlal Nehru. Nehru proposed that Article 24 as existed in the Draft Constitution should be substituted by his amendment, which was as follows:

> (1) No person shall be deprived of his property save by authority of law.
>
> (2) No property, moveable or immoveable, including any interest in, or in any company owning, any commercial or industrial undertaking shall be taken possession of or acquired for public purposes under any law authorising the taking of such possession or such acquisition, unless the law provides for the property taken possession of or acquired and either fixes the amount of the compensation, or specifies the principles on which and the manner in which, the compensation is to be determined.[3]

There were four more subclauses of the amendment proposed by Nehru to Article 24, which covered compulsory acquisition of property. The Constituent Assembly had not seriously discussed the issue of property except for the debate which took place in early 1947 when the matter dealing with the fundamental rights was taken up. So far the Constituent Assembly seemed to be engaged and subsequently divided along lines of community, religion and caste. It was least expected that the mundane matter of acquisition of property could generate a debate which would create divisions among the members as interest groups. It may be reminded that the Raja of Darbhanga was member of the Constituent Assembly and had hardly spoken on any matter. It is quite likely that he might have excused himself from attending the meetings. Nehru, after moving the amendment, pointed out that outside the Constituent Assembly, Article 24 had generated lot of discussions. After making it clear that the clause was controversial, Nehru made an observation whose historical significance could not be ignored. He said,

> It is true that there are two approaches to those questions, the two approaches being the individual right to property and the community's interest in that property or the community's right … . This amendment that I have moved tries to remove or avoid that conflict and also tries to take into consideration fully both these rights—the right of the individual and the right of the community.[4]

Nehru made it clear that 'expropriation without compensation' was made impossible by the proposed amendment. He went on to emphasise fair and equitable compensation for the individual owner of property which would be acquired by the government. He said, 'No community should injure and invade rights of the individual unless it be, for the most urgent and important reasons'. Nehru was aware of the difficult times which the independent India faced at that time. The transition from colonial economy to the economic autonomy of the sovereign state was a painful process. He showed his knowledge and familiarity with the changing conception of property indicating that the right to property could not be regarded as sacrosanct/divine. He made clear that

> Conceptions which had appeared to us basic undergo changes. And I draw the attention of the House to the very conception of property which may seem to us an unchanging conception but

> which has changed throughout the times, and changed very greatly, and which is today undergoing a very rapid change. There was a period when there was property in human beings. The king owned everything—the land, the cattle, the human beings. Property used to be measured in terms of cows and bullocks you possessed in old days. Property in land then became important. Gradually the property in human beings ceased to exist. If you go back to the period when there were debates on slavery you will see how very much the arguments were advanced in regard to the property in human beings as are sometimes advanced now with regard to the other property. Well, slavery ceased to exist.

Nehru went on to elaborate on the changing conceptions of property across time and referred to the contemporary period as the time when a few people tend to monopolise every property. In other words, Nehru talked about concentration of wealth in few hands which had begun in the 20th century in a noticeable way.

Nehru's ideas at the general level seem quite radical almost approximating socialist and communist ideologies. As is evident from the excerpt of his speech above, he almost said (if we use enthymeme) that time could come when there would be no private property. He almost sounded Marxist when he said,

> The small man is crushed out of existence by the modern tendency to have money power concentrated in some hands. Thus the old conception of the individual owner of the property suffers not only from social developments, as we see them taking place and from new conceptions of cooperative ownership of property, but from the development on the old lines when a rich man with capital can buy out the small one for a song.

It was thus important to provide safeguards to individuals, but all individuals are not located at positions of disadvantage. There were zamindars and 'zamindaris' and Nehru made it quite clear that the present government was committed to abolishing both. He attributed central significance to the land question not only in India but also all over Asia.

It may be reminded that land legislation was a state matter and the constitutional provision could only provide for a broader framework for carrying out land reforms. Nehru's socialistic assertion in the beginning of his speech gave way to the question of adequate compensation to the zamindars. The contestation between the individual and the community was far more complex than anybody could have imagined. For example, it was important to acquire land in the public interest and, in such matters, it was not necessary that the land would belong to big landowners, rich landlords and zamindars; it could belong to small and marginal owner. Taking away land of such persons would have implied the taking away of livelihood of such individuals. Justice demanded that such individuals should be duly compensated. However, taking away the land of the zamindars and allotting the same to the tenants offered altogether different parameters of justice. These zamindars had been exploiting large number of tillers of the land by charging exorbitant rent.

Nehru's speech and the amendment he moved led to the division of the members on the basis of class interests and ideology. The amendment evoked tremendous debate and it seemed that class and ideology had taken over all the issues related to community, caste and religion. The debate concluded on 12 September 1949 (forenoon) and when it was put to vote, it was passed by the Assembly by adding one more clause to it. The participation of the members was considerable and they pointed out technical flaws in Nehru's amendment or moved allegedly better amendment than his. Some of them offered theoretical perspectives on the institution of private property, whereas most of them seemed to be taking the position which was favourable to their class interests of the rich. Speeches of various members exhibited their widespread familiarity with legal issues, their breadth of knowledge and their ideological commitments. Some of them who made a difference by showing alternative modes of understanding the external world did hit upon the institution of private property. The proceedings' discussion is confined to some of the speeches.

Criticism of the amendment was initiated by one of the two socialists in the Constituent Assembly, namely Damodar Swaroop Seth.[5] While moving his amendment to amendment 369 on 10 September 1949, he offered a critique of Nehru and the Congress Party. He said,

> If a Socialist Republic has actually to be established in this country, or as the President of the Indian National Congress promises every now and then, that there will be a classless society in this country during the next five years, then a Socialist Republic or a class society are not to be dropped on this land of ours from Heaven like Manna. If they do mean anything, it requires some spadework and clearing of way by dealing property with the question of the economic rights of the people.
>
> We cannot confuse personality with property; nor can we forget the social and functional character of property. Man has no natural right in property. Claim to property is acquired by law recognised by community. The community, sir, has always reserved to itself the right to modify laws with respect to property and acquire it from its owners in the common, social and economic interests of the people. Property is a social institution and like all other social institutions, it is subject to regulations and claim of common interest.

Seth continued to dwell upon the issue of property as a concept which, he pointed out, had been changing over a period of time. He strongly argued that 'development of national economy' and the right to private property could be irreconcilable and the latter must not be allowed to stifle the former. Therefore, compensation for the acquired property must not be treated as sacrosanct. He also emphasised that it was impossible to fully compensate all the owners of properties. Professor Shibban Lal Saxena said that Nehru's amendment would make the Supreme Court judges powerful and asserted that the amendment was 'negation of all that the Congress had stood for'. Saxena, among interruptions, quoted from Gandhi a few lines where acquisition without compensation had been recommended. At this moment, he seemed to have become emotional and concluded his speech by saying that 'Socialists have come and attacked this article that it is not democratic. I oppose this amendment because this is a negation of all I have stood for in my life'.

Brajeshwar Prasad expressed his surprise that instead of Ambedkar, the amendment was moved by Nehru. He said, 'As long as there is poverty and illiteracy in this country no Parliament will be able to play any vital part in Indian politics'. He further added, 'If we do not give compensation and concede justiciability there will be no industrial development in the country'. As a Congressman, he also shared the dream of socialism with other fellow party men, but offered an interesting insight into the peasant psychology wherein he is both Marxist and Platonic. He said,

> There is also the apprehension in our minds that most of the members of the future Parliament of India will come from the ranks of peasant proprietors who will each have their own private property and therefore it would be very difficult for those who have got their own private property to rise to the height of the occasion and take a detached view of things. I hold the view that the system of peasant proprietorship is the greatest hindrance in the way of socialism and progress. There is much truth in the Marxist theory that the state is an instrument of exploitation in the hands of the dominant group in society. Therefore I say that this power should be taken away from the hands of Parliament and vested in the hands of our philosopher-kings.

It is quite clear that divergent voices within Congress as well as the Constituent Assembly touched upon the then available philosophies to articulate different ideas. Kishorimohan Tripathi from CP and Berar moved the amendment and expressed disagreement with Nehru and asserted that the article as moved by him, discriminated between 'industrial property and landed estates', which might create an 'unhealthy atmosphere in the country'. One of the major speakers on 10 September 1949 was H.V. Kamath, who was among the most vocal members of the Constituent Assembly. He observed that Prime Minister's amendment was aimed at protecting the few and he questioned the rationale of such an amendment. He said, 'I was wondering whether this doctrine of protection of the few, should be the foundation of our state'. To explicate his viewpoint he quoted four lines from Shelley's famous poem 'To the Men of England'.[6] And then added, 'Therefore, sir, I would suggest in all humility that the foundation of our State should be that the many should be protected and the few should be justly dealt with'. He then commented upon Nehru's articulation of concept of property:

> I think that ideas about property have ranged from the divine right to property, in other words, the sanctity of private property, to the almost whilst dictum of M. Proudhon that 'Property is

> theft'. The movements for and against property have been based on this whole gamut of conceptions relating to property .... I can only say that it is not the divine right of the individual to property, but it is the right of God himself to all property, and so for *all* His children on earth. All this trouble about property could have been obviated, could have been got over if only men had clearly understood what the divine right meant, that it meant that the property should be utilised justly and wisely in the interests of the whole mankind.

Kamath, the Gandhian, who alluded to the relevance of Gandhi's notion of trusteeship, was followed by Prof. K.T. Shah, the socialist with proposal of numerous amendments. In his long speech on the justification and rationale of the amendments he moved, he offered sociological insights into the notion of property and the role of the state in this regard. The history of all amendments moved by Shah in the Constituent Assembly indicates that his socialist vision of India was rejected by the socialist-minded Congress leaders. One could anticipate the fate of his amendments in the case of property acquisition too. However, he offered an alternative and insightful viewpoint on the issue of property. He made it clear that he disagreed with Nehru's primary position that no property should be acquired without compensation. He raised the issue of 'right to be compensated' implicating justice and ethics with regard to the ownership of property. Referring to the earlier quoted remark of Proudhon that property is theft, he commented,

> I am afraid 'theft' perhaps is very often too mild a word because much of the property has been acquired—if you go into the origins of this—by force, fraud and violence which under any system of ethics can hardly be justified. If you are going to seek to compensate those who have acquired property, no matter how long since, by such means as force or fraud or violence or theft, I am afraid you would not be acting up to the ethical standards which are supposed to animate this Constitution.

Shah referred to the United States where slavery was abolished after the civil war and the owners were not compensated, but he added that the British compensated the slave owners in West Indies to end the institution without violence. He made a general observation that 'nefarious' forms of property had not been compensated in many countries. He pointed out that there is a discrepancy between 'sense of economics and of ethics'. He added,

> Property is not an ethical institution .... It is an economic institution with close connection with ethics. I may say the economics has suffered because of this divergence from ethics, and holding property sacrosanct and demanding compensation even if property is acquired by force or fraud or is used or abused or even unused.

He identified certain 'categories of property' which should not be compensated. First, unused or of poorly used agricultural property, namely zamindari land, land used by private individuals, corporations or firms for public utility and social services and urban lands held by individuals with the hope that its price would increase. Second, added natural wealth in the form of mines and forests which are given to individuals at concessional rates. The third category he identified was industrial and commercial undertakings. He also warned against compensating those industrial and commercial undertakings 'whose assets are much below their liabilities'.

Shah offered an alternative paradigm of making modern egalitarian India by dismantling the foundations of the Indian economy which was essentially characterised by colonial mode of production. In the context of property possession/non-possession, we find two alternative models of Indian modernity whose roots could be traced back to the Western modernity and to achieve it the Indian economy had to undergo the process of modernisation. These two modernities, generally christened as socialist/communist and liberal/capitalist, offer us two alternative models of development and modernisation. In the debate on villages in the Constituent Assembly, we found two alternative modernities within the framework of liberal tradition. Nehru offered a paradigm of property which was primarily rooted in the capitalist path of economic modernity. Shah did not argue for a communist model, but insisted upon the issue of ethics and social morality in the conduct of economic life.

Jadubans Sahay from Bihar followed Shah and moved the amendment that all clauses except the first of the proposed article should be removed. All the three parties, namely industrialists, zamindars and common masses, he argued, were not satisfied with it. Along the changing conceptions of property, he pointed out, the world was also changing and from the divine right of the sovereign the societies have reached a state where the sovereignty of the people had become divine. He said, 'Are we going to hold out hopes for the future that industry in this country will be nationalised or socialised in the interests of the people? No. The Constitution does not hold any hope'. Then B. Das reiterated that there was an immediate need for the removal of intermediaries between the peasants and the state. As a Congressman, he lamented the fact that majority of the Congressmen had already resolved both outside and inside the Constituent Assembly that 'equitable compensation should be paid for properties acquired', but in the end Das went on to support Nehru's amendment. S. Nagappa from Madras characterised the article as non-justiciable and said,

> All these days the State has given protection to the zamindars or capitalists to acquire the properties. Now we are requiring the properties for the State, for the good of the State, for the betterment of the common people in order to maintain the national economy of the country. So we must also take into consideration how these capitalists and zamindars have been responsible for the fall of national economy by not utilising the property in a proper manner, that is to say, by not reducing the required amount value out of the capital that has been in their possession.

Nagappa moved the amendment stating that the provision should not be more than five per cent of the market value of the acquired property.

Pandit Thakur Das Bhargava reminded that the existing law regarding the acquisition of property was contained in Act 1 of 1894 which provided for the compensation prior to the acquisition. He also informed that the rule of compensation was determined in terms of the market value of the acquired land plus '15 per cent for disturbance'. Dr P.S. Deshmukh viewed the proposed Article 24 as half-hearted one because 'it neither protects private property, nor does it confiscate it'. He warned,

> in spite of all our efforts to keep communism away, [it] is getting more and more popular with our people, if we do not want to go back on the off-proclaimed promises held out under different

> conditions and circumstances, it would be necessary for us to go much further than we have been able to go in this particular formula.

On 10 September 1949 when the Constituent Assembly re-assembled at 4 pm after lunch, the contesting stands taken by the socialists and liberal democrats gave way to the defenders of propertied classes of which many were zamindars and businessmen. Naziruddin Ahmad was the first to come in support of the zamindars when he moved the following amendment:

> Provided that when any such law provides for the acquisition by any State of the interests of the Zamindars of various degrees and other intermediaries for the purpose of abolishing the Zamindari system, it shall be sufficient if the law provides for the payment of compensation amounting to not less than twelve times the estimated average net income of the Zamindar of any degree or any intermediaries whose interests are to be acquired.

Naziruddin Ahmad delivered a long speech in justification of his proposed amendment. He pointed out that it was only in Russia that property had been acquired without compensation and made it clear that if it happened in India, then it would be supporting the communist ideology. He identified communists, socialists and the authors and supporters of Article 24 at par differing only in their methods. He stated that whereas the communists would use violence and the socialists would do it through speeches and theories, the supporters of the article would do the same through legal means. He argued that though he was not a zamindar, but it was important that the Constituent Assembly should treat zamindari as a form of property. He said,

> I was a very petty zamindars but I sold away my interests 5 or 6 years ago, for I saw what was coming. Today I am independent, free and dispassionate, a man having absolutely no interest in that question. I am safe and happy. But those poor zamindars who believe in the stability of the law of the land are today sadder, though wiser.

Naziruddin Ahmad was also speaking within the framework of fundamental rights and was raising an important issue of continuity and change. It was quite clear that the legitimacy of the Constituent Assembly existed within the framework of both colonial rule and colonial law. Therefore, it was mandatory politically as well as normatively for new leaders to keep constitutional provisions within the framework of continuity of certain privileges. Revolutionary change was not expected from the then majority party for obvious reasons of the conditions under which India had achieved sovereignty. The socialists were trying within the same framework to work out the revolution forgetting that property relations could not be changed under circumstances when the zamindars and propertied people were members of the Constituent Assembly and had formed an interest group. Ahmad was one of those who publicly supported the cause of the zamindars who were under grave threat of extinction due to political and economic reasons. In case of their vanishing from the economic scene, they wanted to have the best of the bargains.

Who were the zamindars? Were they collectors of rent or owners of land? The matter became crucial due to the simple fact that only the owners of property could be compensated, whereas the collector of the rent could be treated merely as the functionary of the state. Kala Venkata Rao from Madras elaborated on the issue of zamindari rights from the experience of Madras Presidency. He started his speech by quoting Machiavelli that 'one will excuse the murderer of his own father but not the person who will take away his property' to point out the reasons for so much of debate on the matter. He argued that property should not be treated as of a single species and in the case of the zamindari the notion of property did not apply because 'when the *sanad* was granted in 1802, or earlier than that in Bengal when the Permanent Settlement was introduced, the *sanad milkiyat intimrari*, gave the right to the zamindars to collect the rent only'. He asserted that the zamindars never got the proprietary rights under the system. He pointed out how the zamindars did not discharge their obligations according to the provisions of the *sanad*. He said,

> It has been laid down that he must maintain irrigation works, etc. He never did anything of the kind. All the irrigation works are in disrepair and everywhere rent was increased nonetheless without any benefit coming to the ryots. Mr Veblen defined what

> a 'vested interest' in property means as 'a marketable right to get something for nothing'. We could have terminated this authorisation to collect rent by issuing a notice but we are giving compensation.

Rao faced challenge on the matter from the member belonging to his own state, Madras. K.T. Ahmed Ibrahim corrected Rao as follows:

> My friend the Honourable Mr. Kala Venkata Rao said something about Zamindars. He proceeded on the assumption that the whole class of zamindars comprises of only farmers of revenue; but I would remind him that that is not a proposition which can be accepted without any qualification.

He then went on to classify various kinds of zamindars, such as '(a) descendants of rulers; (b) descendants of landowners who had paid the full cost of land; and there are zamindars, who were initially appointed as tax collectors but bought ownership rights'. Ibrahim's observations could be understood in two different ways. First, he was defending the zamindars and secondly, he was pointing out the complexity involved in the zamindari system and pleaded for treating the zamindars according to the merit of the case.

Guptanath Singh invoked Hindu religious tradition to point out that the history of property 'is a tale of awful woes, a story full of fraud, felony, exploitation, expropriation, inhumanity, injustice, treachery, torture, tyranny, and tears'. He concluded that all property belonged to the nation which was represented by society consisting of cultivators and labourers. He quoted Manu that the land belonged to cultivators. He showed his analytical skill by maintaining his position when he said,

> There is some discrimination made as between abolition of capitalism and zamindaries, between nationalisation of factories and other means of production and the abolition of zamindaries. Lands and factories both belong to the same category and both must be nationalised or socialised in the course.

His concluding comments were on Nehru—the mover of the amendment and in certain respects he defined Nehru as national leader and head of the government. He said,

> Panditji has moved an amendment and made a speech. If you give the speech of Pandit Nehru to a person without telling him whose speech it is, as also the amendment moved by him, the man will say that the speech has been made by some revolutionary and the amendment has been moved by someone other than a revolutionary. Pandit Nehru has certainly a revolutionary mind but the article in its present form seems to be framed by brains controlled by some unseen forces.

Lakshminarayan Sahu—a well-known poet, writer and scholar from Orissa—followed Guptanath Singh in invoking Hindu religious tradition by quoting Shankaracharya that 'wealth is evil' and added that 'Those who are after riches are even afraid of their own progeny'. However, Mahboob Ali Baig, in his long speech, made an attempt to reasonably situate the issue of property at its rightful place. He made it clear that the Indian society was based on capitalist system of economy in which the property was owned by private individuals. The Constitution as was being drafted did not provide for abolition of private property. Therefore, the matter before the Constituent Assembly was that the fair amount of compensation and the value of the property should be determined by the court of law. Before concluding the speech he alluded to the speech made by Kala Venkata Rao and expressed his agreement with him on two counts. First, the function of the zamindars as revenue collectors should be abolished and secondly, the zamindari system was anachronism and must be abolished. At the same time, he pointed out that the zamindars were vested with proprietary rights under the regulation XXV of the Permanent Settlement.

The Constituent Assembly met on Monday, 12 September 1949 after the debate on property remained unfinished on Friday despite efforts by the President to conclude the debate. The first speaker at 9 am was H. Siddaveerappa from Mysore state, who argued that under the Ryotwari system the landholdings were small and due to law of inheritance, the holdings had become still smaller and there was a need for a new kind of land reform in such cases. Krishna Chandra Sharma from United Provinces offered his views on the notion of property when he said,

> The present day conception of property is a functional conception. It is its work, its movement. You cannot have property deposited in your house or hold it always in your possession without any regard to question whether it serves any purpose, function or work whatsoever. The old conception of property today is an impossible one … . If the property does not help in its performance of any function or work and has no place whatsoever in the moving changes and structure of society, then the property is nothing; it is a useless thing and nobody can make any claim to it as property.

Sharma treaded along the beaten path and began to touch upon Proudhon's ideas on property, which tended to suggest that the socialists, within and outside Congress, shared ideas of social construction. Despite understanding property as theft, such ideas as and when expressed never came close to the abolition of private property, as was the case with the communists, but insisted upon the superior right of the community over the individual. In other words, socialists' ideas about property were confined to the limited purpose of establishing the moral right of the state to acquire property for the common good, though in the years to come, the acquisition of property for the common good was destined to be interpreted favourably towards the industrial houses. Sharma's amendment was the last in the list of the amendments proposed by various members of the Constituent Assembly after which the President opened all the amendments for discussion. The first to comment was the Raja of Darbhanga—the biggest zamindar of India—Kameshwar Singh.[7] He showed his displeasure with the amendment moved by Nehru and added,

> I am aware of the fact that the Congress party, which is an overwhelming majority in the House, is pledge-bound to abolish the Zamindari system but it is equally pledge-bound to do so on payment of equitable compensation. Now, in implementing the first part of its pledge, is it not fighting shy of implementing its second part, by preventing the question of the abuse of power by State legislature in the matter of determination of compensation from going to judiciary?

It was quite clear that the zamindars and their supporters had accepted the impending abolition of intermediary tenures, but they wanted a settlement and adequate compensation duly adjudicated by the courts. Alladi Krishnaswami Iyer pointed out that many landholders had challenged the validity of the Act.[8] Without the constitutional provision, he pointed out that it would take several years to finally settle the issue by the Supreme Court. He concluded his speech by saying that

> Law according to me, if it is to fulfil its larger social purpose, must serve as an instrument of social progress. It must reflect the progressive and social tendencies of the age. Our ancients never regarded the institution of property as an end in itself. Property exists for Dharma. Dharma and the duty which the individual owes to the society form the whole basis of our social framework. Dharma is the law of social-being and varies from Yuga to Yuga. Capitalism as it is practised in the West came in the wake of the Industrial Revolution and is alien to the root idea of our civilisation. The sole end of property is Yagna and to serve a social purpose, an idea which forms the essential note of Mahatma Gandhi's life and teachings. In the fervent hope that the amendment will further social progress of the teeming millions of the agricultural population of this country, I accord my whole-hearted support to the proposition as put forward by the Honourable the Prime Minister.

The idea that the path of development of India could be possibly tuned to its civilisational experience tended to ignore the more than a century old colonial mode of production, which was essentially capitalist in form and content. Iyer could think of social formations in cultural terms, but economy required a different approach. Despite all this he supported Nehru implying that he accepted the capitalist path. Shyam Nandan Sahay from Bihar was critical of socialists and argued that there was a need for incentives to the private owners without which economic growth was not possible. One of the notable things he told the Assembly was that there was hardly any difference in the conditions of the tenants cultivating land in zamindari system from those of Ryotwari system. Sahaya shifted his focus on the industrialists and said that they were contributing to the development of the country, which would not be possible if the means of production were socialised. He concluded his speech with the following remarks:

> Sir, it is more important for the Legislature and even more so for a Constituent Assembly that we should lay down only such law as

> will appeal to all sections of the people as being fair, just and equitable. I plead with the House to accept my suggestion for deleting Clauses (4) and (6). If, however, I am not able to secure approval of the House for my suggestion I shall content myself by exclaiming with Lord Byron that 'my only solace is that our tyrants are after all our own countrymen'.

Pandit Bal Krishna Sharma shifted to *Bhagavad Gita* to clinch the argument on the notion of property, though he inadvertently supported the view that compensation to the acquired property should be uniformly applied to make the principle justiciable. In the process, he offered his views on property and argued that if a person acquires property for his own comfort, then he is committing a sin. It is important to quote some of the lines of his speech as:

> The one fundamental issue now before the House is what sort of social concept we shall have and what sort of social concept we shall not permit to be incorporated in our Constitution: this is philosophy more than anything else—philosophy behind a certain idea or certain line of action which ultimately influences the conduct of society as a whole. We have seen that in the early nineties the idea brought by Darwin—Survival of the fittest—was accepted as true … . Now, this philosophy, this idea got hold of the mind of the Westerner to such an extent that every one of the notions there tried to be the fittest by way of increasing their armaments, with the result that within twenty-five years or thirty years two devastating wars engulfed them overtook them … Similarly if we today stand up here and say 'property is sacrosanct, property shall not be touched and any attempt to touch property will violate the principles which have been sanctified by tradition', then I would like this House to know that this is not the way in your forebears looked at this question.

Sharma then quotes from *Bhagavad Gita*, and when he begins to interpret the second couplet from *Gita*, the President reminded him that he was becoming too philosophical. Jagannath Baksh Singh from United Provinces spoke in favour zamindars and argued that the amendment moved by Nehru was wrong as it denied judicial redressal to their problems. Pandit Govind Ballabh Pant from the United Provinces offered all clarifications to the efforts of the UP government regarding the abolition of zamindari system and justified the amount of compensation being given to about 20 lakh zamindars in the state. The last speaker, before the mover of the amendment responded to various issues was Maulana Hasrat Mohani. Maulana opposed the amendment. He cautioned, 'Instead of abolishing the zamindari it will tend to establish and perpetuate an evil system of Bhoomidars that you are going to create who will have the same paraphernalia with them'. After Maulana's speech, the President moved the closure motion which was adopted and Nehru was asked to reply. Nehru requested the President to allow K.M. Munshi to reply on his behalf. After his request was granted, Munshi rose to speak. Munshi observed that all amendments could be put into four categories, thus (a) 'there should be no compensation'; (b) 'Parliament should not seize property under the fundamental rights'; (c) Parliament should have power without any judicial review of the compensation fixed by it and (d) with regard to zamindari system, Clauses (4) and (5) should be deleted. Munshi made it quite clear that the Congress would not backtrack from the promises it had made. Munshi told the House that he would accept the amendment of Yadubans Sahai, Kala Venkata Rao and Jaspat Roy Kapoor. After Munshi's reply, all amendments suggested were put to vote.

Among various amendments, when all were put to vote, only two with substantial proposals were adopted. One of these was the substitution of the following subclause in place of Subclause (a) of Clause (5) of the proposed Article 24: '(a) the provision of any existing law and other than a law to which the provisions of Clause (6) of this article apply, or'. In the second case a new clause after Subclause (b) was added which read as follows: '(c) The provisions of any existing law made or of any law which the State may hereafter make, in pursuance of any agreement arrived at with a foreign State or otherwise with respect to property declared by law to be evacuee property'.

After the adoption of the motion, the amended article was added to the Constitution after which the Constituent Assembly adjourned to resume after lunch at four in the afternoon of 12 September 1949 to debate the most emotive issue for the country, that is, national language. However, certain observations on the issue of property may be made by way of conclusion. Acquisition of property for public purposes/good seemed a simple matter for discussion, but to define how an acquisition could be good was a matter of perspective. The acquisition of agricultural land for industrial purposes could be interpreted as good as well as evil depending upon the context in which it would be done. However, the heated debate on property to be acquired in public interest was an indicator of the fact that even if the members of the Constituent Assembly belonged to the dominant party, that is, the Congress, they did not share common perspectives. At the same time, all of them were concerned for and committed to the development of modern India. In such a situation, the natural outcome could be envisaged in terms of what the main leaders thought and how they acted. In the case of property, Nehru's speech betrayed the existing ambivalence among the members with regard to property. The model of modernity got fractured into capitalist and socialist visions of modern India. The outcome was that despite the socialist commitments of many leaders, the path chosen was capitalist. The present scenario is the logical culmination of what was envisioned during the debates of Constituent Assembly by the leaders who could influence the outcome of the debates.

Notes

1. It may be reminded that what ultimately was included in the Constitution is not the concern of this chapter. Rather the focus is to identify multiple perspectives of modernity on property which emerged during the debates.
2. Baba Prithvi Singh Azad (1892–1989) was a freedom fighter from Punjab. He joined the Ghadar Party after reaching the United States in 1911 and after his return he was arrested, tried under the Lahore Conspiracy Case and was sentenced to death, which was later on commuted to life sentence in the Andaman Islands (Singh, 1974). Singh (1974: 411) further informs, 'After six years' stay there, he was brought back to India. Soon after he escaped from the jail and remained underground for sixteen years till he voluntarily surrendered in 1938 at the insistence of Gandhiji'. It seems that he remained a member of the Constituent Assembly for a brief time. However, he remains a legend in Punjab largely

due to his escaping and remaining underground for such a long time.

3. The other four clauses read as follows:

   (3) No such law as is referred to in Clause (2), of this article made by the Legislature of a State shall have effect unless such law having been reserved for the consideration of the President has received his assent.

   (4) If any Bill pending before the Legislature of a State at commencement of this Constitution has, after it has been passed by such Legislature, received the assent of the President, the law so assented to shall not be called in question in any court on the ground that it contravenes the provisions of Clause (2) of this article.

   (5) Save as provided in the next succeeding clause, nothing in Clause (2) of this article can affect:

   (a) The provision of any existing law, or

   (b) The provisions of any law which the State may hereafter make for the purpose of imposing or levying any tax or penalty or for the promotion of Public health, or the prevention of danger to life or property.

   (6) Any law of a State enacted, not more than one year before the commencement of this Constitution may within three months from such commencement be submitted by the Governor of the State to the President for his certification; and thereupon, if the President by notification so certifies, it shall not be called in question in any court on the ground that it contravenes the provisions of Clause (2) of Section 299 of the Government of India Act, 1935.

4. The title of the present chapter has been given from Nehru's idea of individual and community in relation to private property which he mooted while moving the amendment under discussion.

5. Damodar Swaroop Seth (1889–1966) belonged to Bareilly and was educated up to matriculation. He was involved in Kakori case and was imprisoned. He was a committed socialist. (Vyas, 1974).

6. These four lines are as follows:

   Men of England, wherefore plough for the lords who lay you low?

   Wherefore weave with toil and care the rich robes your tyrants wear?

   Rise like lions after slumber in unconquerable number,

Shake your chains to earth like dew, ye are many, they are few.

7. Kameshwar Singh (1907–1962), known as the Maharaja of Darbhanga, was one of the biggest zamindar of India. However, he is known for his charity and for establishing the Darbhanga Sanskrit University.
8. Iyer was referring to the Madras Estates Abolition Act.

6

Fifteen Years that Never Ended

The Language Debate

Diversity in India has been multidimensional, and each dimension requires separate and distinct treatment to make sense of what makes the people so passionate about certain issues that they transgress permitted boundaries of actions. Religion, caste, region and language form the core of the social and cultural existence of Indians. Of all the issues that confronted the Constituent Assembly, language and linguistic identities formed the core as well as the most complex issue, for the subsequent turn of the events showed how people reacted to constitutional provision in almost all parts of the country. English had struck roots in the 19th century as the common language all over the country for various administrative, judicial and academic purposes. Soon after, it turned out to be the language of communication among the educated people belonging to different linguistic zones. Dislodging English from its privileged position was essential for the leaders of the independent country to initiate the process of nation-building. However, if English was to be removed from its privileged position, then the identification and acceptance of an Indian language was a matter that offered tremendous challenges. There was the possibility of the language question remaining the subject of continuous contestations, whereas certain degree of consensus was a prerequisite for building the nation characterised by linguistic diversities.

Three issues began to reverberate right from the beginning of the meeting of the Constituent Assembly and remained postponed till the end. These were: name of the nation-state/country, national anthem and national language. Interestingly, only the issue of national language was debated by the Constituent Assembly thoroughly and passionately, but without coming to any decisive moment. As it turned out, the debate seemed inconclusive and the decision a compromise. The significance of the debate on national language lies in the way the members imagined India as a nation, articulated regional and linguistic identities and sought to build unity of purpose to lay the foundation of modern India.

In the Constituent Assembly, the debate on language did also involve the question of script, for the members were awfully aware of the significance of script in creating a homogeneous national identity. The unprecedented nature of the debate was evident from the fact that for the first time in the debates in the Constituent Assembly, unity instead of diversity, homogeneity instead of heterogeneity and mono-culture instead of plurality were on the agenda of the Assembly. Therefore, the objective of the debate was not only to arrive at a compromise language formula, but also to protect regional–linguistic identities. The divide between North and South was known, and the fate of English was inseparably linked with how far the members from South India could resist the pro-Hindi majority from the North.

With this general introductory background, we may now move to the actual debate which has been discussed at length in this chapter. Within the framework of the premise that India needed indigenous language to be the national language by displacing English from its high citadel, the discussion in the present chapter has been divided into three parts. The possibility of building a consensus on language for the nation implied overcoming difference within the party. The first part takes cognisance of this search for consensus. The second part takes stock of how the language question got delinked for various secular ideologies and replaced by regional and religious considerations. The third part is a narrative of a significant part of the debate when Purushottam Das Tandon,

Maulana Abul Kalam Azad and Raghu Vira spoke on the language issue.

I. Search for Consensus

Seth Govind Das had raised the issue of national language on 30 July 1949 when the Constituent Assembly met and he said that there were apprehensions that the matter of national language would be decided by the parliament. The President of the Constituent Assembly assured him that even the question whether the issue of national language could be left to the parliament was to be decided by the Constituent Assembly. Finally, the debate on language question as Part XIV-A of the Draft Constitution began on 12 September 1949. There were 178 amendments moved by the members of the Assembly due to which the President had some preliminary discussion with the members regarding the modus operandi of the debate to be followed. Interestingly, he invited N. Gopalaswami Ayyangar from Madras (though he had spent some time in north India) to move his Amendment No. 65. Ayyangar informed the House that that there had been series of discussions among the members in small groups and pointed out that there was unanimity among them with regard to the view that the language of the country should be a substitute to English. He said,

> The decision to substitute Hindi in the long run for the English language having been taken, we had to take also two subsidiary decisions which were involved in that one decision. Now the subsidiary decisions were that we could not afford to give up the English language at once. We had to keep the English language going for a number of years until Hindi could establish for itself a place, not merely because it is an Indian language, but because as a language it would be an efficient instrument for all that we have to say and do in future and until Hindi established itself in the position, namely that for a period of about fifteen years English should continue to be used for all the purposes for which it is being used today and will be used at the commencement of the Constitution.

All these lines spoken did not only have the historical significance, but also had symbolic importance. The amendment was proposed by a member from the Madras Presidency where anti-Hindi feelings were strong. However, nobody raised an issue that there could be consensus on two national languages, as has been the case with Canada. Bilingualism could not have been unnatural for a country like India's size. However, with the domination of English as the elite language, the idea of any other language would have further complicated the matter. The conditions prevalent at the time made it necessary that those who opposed Hindi had the choice of English as an alternative even if it was meant to be for 15 years. Ayyangar identified various challenges associated with the adoption of Hindi as the national language: (a) question of numerals, (b) issue of language of states and communication between states and between centre and states, (c) language used in legislatures and High Courts and Supreme Court and (d) whether Hindi could develop capacity to absorb ideas. He suggested:

> Our basic policy should be that the common language of India for Union purposes should the Hindi language and the script adopted should be the Devanagari script. It is also a part of this basic policy that the numerals to be used for all official Union purposes should be what have been described to be the All-India forms of Indian numerals ... We consider that to the same extent the Hindi language and the Devanagari script for letters in that language should form a permanent feature of the common language of this country, to the same extent should the international forms of Indian numerals be part of this basic policy.

Ayyangar then moved on to identify various problems in replacing English by Hindi at the various levels of administration and legislatures. He moved his amendment by suggesting that it should be added to Part XIV as the new Part XIV-A. The contents of the amendment proposed were quite comprehensive and consisted of four chapters. The first chapter of the proposed amendment covered the recommendation to have Hindi in Devanagari script and to keep English for 15 years and to keep the international numerals. However, it also recommended that the President might appoint a commission to make sure that Hindi was progressively used and the use of English was to be discouraged. The second chapter dealt with regional languages in which it provided for autonomy to each of the states to enact law to adopt any language to be used in the state for official purposes. Interestingly, Chapter III entitled 'Language of Supreme Court and High Courts, etc.', was important because it clearly acknowledged the incapability of Hindi Language, as it existed at the time, in handling technical use of the various aspects of Law.

Chapter IV, titled 'Special Directives', of the proposed amendment consisted of two clauses. Following were the provisions suggested:

> 301 H. Every person shall be entitled to submit a representation for the redress of any grievance to any officer or authority of the Union or a State in any of the languages or in the State, as the case may be.
>
> 301 I. It shall be the duty of the Union to promote the spread of Hindi and to develop the language so as to serve as a medium of expression for all the elements of the composite culture of India and to secure its enrichments by assimilating without interfering with its genius, the forms, style and expressions used in Hindustani and in other languages of India, and drawing, wherever necessary or desirable, for its vocabulary on Sanskrit and secondarily on other languages.[1]

Hermeneutics of the above-mentioned clauses were quite obvious. Without touching Persian and Pali and Prakrit, the proposal was to remind the Hindu ancient past through the Sanskritic tradition. Seth Govind Das—the major exponent of Hindi—was the first to speak and express his happiness, but wavered in the choice of the language of his speech, for he wanted to speak in English to perhaps show his gratitude to his South Indian colleagues in the Assembly. In the end, however, he spoke in Hindustani and strongly argued against the adoption of international numerals. Seth Govind Das began his defence after it became clear that the national language would be Hindi.

II. Ethnic and Communal Identities Override Secular Ideologies

It was important to note that the Constituent Assembly with the leadership which was predominantly from North India was more worried about the reaction of the members from South India. In this regard, the controversy and contestations over national language were leading towards North–South divide. It was natural because despite the status of Hindi as the language spoken by the majority of the people in India, there was no consensus over the issue. The relationship between religion and language could be vaguely established in terms of the original language of the sacred text of each religious community. Extrapolating it to make religion and language coterminous was a serious attempt at communalising the issue of language even after the partition of the country on communal lines. The supporters of Hindi were accused of being communal, and Seth Govind Das was aware of such accusations which did emanate not only from ordinary members but also from some major leaders. He refuted all such charges and challenged his accusers to show whether in his life he had done anything to establish such an accusation. He clarified that he never thought that Urdu was the language of the Muslims, but the source of inspiration of Urdu was from outside the country. He said, 'Ours is a secular State and we all are one on this point. We treat every religion equally. We do not want to stand in the way of the development of any religion. But we do admit the fact, that in spite of our secularism there are different cultures in the country'. He also made it clear that he was not against regional languages.

In between the justification and arguments in his defence, Seth Govind Das also emphasised the ancient traditions of the country without underlining the importance of Islamic influence on India. For him *Koh Kaf* and Rustom were alien to Indians. While concluding his speech, he quoted from a letter written by Nehru in 1931 in which Nehru had mentioned that Hindi was spreading in Tamil Nadu. Naziruddin Ahmad, a Sanskrit scholar, was the next speaker. He made it clear that Hindi could not be established as the national language immediately due to which it was necessary that English should continue for some time. He pointed out that the issue of national language could not be decided through legislative vote. For a language to be suitable for being the national language, it must fulfil certain conditions. Ahmad said, 'It requires great writers, great thinkers, great men, scientists, politicians, philosophers, litterateurs, dramatists and others'. However, he argued that the selection of the national language should be based on two conditions. First, the people must be made literate in their own language. Secondly, there must be the re-grouping of the states on a linguistic basis.

Ghanshyam Singh Gupta asked Ahmad to express his views on Sanskrit and he began to quote various authorities on Sanskrit. When he was asked to specify his stand whether Sanskrit could be the national language, Ahmad was non-committal, but in the process he, by referring to C. Narayana Menon (a professor from Banaras), told the House that Hindi:

> is the most erratic. It has hands and feet proceeding in all directions like an octopus. The script is not smooth and rounded and the language is not capable of being speedily or easily written. Sir, this ease in writing is also one of the factors to be considered in the modern language.

In contrast to Hindi, Sanskrit was impartially difficult and should not be adopted as the national language, he added.

S.V. Krishnamoorthy Rao, who had learnt Hindi when he was in jail and at that time, as he informs, Hindi was called the language of the Muslims in South India, suggested that the matter regarding language should be decided by the parliament and the international numerals should remain. He then went on to show his knowledge of Hindi and argued that there was vagueness in using various English terminologies in Hindi translations. He then made a profound remark, 'If Hindi is going to be the common language of India and meet the needs of growing nation, it should develop itself borrowing freely from all languages'. The subsequent developments in the growth of Hindi did not show any such trajectory resulting into a general apathy towards the national language in non-Hindi-speaking areas.

Mohd. Hifzur Rahman from United Provinces invoked Gandhi to argue that Hindustani should be the national language. Hindustani written in two scripts: 'Hindi and Urdu', which implied Devanagari and Persian scripts. He said,

> This will have to be accepted in clearest terms that the present Sanskritized form of language which is being proclaimed as the lingua franca of India can never be the national language of our country. Similarly that form of Urdu which is encrusted with Arabic and Persian words can never be the language of our day to day life, market place and business.

He was the last speaker on 12 September 1949.

On 12 September 1949—the day the debate on national language began—it was quite clear that the members did not have any unanimity on the issue, though the member who moved the historic amendment hailed from South India. Various issues that came up for discussion were as follows:

1. Hindi in Devanagari script should be the national language, but English should remain in operation for 15 years.
2. International form of numerals should be adopted.
3. Those who disagreed with the above argued that (a) English should remain as it is, (b) Hindustani should be the national language which could be written either in Devanagari or Persian script, and (c) Sanskrit should be made the national language.
4. There was an agreement on the question of language, but there was disagreement on the issue of numerals.
5. Some members indicated that the language question had been communalised.
6. There was a clear-cut North–South divide on the question of language.

It became clear to all that language was as emotional an issue as was religion, but the best way to resolve it was to debate it thoroughly and as indicated earlier, it could not be decided through votes. Consensus was the prerequisite for nation-building with which the matter of national language seemed to be inseparably linked. The most remarkable aspect of the debate was the tacit acceptance of the fact that Hindi as a national language was not sufficiently equipped with terms, and technical and legal expressions to handle all aspects of the running of the state apparatus. Metaphorically, nation-building could not have occurred immediately; it required time and the members of the Constituent Assembly thought in their prudence that 15 years was a reasonably sufficient time to make English vanish.

When the debate resumed next day, that is, on Tuesday, 13 September 1949, R.V. Dhulekar from United Provinces was the first speaker and his speech ostensibly suggested that the pro-Hindi lobby had come prepared to push Hindi through. Dhulekar was reminded, during his speech, that Hindi had not yet been declared as the national language, but he kept on praising and glorifying the rich tradition of Hindi in India and then spoke the unspeakable:

> For the last thirty-eight years, during the period I have been in the Congress, the history of this appeasement policy or this friendly policy or the Hindustani business has to be recollected a bit. I may ask in the name of Lokamanya Tilak, in the name of Surendranath Banerjee, in the name of Mahatma Gandhi, why not have separate electorates also? I may say that except for them, the bulk of the Muslim population was not with us. They did not feel that this country was theirs. And therefore they wanted to separate. They wanted to have separate electorate. And the Congress knew as far back as 1916—and even before—that they could not fight against the foreign rulers by fighting a triangular fight and therefore … .

He would have continued to speak his mind had he not been interrupted by a member, but after the first hiccup he continued to speak and embarrass the Congress leadership. Nehru intervened, 'May I enquire whether all this is relevant?' President responded, 'No, I have reminded the Speaker more than once'. Dhulekar concluded his speech by emphasising the Hindu–Muslim unity for nation-building, but by that time he had not only argued his case against Hindustani, but also established the link between religion and language.

While accepting the suggestion that English should continue for 15 years, Pandit Lakshmi Kanta Maitra argued for Sanskrit to be accepted as the national language and told the House that the best example to emulate is that of Israel where Hebrew had been recognised as the official language. Frank Anthony from CP and Berar proposed an amendment which provided for replacing Devanagari script by the Roman script. Anthony made two interesting remarks which suggested how things had changed during more than a century's British rule. He said,

> if India is to achieve real unity, a real sense of Indian nationality, then every one of us must accept this premise that we must have a national language, English is my mother tongue. Because I am an Indian, because English is my mother tongue, I maintain that English is an Indian language.

The second point he made was that there were views that if you spoke against Hindi, then communal feelings would flare up. Qazi Syed Karimuddin was the next speaker who speculated that Pakistan's decision to have Urdu as the national language might have been triggered by the fact that India had declared Hindi in Devanagari script as the national language. His speculation was based on too many notions of the existing state of affairs. It was becoming obvious to most of the members that the partition of the country had significant bearings on the way Indian nation was being defined (not imagined) and its evidence was the decision to end all kinds of separate electoral systems. The decision to declare Urdu by Pakistan could have been in accordance with the perception of the leaders that Urdu and Muslim were coterminous and the only part of Pakistan which might have objected to it (and as it turned out to be) could be the Bangla-speaking area. The implications of such a decision of Pakistan in India were difficult to assess at that time. While campaigning for the cause of Hindustani, Karimuddin also made an attempt to refute some of the assertions of Dhulekar one of which was that Urdu was the mother tongue of Muslims. He further tried to correct Seth Govind Das that Sohrab and Rustam were Parsis and narratives of various kinds could be written in any language.

Lakshminarayan Sahu from Orissa made an attempt to identify primary reasons for the dispute over national language and said,

> We should first think over the cause of the dispute. It is whether there should be a national language or not. It is the view of some people that they cannot recognise any language as the national language, though they may agree to accept one language as the official language.

He further proposed that along with the promotion of Hindi, other regional languages should also be promoted. Sahu made an interesting observation on the issue of numerals:

> A new dispute regarding the numerals has also cropped up and the issue is whether the numerals should be international form or Devanagari form. The crores of our South Indian friends are insisting that they would not yield on this point, even though they may concede other points. What should be done? They have become obstinate, for the world does not go by logic; sentiment also prevails. We should therefore accept the foreign numerals.

The location of Hindi as a language was first indicated by N.V. Gadgil from Bombay, when he pointed out that Hindi was provincial language and some other languages in India were richer in literature than Hindi. He was of the view that there was no Indian who would vote for English, but the subsequent developments showed that he failed to assess the stronghold of English in India, though he was not the only one in this perception. Gadgil made an important point that the language issue could not be decided through votes, but it required consensus. In this context T A. Ramalingam Chettiar—a lawyer from Madras and is still remembered in Tamil Nadu for his comments on the issue of language—hit the nail on the head:

> Mr President, Sir, this is a very difficult question for us from the South to solve. It probably means life and death for the South unless it is going to be handled in the way in which it ought to be done. Well, Sir, for us coming from the South to go back and face our people with any decision you are going to make here, you will see what it will mean.

Chettiar's speech carried two interrelated matters. The first was the divide between the North and the South on the question of Hindi. He also added that some of the South Indian languages were better developed than Hindi. Secondly, in democracies people's opinion carried lot of weight and the leaders could not make decision by sacrificing their political careers.

When Chettiar pointed out the superiority of some South Indian languages, the President of the Constituent Assembly intervened and told the House that members should abstain from comparing literatures of different languages. Professor N.G. Ranga from Madras objected to the President's comment and when the latter insisted on maintaining the decorum in the House, Ranga told him that he was not reasonable. Chettiar continued to emphasise that Hindi was not the greatest of Indian languages. He added that Hindi in Devanagari script might become official language, but could not be recognised as national language. He said, 'When a man has to come two thousand miles and do his things here, he naturally feels that he is not in his own land'. As if he was offering a middle path, Satish Chandra Samanta from West Bengal was candid enough to propose that Bengali should be accepted as the national language.

Opposition of the members from the South and non-acceptance from the members from the East did not make the North Indian supporters of Hindi hostile towards them. Algu Ram Shastri from United Provinces delivered a long speech extolling the virtues of Sanskrit and at the same time underlining its becoming extinct as a spoken language. He pointed out that Sanskrit was the mother of all Indian languages with so many common words among them. Hindi was one such language. Shastri was followed by Dr Syama Prasad Mookerjee[2] from West Bengal. He began his speech by emphasising the multilingual character of the Indian subcontinent and opined that 'If we dig into the past, we will find that it has not been possible for anybody to force the acceptance of one language by all the people in this country'. He pointed out that achieving 'unity in diversity' was possible only by involving people and getting their consent, for it could not be achieved through coercion. Such an objective required a favourable environment. He expressed his personal view by stating that Sanskrit should be the national language owing to its greatness and richness, and also pointed out that he loved his mother tongue. He then argued for Hindi:

> Why do we accept Hindi? Not that it is necessarily the best of Indian languages. It is for the main reason that that is the one language which is understood by the largest single majority in this country today. If 14 crores of the people out of 32 crores today understand a particular language, and it is also capable of progressive development, we say, let us accept that language for the purpose of the whole of India, but do it in such a way that in the interim period it may not result in deterioration of our official

> conduct of business or administration and at no time retard true advancement of India and her other great languages.

Mookerjee was the last speaker in the morning session of the Constituent Assembly and when the session resumed at four in the afternoon, the form and content of the discussion remained unaffected by what was being argued earlier suggesting that on the language issues the members had already taken the positions and they were prepared to fight for what they thought was appropriate. P.C. Chacko from Travancore and Cochin insisted that English should continue for a fixed period and the matter pertaining to national language should be decided upon developing a consensus and by the parliament. He said,

> After having seen a sort of fanaticism in action in the matter of a comparatively smaller question of the numerals and after having heard a section of the people of this House speak as if all that mattered in life was the Devanagari system of numerals. I feel that it would be better for us to leave the decision on this question to soberer men. We can hope that our posterity will be more tolerant and wiser and hence may be able to find an agreed solution for this problem. Our intolerance has already divided India. Let us not divide it again.

Divisions among members on language issue had not occurred along ideological and party lines. Question of language implicated identity in cultural and regional sense. Hindi as a language could not claim to be the most developed language. Dr P. Subbarayan, who was the chief minister of Madras Presidency during British rule and then Union Minister of Transport and Communication in Nehru's Cabinet among other things and had law degree from United Kingdom, proposed the amendment that the national language should be Hindustani in the Roman script, which, he stressed, was the 'acceptable solution'. Then he commented, 'What is all this nonsense about numerals, I say. Do you want to be archaic and go back to things which have been forgotten for a long time?' Subbarayan's speech created heat in the House, and there was an exchange of sharp words between him and Pandit Balkrishna Sharma. It seemed that the President was also unhappy with him. Subbarayan showed his aggression by telling the pro-Hindi lobby that 'I am reminded of the other Tamil proverb which says, if a man comes and asks for a little place on the verandah and if you grant it, he will next ask for entry into the house itself. That is the position of most of you gentlemen, today'. He then narrated the effect of introduction of Hindi in Madras and told the House that there was strong opposition to the introduction of Hindi. At this moment, the members of the House started speaking at once and there was pandemonium, but order was restored quickly. The most memorable part of the speech of Subbarayan is quoted as follows:

> Sir, I will give information for the edification of my colleagues from the United Provinces. The Congress Bulletin is published both in English and in Hindi. If you compare the number of subscribers for these two editions you will be surprised. Only 1/40th of those who subscribe for the English edition, subscribe for the Hindi edition. This shows that in spite of Gandhiji's attempts and in spite of everything that has been done, we have not been able to make even those who seem to be jealous of Hindi language buy the Hindi edition of the Congress Bulletin.

He further proposed an amendment that 'English should be added as the fourteenth language in the Schedule'.

Kuladhar Chaliha from Assam characterised the speech of Subbarayan as the most rational speech. He supported Ayyangar's amendment because he thought that as a compromise solution it was good for India. B.M. Gupte from Bombay expressed the view that Sanskrit could not be the language of masses. Nehru was next to Gupte to express his views on the issue. Nehru delivered a long speech combining the issue of language with various dimensions of personal and collective living. He made it clear that he was supporting Ayyangar's proposed amendment amongst cheers. After making his position clear with regard to language, he began his discourse on the question of language. Let us begin with one of the best specimens of this discourse:

> Language is a most intimate thing. It is perhaps the most important thing which society has evolved, out of which other things have taken growth. Now language is a very big thing. It makes us aware of ourselves. First, when language is developed it makes us aware of our neighbour, it makes us aware of our society, it makes us aware of other societies also. It is unifying

> factor and it is also a factor promoting disunity. It is an integrating factor and it is a disintegrating factor as between two languages, as between two countries. So it has both these aspects and when therefore you think in terms of a common language here you have to think of both those facts.

After stating his position with regard to the significance of language in uniting and disuniting people, Nehru invoked Gandhi to support his contention and he argued why Hindi could be the uniting and integrating language in India.

While invoking Gandhi, Nehru identified three crucial aspects of the language meant for India as a nation.[3] First, despite its greatness English could not be the language of the country because a foreign language should not be the language of the people. Secondly, as a corollary to the first argument, the national language must be the language of the people. Finally, the language should represent the composite culture of the country. Gandhi used the word 'Hindustani' in a broad sense of the term. After making it clear that Gandhi used the expression 'Hindustani', it was important for Nehru to interpolate the argument to establish that what Gandhi said Hindustani was in fact Hindi. Instead of making logical claims, he took the help of his charisma and focussed on Ayyangar's proposed amendment and said,

> 'Now, we stand on the threshold of many things and this Resolution itself is the beginning of what might be termed as a linguistic revolution in India, a very big revolution of far-reaching effects, and we have to be careful that we give it the right direction, the right shape, the right would lest it go wrongly and betray us in wrong directions. Men shape a language, but then that language itself shapes those men and society.

Nehru rejected Sanskrit as the possible or probable choice as the national language. By the content of subsequent speech of Nehru, it appeared that he had come well prepared to deliver that speech to make a case for Hindi by putting his weight behind the resolution. It is important to have some degree of familiarity with his sense of history and culture in a larger context:

> Till very recently—in fact, I would say a generation ago—French was the recognised diplomatic and cultural language of Europe

> and large parts of the earth's surface … . Nobody objected to French. No Englishman, or Russian, or German or Pole objected to French. So all those other languages were growing and today it might be said that English is perhaps replacing French from that proud place of diplomatic eminence.
>
> Before French, in Europe the language of diplomacy was Latin just as in India the language of culture, and diplomacy for a vast period of time was Sanskrit. …
>
> After Sanskrit Persian became the language of culture and diplomacy in India and over large parts of Asia.

After giving the reasonably coherent and historically accurate picture of the history of languages, he shifted his focus on English as the language of the colonial masters and made it clear whatever might be the richness and advantages of English, it was not the language of the masses. He agreed with some of the earlier speakers that English would continue to be most important in the affairs of the world in times to come and was unsure whether it would be possible to completely discard English. Importantly, Nehru expressed his displeasure to the enthusiastic and aggressive supporters of Hindi in the House as well as outside and tried to convey to them what democracy was really about. He said,

> Is your approach going to be a democratic approach or what might be termed as authoritarian approach? I venture to put this question to the enthusiasts for Hindi, because in some of the speeches I have listened here and elsewhere there is very much a tone of authoritarianism, very much a tone of the Hindi-speaking area being the centre of things in India, the centre of gravity and others being just the fringes of India. That is not only an incorrect approach, but it is a dangerous approach. If you consider the question with wisdom, this approach will do more injury to the development of the Hindi language than the other approach. You just cannot force any language down the people or group who resist that.

He then moved on to express his views on the issue of Hindi vs Hindustani and he made it clear that the word Hindi was better and could be used as an inclusive language. He supported international form of numerals explaining that if we did not do that, we might land ourselves in trouble. He concluded his speech with the following words:

> What sort of India do we want? Do we want a modern India—with its roots steeped in the past certainly in so far as it inspires us—do we want a modern India with modern science and all the rest of it, or do we want to live in some ancient age, in some other age which has no relation to the present? You have to choose between the two. It is a question of approach. You have to choose whether you look forward or backward.

Nehru had many memorable moments and speeches in the Constituent Assembly, but it seems that after his Independence Day speech in the Assembly when he said 'We had tryst with destiny', his concluding remarks in his speech on the language issue could be considered historic. He was unambiguous in his position with regard to India's future which according to him should be modern, for past and ancient India was worthy of remembering but not emulating. The present India had to look forward to future with the help of modern science. Could Hindi become the pedestal of launching the dream of modernity, of modern India? Nehru believed that it was possible, but the national language, Hindi, had to become the language of masses and should be democratically accepted by all Indians.

The charisma of Nehru failed to impress the diehard supporters as well as opponents of Hindi. Still two important interventions were to occur in the form of Azad and Vira. But it was Pandit Ravi Shankar Shukla from CP and Berar—who became the first chief minister of Madhya Pradesh, later on—spoke after Nehru completed his speech. Despite his commitment to Hindi, he pointed out various problems of working in Hindi due to paucity of translation of technical and scientific words.

On the morning of 14 September 1949, G. Durgabai from Madras was the first speaker to express her views and she argued for Hindustani which was Hindi and Urdu combined. While referring to Gandhi, she said, 'The official language of India should be only that which is commonly understood and easily spoken and learnt'. After giving her opinion, she gave interesting information:

> Long before the Pandits of Hindi Sahitya Sammelan realised the importance of having national language for India, we all in the South obeyed the call of Mahatma Gandhi and carried on Hindi propaganda in the South. We started schools and conducted

> classes in Hindi. Thus with great inconvenience we dedicated ourselves very long ago to the propagation and learning of Hindi.

Durgabai was essentially mentioning the efforts of the Dakshina Bharat Hindi Parcharak Sabha of which she was a part. She said that the Hindi-speaking people should compulsorily learn any one of the provincial languages. Shankarrao Deo from Bombay commented that Gopalswami Ayyangar's amendment was a compromise formula and it did not guarantee total success. Ravi Shankar Shukla intervened and told Deo that the amendment was not a compromise. Deo began with the core of what was causing a degree of narcissism among the members of the Constituent Assembly when he apparently responded to Shukla's interruption. He said,

> Sir, as you have yourself said, this question of language has agitated our minds most, in my opinion, next only to freedom, because this question is vital for future development and growth of this nation. Those who have preceded me have already spoken so much about the importance of language in the building and growth of an individual or nation. To me, next to my mother, it is language which is ear, because my mother has given me birth, no doubt, but it is the language which has made me what I am today. That is why though many of us do not like it, this controversy has stirred our passions to their depth and sentiments have been roused and many a time, it blurs our judgement. I would request my friends from the South as well as from the North not to look at this question from an emotional or sentimental point of view.

It becomes clear that the debate on language was arousing passions among the members and Hindi as the national/official language of the country was not acceptable to all. One of the arguments being used in support of Hindi was that it was spoken by a majority of the Indians. Deo tried to put the contention in its right place when he commented,

> After all, what is the claim that is now being put forward? The claim is that this language is spoken by a majority—I am not sure about that even I know when I go to Rajen Babu and people from Bihar come to him they do not speak Hindi. If I am not wrong, neither Tandonji speaks Hindi at home. So when you say that Hindi which is spoken by the majority of the country I doubt it. I can only concede that it is perhaps understood by the majority, and that too, not the present high-flown Sanskritised Hindi which is understood by Pandits only.

Deo's long speech had not yet been concluded. He had already identified the problems in the case for Hindi as the language. Notwithstanding passion and sentiments bordering on to extremism and fundamentalism, the support to Hindi as a language spoken by majority faced two major issues. First, Deo almost demolished the assertion that Hindi was spoken by a majority in the country, the criterion could be the number of people understanding a particular language. Second, as a corollary to his assertion, he advocated that to suit the composite culture of India, the language should evolve so that each culture found expression in that language. He reminded that our forefathers accepted 'English for its superiority', as 'it opened a new world for the people of India. At the same time, he made it clear that there was also an economic dimension of language and added, 'And if today Hindi is so much valued and people prefer it to any other language, it is not because it is superior to other languages but it is a means to get a job'. Deo's speech was frequently interrupted, but he took his time and concluded with the remark that 'I admit that the amendment of the Honourable Shri Gopalaswami Ayyangar is not an ideal one; still it is the only formula on which unanimity is possible'.

Hukam Singh, who had earlier supported Hindi in Devanagari script, changed his stance to Hindustani in Roman script when he rose to speak after Deo concluded his speech. He said that he was doing so after watching the fanaticism and intolerance of the supporters of Hindi in Devanagari script. He reminisced the pre-partition times when there was strong contest between Hindi and Urdu to become national language. He then identified six points to support his contention. These were: Hindustani in Roman script was already in use in the armed forces and it was convenient to learn, the people familiar with Roman script were large in size, Devanagari script is tedious even for printing, Roman script could be modified to suit the purpose and will also be convenient for railway time tables and telegraph codes, it will connect India with the outside world, and it will help in ending conflict between North and South. Hukam Singh's amendment was interesting, but in the prevailing environment in the House it was not possible to push through such an idea. He went on to take the question of language little further by linking it with religion and defining it in terms of communalism. He said,

> Communalism has not been correctly defined anywhere, but a convenient definition may be that whatever is said and done by majority in a democratic country or at least in India is pure nationalism and whatever is said by a minority community is communalism. This is also the basis on which we are proceeding. As there were fears in the minds of the minority that Punjabi might be swept away altogether, they advocated its adoption as one of their demands to the majority community, but I fear that just as the protagonists of Hindi have done a disservice to that language so have the Sikhs by taking up the cause of Punjabi done it a great disservice because this demand has been dubbed as a communal demand.

He then described the situation in Punjab where the language issue was getting inseparably connected with religion. He stressed, 'I might make it clear that now after Partition no minority can be communal'.

It was thus clear that the language question was not only the matter of North–South divide, but also linked with religion, making the matter more complicated than it was thought. Jaipal Singh, from Bihar, joined all those who strongly opposed the fanaticism of Hindi supporters after suggesting that Mundari, Gondi and Oraon (all tribal languages) should be added to the list of languages. He also pointed out that 'Devanagari script has given headache to all the producers of printing machinery. In the time you can print something like fifteen thousand copies or twenty thousand copies in English, you cannot print even one-tenth of this number in Devanagari'.

III. Twist in the Debate: Tandon, Azad and Vira

Amidst ambivalent reaction to Hindi in Devanagari script even after Nehru had already supported it, Purushottam Das Tandon from United Provinces rose to speak. He was logical and reasonable in the presentation of argument in favour of Hindi in Devanagari script, but he provoked many members in the process. What he said could be understood as an exercise in semantics and semiotics of language. Let us see how it happened. First, he used the expression 'Hindi provinces' to argue that since Hindi was the official language in United Provinces, it was quite possible that by the time 15 years are completed the much needed terminology would be available for others to adopt.

Maulana Hasrat Mohani lost no time in asking Tandon, 'What do you mean by Hindi provinces?'

Tandon replied, 'I am referring to those provinces which have adopted Hindi as their language; for example, the United Provinces has formally adopted Hindi as its language: so has Bihar ...'

Maulana interrupted him, 'The United Provinces is either a Urdu province or a Hindustani province. It cannot be a Hindi-speaking province'.

Tandon told Maulana that he did not want to get into controversy and then he shifted to the issue of numerals and said, 'I know that our Madras friends want to change the Hindi numerals'.

Many members shouted, 'Bengal also'.[4]

Tandon responded, 'If I am wrong you can correct me; but I never heard that from my Bengal friends'.

Many members snapped back, 'Bombay also. As a matter of fact, all non-Hindi speaking people'.

Tandon responded again, 'My submission is that it is not correct. ... . I ask Mr. Shankarrao Deo and Dr Ambedkar, who are sitting here to tell me whether the people of Maharashtra are going to accept it'.

Ambedkar kept quiet but Deo responded, 'I say that whatever stand I take the Maharashtrians will take that stand too'.

Tandon was insistent, 'From my knowledge of Maharashtra I submit, because the script is the same, that if there is referendum there, the people of Maharashtra will not accept the so-called international numerals'.

Many members said in one voice, 'If there is a referendum in India Hindi will go!'

Tandon said, 'I would beg of honourable Members to interrupt me one by one and not many at a time. I shall be happy to hear Shankarrao Deo and Dr Ambedkar'.

Instead Dr Syama Prasad Mookerjee intervened, 'Why not refer to a referendum'.

Tandon kept on speaking in an argumentative style, as if substantiating what later on Amartya Sen had to say about an argumentative Indian, provoking many members. Maulana Mohani repeated his demand for referendum in United Provinces. The President clarified that the Constituent Assembly's function was to make Constitution and not to organise referendum. He further added that the Constituent Assembly represented and reflected the will of people. Tandon who was awarded Bharat Ratna in 1961 did not say anything so controversial that it should have evoked such a response. Interestingly, there was nothing new in his arguments and the posterity would remember him as one of the major exponents of Hindi as the national language. The message was loud and clear that the fate of a language to be the national language would be decided through a majority vote. Two important personalities were yet to speak, namely Maulana Abul Kalam Azad and Raghu Vira.

Azad, despite his reputation as a major Muslim leader in the Congress, seldom spoke in the Constituent Assembly. He was not vocal on the issue of minority rights and privileges. He did not intervene when the Constituent Assembly decided to withdraw provision of reservation for religious minorities as moved by Sardar Patel. Similarly, Vira was hardly known through any eloquent intervention in debates. Vira was well educated with masters from London and PhD from Leiden, Netherlands. He was an indologist and linguist. Born in Punjab (Rawalpindi), his mother tongue was Punjabi, but he was multilingual and was passionately opposed to English as the national language in India. He began as a Congress activist but died as the leader of the Jan Sangh. Let us know what these two illustrious personalities—one highly educated and the other the maker of modern education in India—had to say on the issue of language.

Azad's speech could be divided into two parts. The first part of his speech is devoted to the decisions taken by the drafting committee with regard to language. He was part of the committee. In the second part of the speech, Azad expressed his personal views on language. It has already been noticed that language was the only issue in which the party affiliation did not influence the views and opinions of the members.

He began by informing that the members of the committee began with the objective of removing English from its position in administration and education. It was thought that it would be done in five years. However, the members belonging to the South and Bengal argued that more time was required and he agreed with them. He expressed his unanimity with Ayyangar's amendment that 15 years were required to erase English from the position it was holding. Azad then identified two problems and challenges faced in order to remove English. First, there was no national language which could immediately replace English. Secondly, there was no common language in India. He candidly admitted the divide between the South and the North on the question of language. He made it clear that there was a need for consensus and the matter should not unnecessarily be pushed through. Since the University Commission had been constituted. it was important that the changes should be introduced without affecting the students' capability. States should have waited for the recommendations of the Commission before introducing changes in the medium of language. Ravishankar Shukla interrupted his speech and commented that the decision to introduce Hindi was taken three years before the setting up of the Commission. Azad reiterated that the decision could have been taken after some time. Then he spoke on the issue of national language,

> So far as language is concerned, this has been admitted on all hands that the language spoken in Northern India can only be made the Lingua Franca, but it has got three names—Urdu, Hindi and Hindustani. Now the point of dispute is as to what name should be given to it. Naturally, with different names are associated different forms and styles of the language; so in reality it is not a quarrel about names but about the form or style. I want to give you a brief resume of the points of difference in these three names.
>
> The general framework or setup of the language spoken all over Northern India is one and the same, but in its literary style it has got two names—a style resplendent with Persian is called Urdu and a style leaning towards Sanskrit is known as Hindi. The term 'Hindustani' has developed a wider connotation: it embraces all forms of the language spoken in Northern India. It includes 'Hindi' as well as 'Urdu' and even more than that. It includes each and every shade of the spoken language of the North. It does not exclude any. It covers all.

Azad's message was loud and clear: whatever name you give to the national language, it should have two things. First, it should be one of the languages spoken in North India and secondly, it should be inclusive. He also insisted that the international numerals are primarily of Indian origin. He expressed hope that the prevalent narrow-mindedness would disappear in due course of time when the past would no longer influence them and the issue of language would be seen in right perspective.

Dr Raghu Vira from CP and Berar was the last member to speak on the issue. It is quite possible that seen as an expert in linguistics, he was trying to settle the issue of language in a manner favourable to Hindi. Interestingly, he spoke largely in opposition to Azad. Azad talked about commonalities, Vira showed differences there. Here is an instance of his difference:

> In the beginning the difference between Hindi and Urdu literature was not great ... While they [Urdu writers] took the grammar and construction of the language from India, the literary inspiration and other factors were taken from Arabic and Persian ....
>
> So, the tradition was developed in the 19th century whereby Urdu became the repository of Persian and Arabic words and culture. There was a reaction in the 19th century and hence developed the Hindi literature which had for its basis and structure the same language which was the basis of Urdu but whose literary tradition was native to the soil. This difference kept in developing and developing until today we find two literatures, which though they had the same basis have developed differently.

After this he kept on underlining how there were two different traditions and both had become divergent with the passage of time. Vira might have continued for long had he not been interrupted at about 1 o'clock—the lunch time. When Vira was asked how much time he would take, he said that he would take half an hour. At that moment, the President closed the debate and when the Assembly re-assembled at 5 o'clock, the President asked Vira to complete his speech in two minutes. It is in the fitness of the things to quote his last lines he spoke on the subject of language:

> Mr President, I join other Members of the House in expressing our great satisfaction that a satisfactory arrangement has been reached between the different view-points on the question of the numerals. Now discussion may be concluded in a friendly manner. This is a matter in which I should congratulate the House. As there is no controversy now, the discussion may be closed.

After the motion for closure was moved, Maulana Mohani expressed his disgust with the attitude of the Prime Minister and policy of appeasement of Maulana Azad. Finally, the language issue was considered decided and chapter on language seemed closed. It did not happen in that way, partly due to the protocol in matters of deciding the matter through votes. Befóre N. Gopalaswami Ayyangar could respond to all other amendments and issues moved and raised in the House, Mohamed Ismail pointed out that the amendment which he had put forward had not been debated, for he was not asked to speak. When he was allowed to speak, he moved that Hindustani with Devanagari and Urdu scripts should be the official language and the international form of numerals should remain in use. He quoted Gandhi to support his contention. He also pointed out that Tamil was rich language and among the oldest spoken in India and the Tamilians were prudent enough not to insist on one of the ancient language of India as the official language.

Ayyangar was invited by the President to reply to the whole debate. He did not seem to be in the mood to respond with a long speech, which was evident from his opening statement:

> Sir, we are in a happy mood just at the moment and I do not want to mar this happy mood by anything like a long speech from me. I have formally, as mover of the major amendment, to accept the amendments to that amendment which have been moved by my honourable Friend Mr. Munshi. I accept them *in toto*.

After his short speech, the rest was just a formality and Amendment No. 65 with certain amendments accepted by Ayyangar was passed to be put as new Part XIV-A of the Constitution.

The historic day of 14 September 1949 would remain as one of the most important days in the history of not only the

Constituent Assembly but also of India. The day's debates were over, but still what remained was the speech of the President who in earlier debates never felt motivated/compelled to deliver a speech. His were the final words on the matter and it would be of interest to have the feeling of what Dr Rajendra Prasad thought of the language question. He said that 'I think we have adopted a Chapter for our Constitution which will have very far reaching consequences in building up the country as a whole'. After pointing out the richness of Sanskrit literature, he admitted that it was not used for administrative purposes. He then talked about Hindi:

> I do not claim to be scholar of Hindi or any other language. I do not claim to have made any contribution to literature but this much I can say as a layman that it is not possible today to foresee what form this language, which we have adopted as the language of administration of the union, is going to take in future. As it is, Hindi has undergone change in past so many many occasions and we have several styles of it, we have had literature written in Braj Bhasha. Khari Boli is now the prevalent style in Hindi. I think its contact with all the other languages in the country will give it opportunities for further development. I have no doubt that Hindi will benefit rather than lose by absorbing as much as it can of the best that is to be found in other languages of the country.

For him it was an achievement of unification of the country and then he recalled his association with the propagation of Hindi in South India which was initiated by Gandhi in 1918. He concluded his speech by saying that,

> If in place of English we have adopted an Indian language, it is bound to bring us closer together, particularly because our traditions are same, our culture is the same, and everything that goes to make our civilisation is the same .... I hope posterity will bless us for this.

No doubt, the debate and decision on national language was one of the major events in the history of postcolonial India. Language being associated with national identity was an important issue for the people and leaders of India. In the Constitution of India, official language has been covered under Part XVII of the Constitution and Articles 343 to 351 pertain to language issues. It is important to cite Clause 3 of Article 343, which states, '(3) Notwithstanding anything in this article,

Parliament may by law provide for the use, after the said period of fifteen years, of—(a) the English language, or (b) the Devanagari form of numerals for such purposes as may be specified in the law'.

The fate of two constitutional provisions could be predicted right from the time the Constitution was being finalised. The first pertained to the matter of reservation in legislatures and the Lok Sabha which was meant for 10 years, but could be extended further by the parliament. The second was the discontinuation of English after 15 years, but its use could be allowed by the parliament. Ironically, both the political reservations and the use of English still continue and any effort to create compulsion for the use of Hindi has met with tremendous resistance from many corners and classes of India. Subsequent developments with regard to language implicated numerous issues. One of them pertained to the linguistic reorganisation of the states which was a matter of policy and an outcome of the enactment of the parliament. Formation of states on the basis of common language could be seen as an attempt towards uniformity instead of diversity. However, the language issue was turned into communal matter with the identification of a particular language with a religious community in certain cases. It was a kind of an unintended consequence of taking up language issue in the reorganisation of states. The classical example has been that of Punjab where Punjabi was identified with the Sikhs. As Rajivlochan has informed that the Hindi agitation in Punjab was primarily organised by the Hindu leaders and interestingly most of them did not know Hindi[5] as most of their press statements used to be in Urdu. Communal overtone with regard to language could be observed in various speeches in the Constituent Assembly. Despite the fact that Hindi is understood in most of India, any attempt at formalising the use of Hindi still arouses passion. The popularisation of Hindi in India has not been the result of a political act, but the popular cinema. The language used in Indian cinema is close to Hindustani and due to common grammar of Hindi and Urdu, there is no strict boundary between the two in the world of entertainment. However, the protagonists of Hindi have not learnt from this fact and still pushing Sanskritised Hindi as the lingua franca. In this regard, the only rational and courageous vice to identify the problem was Hukam Singh.

Notes

1. Under Schedule VIIA following languages (regional) were recommended: 1. Assamese, 2. Bengali, 3. Canarese, 4. Gujarati, 5. Hindi, 6. Kashmiri, 7. Malayalam, 8. Marathi, 9. Oriya, 10. Punjabi, 11. Tamil, 12. Telugu, 13. Sanskrit and 14. Urdu.
2. Syama Prasad Mookerjee (later on, the suffix was spelled as Mukherjee) founded the Bhartiya Jana Sangh with the active cooperation of Rashtriya Swayamsevak Sangh (RSS) in 1951 after his disagreement with Nehru on inviting the Pakistani leader. He was a member of the Congress at the time of debates of the Constituent Assembly.
3. In this speech, Nehru used the signifier Father of the Nation for Gandhi.
4. Both Madras and Bombay provinces were covering large areas which were later on divided into many states after the linguistic organisation of the states.
5. With permission from M. Rajivlochan to refer the fact from his unpublished work entitled 'Hindi Agitation and Kairon' (2014).

7

Elusive Consensus

The Sikh Issue

There is twofold purpose of dealing with the Sikh issue in this chapter separately despite having covered the issues of minority rights (see Chapter 3) and the partitioned states (see Chapter 4) in which the Sikhs figure prominently. First, the earlier stages of discussion on minorities occurred by putting Muslims in the centre of discourse. Secondly, most of the decisions were taken by keeping Muslims and partition in view. The Sikh members except Gurmukh Singh Musafir reacting to a comment of a member on the Sikh identity (see Chapter 4) hardly spoke on the issue. It is also important to inform that the Sikh issue surface towards the end of discussion on the Draft Constitution.

The Constituent Assembly, dominated by the Congress led by the influential and charismatic authority of Nehru, Patel and Rajendra Prasad, remained a divided house on various issues. We have discussed in detail the debate on language in which people got divided by ethnic and religious identities. When the issue of property was examined, there was no unanimity among the members of the Congress, for the members of the Congress were guided by their class interests and/or ideologies. I have discussed in detail how the issue of minorities was debated and settled.[1] There was an obvious departure from the provision of separate electorate which was considered the root cause of partition of the country. After some indications of reservation for religious minorities in the earlier period, it was finally decided to end the provision of reservation for all minorities except the scheduled castes and four castes among the Sikhs. During the earlier debate on reservation for minorities, the Muslim members voiced their opinion and views strongly and unsparingly and sometimes politely, but the Sikh members kept quiet except for two occasions. First when Gurmukh Singh Musafir reacted to Jaipal Singh's comment and again when Musafir recommended the inclusion of two members for the Sikh community in the Constituent Assembly.[2]

When the article-wise discussion of the Draft Constitution was approaching its conclusion, the Sikh members seemed awakened from the long slumber. It seemed strange that the Sikh members did not raise the Sikh-specific issue when the minorities were discussed in the House. It is quite reasonable to argue that the Sikh members did not want their issue to be linked with other religious minorities, particularly the Muslims. On 25 May 1949, it was decided that there would be no reservation for religious minorities except four castes among the Sikhs. At that time, there was no protest among the Sikh members. On the contrary, they praised the Congress leadership. Within six months the position of the Sikh members belonging to the Shiromani Akali Dal changed, whereas Gurmukh Singh Musafir, the Congressman, did not speak on the issue. The present chapter deals with the debate on the Sikh issue in the Constituent Assembly.

This chapter in two parts takes cognisance of how the Sikh issue resurfaced largely due to a speech of an Akali leader and the way it spilled over to the next phase of the third reading of the Draft Constitution. The underlying assumption of this chapter is that even when the Constitution was ultimately passed by the Constituent Assembly, consensus on various issues remained an illusion. In the end, in concluding remarks an attempt has been made to make conjecture on the possible relationship between these debates and the Sikh separatist insurgency in 1980s.

I. Minority Issue Resurfaces

The context of the Sikhs raising the issue was remotely connected with the religious minorities. Since the Constituent

Assembly recognised the scheduled castes as a minority, the discussion on them was turned into the Sikh issue by Hukam Singh. At this juncture, it is important to introduce Hukam Singh by digressing from the main point of discussion, for he becomes the main actor in the debates of the Constituent Assembly on the Sikh issue. The expression 'speaking truth to power' may be applicable to him. Interestingly, he did not vanish from the political scene afterwards.

Hukam Singh (1895–1983) belonged to Montgomery (now Sahiwal in Pakistan) from where he did his matriculation and then he did his graduation from Khalsa College, Amritsar, in 1917. After completing LLB in 1921 from the Law College, Lahore, he started his legal practice at his native town. However, he became an Akali activist in the Gurdwara Reform Movement. After partition, with the recommendation of an influential Akali leader, Giani Kartar Singh, he was appointed the Judge of the High Court of the Kapurthala state. Giani Kartar Singh again helped him in getting elected to the Constituent Assembly in 1948. However, after independence, he joined the Congress. He was elected to the Lok Sabha thrice from 1952 to 1962. In 1962, he was elected speaker of the Lok Sabha. In 1967, when he did not fight election he was appointed governor of Rajasthan till 1972. During his tenure as member of the Constituent Assembly, he spoke on a number of issues including language and governance, but his intervention on Sikh cause has been outstanding due to his ability to logically argue the issue (Singh, 1996). There were also other Sikh members of the Constituent Assembly, who shared the same concerns with Hukam Singh so far as the Sikh community was concerned, though they might have had different viewpoints. In total four from East Punjab and three from Patiala and East Punjab States Union (PEPSU) were Sikh members of the Constituent Assembly. Only Hukam Singh was able to articulate the Sikh perspective. It required a minor pretext to initiate the debate on the Sikhs and Hukam Singh did it when the issue of reservations came for discussion again.

One of the hotly debated issues earlier in the Constituent Assembly resurfaced on 14 October 1949, when the amendment of the Article 296 was moved in the House by Dr B.R. Ambedkar, which was as follows:

> The claims of the members of the Scheduled Castes and the Scheduled Tribes shall be taken into consideration consistently with the maintenance of efficiency of administration, in the making of the appointments to services and posts in connection with the affairs of the union or of a State.

The proposed amendment did not exactly deal with reservation, but with the additional qualifying condition that if the members of the scheduled castes and the scheduled tribes were given preferential treatment in the government jobs, then standards must not be compromised. First, Bhupinder Singh Mann and then Naziruddin Ahmed raised the point of order that the issue had already been settled. The President told the House that according to the Rule 32 of the rules governing the conduct of the Constituent Assembly, there was provision that any issue could be reopened if one-fourth members had given their consent. The President then moved the resolution: 'Is the House in favour of reopening the question?' The resolution was adopted and the matter was reopened for discussion.

The first amendment was moved by Hukam Singh. In his proposed amendment, he replaced the words scheduled castes and scheduled tribes by 'all minority communities' and then added a caveat entitled 'Explanation' stating that 'Among others Muslims, Christians, Sikhs, Anglo-Indians and Parsees shall be recognized as minority communities'. Hukam Singh brought everything back to what was happening in 1947 and how all minorities except scheduled castes were dropped from any provision of reservation. He, in his considerably long speech for the occasion, made two important points:

> It is very unfortunate that the Sikhs for the present cannot persuade themselves to have implicit faith in the party in power. They have reasons for that, for they think that the past is a record of repudiated promises and broken pledges. Suppose for the sake of argument, that I am wrong, that this is incorrect, and that the present leaders can be trusted to do justice to everybody; then is there any guarantee that the present leaders will continue for all time to come? Are there not indications, even now apparent, that men with different ideals and aims might come to power very soon? This House should take a detached view and not consider the fears of the minorities as necessarily a disparagement of the present party or its leaders.

> Then my second point is that the Honourable Members should place themselves in the position of the minorities, and then try to appreciate those fears that they have expressed from time to time.

Between 26 May 1949 and 14 October 1949—four months' time—no change had occurred in the position held by the Sikh members. If we assume that Hukam Singh represented the Sikh community in general and as an Akali he had the right to think so, then it becomes clear that either the nightmares of partition were still weighing on the minds of the members or due to certain reasons the Akalis got disappointed from the Congress leadership. Punjab was a state which was partitioned and it had a sizeable population of Sikhs. For Hukam Singh, the situation was clear in the sense that any act of aggressiveness of the majority community could be taken as the sign of nationalism, whereas the minority could always be accused of communalism even if it had made modest demand. He made it clear that 'nationalism is an argument for vested interests'. He then reiterated his stand:

> When the question of safeguards for minorities was decided in 1947, the question as regard the Sikhs was kept pending as it was said that the result of the partition was not known very clearly then ... . The Sikhs were leaving the West Punjab under circumstances which are well known to everybody here. They had willingly suffered themselves to be vivisected and they elected to remain with India. They were marching on foot, leaving behind everything they loved. They were not coming alone. They had saved and brought seven districts to the Indian Dominion. The full significance of leaving open the question of Sikh minority on 28th August cannot fully be understood when we look at those events.

Ostensibly, there was a shift in the emphasis of the content in the speech of Hukam Singh. In the earlier speeches of most of the Sikh members, there was no mention of the choice they had exercised in remaining with India. Moreover, they did not seem to be allied with the position that the Sikhs were part of the minorities in general. It may be recalled that on various issues of minorities, the Muslim members were more vocal than others in matters related to separate/double electorate and reservations. On certain occasions when the Sikh members raised the community-specific issues, Patel had snubbed them and none of them raised the issue of their being part of the Indian Union by choice for which they needed to be acknowledged. Hukam Singh raised certain issues which had tremendous ramification for the future. First, the minorities never gave their consent to forego all privileges earlier provided in the fundamental rights. Second, in the proceedings of the Minorities Subcommittee, there was no mention of Articles 296 and 299. Three, the Sikhs gave no undertaking that if the Mazhabis, Ramdasis, Kabir Panthis and Sikligars were recognised as scheduled castes, they would not demand any other safeguards in the Constitution. He said,

> There is one very important factor that has gained currency during the last three or four days. It concerns the Sikhs alone. It has been given out that the Sikh representatives on the Minorities Committee gave an undertaking in writing that they would not put forward any demands for any safeguards in the Constitution if—that was very big if—their backward classes the Mazhabis, Ramdasis, Kabirpanthis and Sikligars were recognised and calculated as Scheduled Castes. That may be true. In May last, as I have said, the position was that these two Articles 296 and 299 had been accepted by the Constituent Assembly. The reservation was there also, but they agreed on that date that they would give it up. The Instrument of Instructions is gone. So far as I have been able to ascertain from the proceedings of the Minorities Sub-Committee, I do not find any mention anywhere that 296 and 299 were referred to that the minorities were asked to give up this as whole. The Minorities Committee decided to abolish reservation only in the legislature. I must point out there that there is no reservation in Articles 296 and 299.

The above observation of Hukam Singh is crucial. Any reader of the Constituent Assembly debates would look for a comprehensive debate on the provision of reservation for the minorities as a complete package. One begins to realise that most of the discussion is related to the reservation of seats in the legislatures, whereas the issue of reservation for jobs and in educational institutions seems subsumed under the discussion on political reservations. Hukam Singh's comments clarify the matter that the political reservation was an issue on which the Sikhs agreed to forego any claim if four castes mentioned in his speech were made eligible for reservation. Secondly, the issue of Sikhs could not be equated with the Muslims or other minorities. Third, the Congress leaders betrayed the Sikhs. What was the nature of this betrayal? Hukam Singh went on to outline the alleged betrayal,

> The Sikhs are told, when they remind the Congress of their past pledges in 1929, 1946 and again in 1947 that circumstances have changed. The Sikhs were recognised as one of the three main communities in the Cabinet Mission Plan of which this Constituent Assembly is the creature. The only changed circumstance is that the Muslims have got Pakistan. Does it stand to reason that because Muslims have secured Pakistan therefore the Sikhs have ceased to be a minority?

Hukam Singh did not specify the exact content of pledges or promises of the Congress. It was clear that the Sikh were largely concentrated in Punjab where they constituted a sizeable minority in addition to which they were living in the princely states some of which were ruled over by the Sikh princes.[3] Keeping in mind their more than half century's rule in Punjab in the 18th and 19th centuries, the Sikhs were not an ignorable community. Most of the 19th century aristocracy of Punjab was the creation of the Sikh rule and it was not destabilised from its elite positions by the British. In such circumstances, the Sikhs had high expectations of fair treatment. The discourse of the Sikhs in terms of their demand for more privileges did not emanate from their being in minority in the sense of deprivation and denial. As a representative of the Shiromani Akali Dal, Hukam Singh made his case clear that the Sikhs were being denied the rightful place in the independent nation.

Brajeshwar Prasad from Bihar in his proposed amendment moved that efficiency should be the only basis of appointment in the administration. He stated that he believed that there was no minority in the country. With regard to the scheduled castes and Scheduled tribes, he said, 'I hold the opinion that those persons who are clamouring for these seats, for reservation, for consideration, represent a handful of people, constituting the cream of the Harijan society'. He dismissed the argument of social oppression wondering why for all these centuries they never got organised. He further added that others were also suppressed due to the foreign rule in India and stated categorically, 'I cannot accept the proposition that the Caste Hindus have perpetrated any wrong on anybody'.

Guptanath Singh, also from Bihar, moved his amendment which included the expression 'such other castes who are educationally and socially backward' in addition to the scheduled castes and scheduled tribes. It was not the first time that the idea of backwardness independent of untouchables and tribals was moved in the Constituent Assembly. Such an argument met with a general response that the whole of India was educationally backward. That was true. With low literacy rate, it was not possible to locate certain distinct castes which could be covered under the term 'backward'. Singh, after pointing out that communalism had proved to be curse for the country, stated that there were other castes whose conditions were no better than the scheduled castes and scheduled tribes. He then referred to some cases one of which was regarding a Brahmin student who applied for the scholarship meant for the scheduled castes claiming to be so and another of a brilliant student who was terminated after appointment as he belonged to a 'very backward class'. It seemed that Singh would have continued to narrate case after case of such kind had the President not cut short his speech. However, R.K. Sidhwa, who was the first speaker after all amendments had been moved, proposed that Article 301 in which backward classes have been mentioned should be deleted. He made it clear that the amendment proposed by Guptanath Singh was not acceptable and should be rejected.

R.K. Sidhwa[4] also opposed the amendment moved by Hukam Singh in which Parsis were also included. He said,

> My community has never asked for special rights in any legislatures or in services … . Merit alone should count in our future Constitution and nothing else … . This method has been started by the British Government of favouring one community or the other.

Sardar Vallabhbhai Patel was the next speaker and he made it clear that he had no intention of speaking on the matter, but Hukam Singh's speech prompted him to make an intervention. As a matter of fact, the Sikh issue had been settled earlier and the matter had seemed closed for good, but Hukam

Singh's speech surprised everybody. Patel was shocked that the Congress had been accused of breaking the promise. He said,

> If he refers to 1929 and then again to the Partition of India and Pakistan, I wish to point out to him that there was not a single Sikh voice against the partition; on the other hand they are probably in the forefront in demanding the partition of the Punjab. After the butchery and bloodshed that took place in Rawalpindi and Multan, the Sikhs were terribly upset and they had considerable sympathy from the Congress. At the same time there were other tragedies happening in other parts of the country and then came the conflagration in Lahore, Amritsar and other parts of the Punjab. It was at that time with the concurrence of the Sikhs—unanimously, with one voice they agreed—we agreed to the Partition of India. Now to turn round and charge us with a breach of faith is a charge which I cannot understand and it is not right for the Sikh community—a brave community like the Sikhs—to fling these charges at us. Who were we to agree to the partition of India and partition of Punjab if the Sikhs were opposed?

There is a reasonably valid evidence to substantiate Patel's remark only on the issue of partition of Punjab. On 4 June 1947, Lord Mountbatten had stated the following in a press conference:

> There are two main parties to this plan [partition]—the Congress and the Muslim league—but another community much less numerous but of great importance—the Sikh community—have of course to be considered. I found that it was mainly at the request of the Sikh community that Congress had put forward the resolution on the partition of the Punjab, and you will remember that in the words of that resolution they wished the Punjab to be divided between predominantly Muslim and non-Muslim areas. (cf. Singh, 1999: 275)

The excerpts from the speech of Patel dealt with what Hukam Singh had said about the promise of 1929. However, Patel's position that the Congress agreed to the partition of India only if the Punjab was also partitioned and it was done due to the insistence of the Sikhs and in the process he accused Sikhs of demanding the partition of India. In the light of the press statement by Lord Mountbatten, it becomes clear that the Sikhs asked for only the partition of Punjab if India were to be partitioned. It seems that Sardar Vallabhbhai Patel missed the same point made by Hukam Singh about partition. He has also commented that seven districts of Punjab became part of India in the partition due to the Sikhs. Interestingly, every time the Sikh leaders raised any issue, the final response would come from Patel. After his response to the 1929 issue, he turned his attention to 1946 as mentioned by Hukam Singh. He said,

> Then again he says about 1946. If he refers to the Minorities Committee recommendations, I can understand it. I propose to explain it in detail as to what has taken place. But I do not know what he meant by 1946 promise. If I can have any concrete expression of a promise given by Congress leaders, I might, and if so I do not think there is any Congressman who will go against that promise. I have not however understood the psychology of the Sikh leaders—some of them—who often charge everybody with breach of faith, and always complain of minorities being ill-treated.
>
> Look at the army. Are they not very heavily over-weighted? What have we done? We are under their protection and we trust them and not a single army officer is disloyal to us. Why do you create this feeling for nothing? What is it that you want?

Clearly, Patel was flabbergasted over the perseverance of the Sikh leaders in insisting on the core Sikh issues. Patel said something questionable and communal without anyone protesting his creating the categories of 'we' and 'they'. He said, 'we trust them' and 'not a single army officer disloyal to us'. One may argue that it was exactly the kind of perception that Patel and others like him had had about religious minorities to which the Sikhs were now reacting. The Sikh position, personified by Hukam Singh, indicated that the Sikhs did not believe the Congress and were suspicious of its designs. Hukam Singh clearly pointed out that if they had accepted reservation for certain untouchable castes among the Sikhs, then it never meant that they would not ask for more.

It was clear to everybody that the construction of modern India was a twin project of socio-economic development and nation-building. Partition and religious nationalism created trust deficit between the Muslims and the Hindus, whereas all other religious minorities were significantly marginal in terms of numbers that their fears as well as their noise could not have been audible enough to disturb the power that might be. The

Sikhs, however, were different from other non-Muslim religious minorities. First, they were largely concentrated in Punjab and PEPSU, though in 1949 they were not in majority. Second, they were visible in the nationalist struggle. Patwant Singh has the following facts, which may be questionable, to underline the contributions of the Sikhs to freedom struggle:

> Out of 2,175 Indian martyrs for freedom, 1,557, or 75 per cent, were Sikhs. Out of 2,646 Indians sent to the Andaman for life imprisonment 2,147, or 80 per cent, were Sikhs. Out of 127 Indians who were hanged 92, or 80 per cent, were Sikhs. Out of 20,000 who joined the Indian National Army under Subhas Bose, 12,000 or 60 per cent, were Sikhs. And the Sikhs comprise only 2 per cent of India's total population! (Singh, 2002: 253–254)

The Sikhs were in significant numbers in the Indian army. Despite being the third largest religious minority (after Muslims and Christians) and less than 2 per cent of the total population of the country, the Sikhs became important players in the nation-building process. However, Hukam Singh had different perspective on nationalism because nationalism for him was contextual. The same day, that is 14 October 1949, he commented in the same speech that

> I might be accused of communalism when I sound the discordant note. But I hold that this nationalism is an argument for vested interests. Even the aggressiveness of the majority would pass off as nationalism, while the helplessness of the minority might be dubbed as communalism. It is very easy for the majority to preach nationalism to the minorities, but is very difficult to act up to it.

Obviously, the reason for Patel getting provoked could be located in the way Hukam Singh presented the case of the Sikhs.

Patel insisted that the Sikh leaders both in Congress and outside always argued that they should be treated at par with other religious minorities. They did not want any 'special arrangement'. He further added that the Sikhs asked for special treatment to certain castes at par with their Hindu counterparts. Interestingly, Patel revealed the views expressed by some Sikh leaders which he earlier refrained from doing so in his speech on 16 May 1949 that the Sikhs said that 'if you do not recognise these concessions, then they will go back to the Scheduled

Caste Hindus and we will lose'. Apparently, the scheduled caste members of the Constituent Assembly were against giving any concession to caste/community other than belonging to Hindu religion. Patel emphasised that he was instrumental in changing that decision and included certain Sikh castes for the eligibility of reservation policy. He said,

> What is the use of charging the Congress with having broken promises? Do not break the promises you have given, and do not charge others with breach of promises.
>
> What is it that you get in the Services? Even at present, what do the Sikhs do? What do other communities do? … . You are quarrelling or asking for the minor posts—Chaprasis and clerks. Is it the Sikh position now that we have not got enough Sikh Chaprasis and clerks? Are you going to raise the community in that manner? If that is so, tell me, and if you leave what you have got for the Scheduled castes, I shall persuade the Constituent Assembly to give you what you want, but you will repent afterwards.

Looking at the times and situations in which the debates were going on it emerges that Patel might have been justified in his assertion so far as the Sikh issue was concerned. He seemed annoyed with their inconsistency and unpredictability with regard to the decision taken with their consensus. They were consistently reverting back to what had already been decided with their consent. However, looking at present could lead us to many doubts. Castes are struggling to be recognised as backward classes to reap the benefits of reservation policy. Sikhs remained agitated and felt betrayed—a feeling that never vanished. Sikh grievances were hijacked by the extremist elements within the community and Punjab witnessed a violent militant movement for Khalistan in 1980s. Patel's advice might have been justified in the light of subsequent events, when he told the Sikh members of the House that 'Do not break that spirit by continuously saying, "We are injured, we are helpless, we are a minority, we are hopeless, we cannot do anything"'. For him, Sikhs were brave and virile and could fend for themselves. Patel told the House that the atmosphere for the Muslims was not pleasant and there were reasons for which the Congress was not responsible. He expressed hope that the things would finally settle peacefully. He assured the Sikh community that the

Congress had done nothing to harm their interests, but that was one way of understanding the perspective on Sikhs, whereas the Sikhs' perspective was different.

After Patel's speech, Article 296 as amended was adopted by the Constituent Assembly to be the part of the Constitution. The issues raised by Hukam Singh had caused ripples in the Congress camp. When the Constituent Assembly met in the afternoon on 14 October 1949, the first thing that the President did was that he read the document containing the proceedings of the meeting of the Sikh members of the East Punjab Legislative Assembly as well as the Constituent Assembly held on 10 May 1949,[5] which was presided by Sardar Kapoor Singh. The following were the recommendations made by the Committee:

1. The Sikh backward classes, namely, Mazhabis, Kabir Panthis, Ramdasis, Baurias and Sikligars should be given the same privileges with regard to representations in the legislatures and other political concessions in the East Punjab and PEPSU as may be provided for the scheduled castes. For this purpose, either these classes may be included in the schedule of scheduled castes enumerated in the Draft Constitution or seats may be reserved for them on population basis out of the quota reserved for Sikhs.
2. In the East Punjab, seats should be reserved for Sikhs according to their population with right to contest additional seats.
3. In provinces other than the East Punjab and the centre, the Sikh minorities where they are entitled to representation on the strength of their numbers should have seats reserved for them and when adequate numbers are not returned by election, their strength should be made good by nomination.
4. The Sikhs will be prepared to give up reservation in the East Punjab if Sikh and Hindu scheduled castes are lumped together and seats reserved for them on the strength of their population

In case these proposals are not accepted, the whole question of safeguards for Sikh minorities may be referred to arbitration in accordance with the assurances given by the Congress.

It seemed that the matter was solved so far as the Sikh issue was concerned. By 16 November 1949, the discussion on the Draft Constitution was complete and most of the articles were either adopted or after certain amendments were passed by the Constituent Assembly. The vision and mission of the Assembly was achieved. Obviously, modern India was not merely imagined on rational basis but also decided on the basis of majority vote. What was the most notable aspect was that with tremendous patience and perseverance the President of the Constituent Assembly allowed the debates to take place till all aspects of the matter were covered. The next step was to have the final reading of the amended Draft Constitution and it was christened as third reading. When the third reading began on 17 November and concluded on 26 November 1949, the Sikh issue emerged again.

II. Third Reading and the Sikh Question

We may begin with the speech of Bhopinder Singh Man, who spoke on 21 November 1949, on the Constitution. After suggesting that Kashmir had been given 'very enviable position', he began to build his argument to bring out the issue of the Sikhs: 'I will be failing in my duty if I do not give you the reactions of my own community, the Sikhs of the East Punjab, so far as this Constitution goes'. He further added,

> it was agreed originally that all the minority groups will be given due representation in the Services compatible with the efficiency of the administration and that there will be a special Officer at the Centre and in the provinces to watch the working of the Constitution so far as these minorities are concerned. They [Sikhs] feel that towards the later days of the framing of this Constitution, that attitude was changed and different articles incorporated in the Constitution brushing aside all minorities except the Scheduled Castes. We felt that this change was very lightly brought about in spite of the advice of Sardar Patel who said in the draft Report that decisions arrived at should not be lightly changed.

Bhupinder Singh Mann was expressing his anguish over the way the Sikh depressed classes were treated at par with their Hindu counterparts. He said that it should have been done without any contestation. H.J. Khandekar expressed his astonishment that there were scheduled castes among the Sikhs. He said,

> I remember when Dr Ambedkar wanted to denounce the Hindu religion. Sikh friends and Sikh leaders came to Dr Ambedkar and his party to embrace Sikhism. But, today, I hear from this platform a Sikh friend of mine saying that there are untouchables in the Sikh community. On these grounds the seats of the Scheduled Castes in the East Punjab have been taken by my Sikh friends. If at all they wanted to take their share in the name of untouchability, they ought to have taken it from the general seats.

Strangely enough if the percentage of the seats reserved were to be decided in terms of the population proportion, then Khandekar's argument was not making any sense. He could be only logically meaningful if the reservations were to be made on the basis of the fixed quota. Therefore, his argument that the Sikhs had encroached upon the rights and privileges of the Hindu scheduled castes in East Punjab was somewhat misplaced in one context. It should also be seen from an altogether different perspective. In the face of domination of the Sikhs in the state, the probability and possibility of choosing from various reserved seats could get biased due to which the Hindu scheduled castes faced the threat of underrepresentation

Hukam Singh was the first speaker on 21 November 1949, when the Constituent Assembly resumed its business after lunch. He began his speech with comments on the Constitution and specifically mentioning Article 19 as not clearly guaranteeing the Right to Freedom. He said, 'Unless material insecurity is eliminated personal freedoms are paper safeguards'. However, the major portion of his speech was focussed on the issue of Sikhs. It seemed that he had come prepared to respond to what Patel had said in reaction to his speech few days back. He began with the matter which is still being articulated in terms of discrepancy between the contribution of Sikhs to the Indian freedom struggle and the privileges they got after independence by the Akali leaders. The articulation of the Sikh sacrifices for freedom ignores and decentres the contribution of the Sikh soldiers, who constituted a large minority much more than their proportion in the total population of India, to the perpetuation of the British hegemony in India. Let us see what Hukam Singh had to say, later on, which became the buzz word of the Akalis, that is, 'sacrifices'. He said,

> If the sacrifices for freedom were to be looked back upon, the Sikhs can feel well proud of their contributions. In 1872 in the well-known Kuka rebellion more than 68 Sikhs were blown off with cannons. In 1907 S. Ajit Singh, Kishen Singh and others played a very important role in the movement. During 1912–16 the Ghadar movement got considerable momentum by the advent of revolutionaries brought in by Kamagata Maru and other ships. Most of them were Sikhs who died cheerfully on the gallows for the love of their country. During the Martial Law Regime in 1919 the Sikhs raised a bold and open revolt against the British and underwent many hardships.

The assertion of Hukam Singh could be challenged on various grounds. Nobody asks a martyr whether he sacrificed his life due to his religious affiliation or as an Indian. Was Kuka rebellion a nationalist upsurge? If so, then why did the Kuka militants attack and kill Muslim butchers in certain cities of Punjab and then moved on to attack Malerkotla state ruled by a Muslim Nawab? The family of Shaheed Bhagat Singh was Arya Samaji. The movement to which Hukam Singh made reference in the House was agrarian movement that emerged in the Canal Colonies because the farmers who had been allotted land were informed that their proprietary rights were temporary. It goes without saying that both Kishen Singh and Ajit Singh were big landowners. The voyage of Kamagata Maru is the story of those Punjabis who wanted to do big in Canada. They were not freedom fighters and in the return journey no Ghadar activist joined them. Hukam Singh continued his commentary on the Sikhs and the Congress party and in the process gave sufficient material for his party men to construct the Congress as anti-Sikh party. Subsequently, though he joined the Congress to become the Speaker of the Lok Sabha. He said,

> The Congress is announcing again and again that all minorities shall have proper safeguards. The Muslims refused to be contented with any safeguards, but insisted on having a home for themselves. They got Pakistan and can have no further grievance. The Anglo-Indian community has been sufficiently protected. They can have no grouse. The Parsees and the Christians are far

> more advanced educationally and economically and have declared that they do not want any safeguards. It is only the Sikh community that earnestly desired, repeatedly requested and constantly cried for safeguards but have been denied any consideration. They fail to understand why they have met this treatment. The majority can oppress, it can even suppress the minority; but it cannot infuse contentment or satisfaction by these methods.

As the end of his speech on the Sikh question, Hukam Singh responded to Khandekar's objection to the provision for the depressed classes among the Sikhs. He pointed out that despite the absence of untouchability, the same castes could not be denied the benefits of reservation and then added that the Sikh depressed classes did not take any share of the Hindu untouchables because reservation was based on population. As if speaking on behalf of the Sikh community by having its mandate, he said, 'My community cannot subscribe its assent to this historic document'. True to his comment he did not sign the Constitution.

Two days after Hukam Singh's speech, that is, on 23 November 1949, Gurmukh Singh Musafir spoke on the Constitution and he began by saying that the provision of separate electorate was a curse. After showering praises on the top leaders of the Congress, such as Nehru and Patel, he started saying all the good things about the Constitution. Towards the end of his speech, he turned to Hukam Singh's speech:

> Sardar Hukam Singh and some other friends have said that deletion of the provision relating to reservation in services has created dissatisfaction among the Sikhs. As I have said, the minorities have given their common consent to the abolition of separate electorates, but I must confess that the Sikhs and other minorities in some places are dissatisfied because reservation in services has been removed. But to incorporate such a thing in the Constitution would have been contradictory to other Articles. Now when the reservation has been abolished, every man shall be appointed on his merit and thus everybody will be inspired with the desire to make himself accomplished.

It was a remarkable piece of argument bordering on to buffoonery in retrospect. It was so clear that Musafir was going out of the way to please the central leadership of the Congress.

On the other hand, Hukam Singh, as an Akali, was taking a position which was out of tune with the facts and reality. Both were important political leaders and both became successful politicians afterwards. The last Sikh speaker to raise the issue of minorities was Sardar Sochet Singh from Patiala and PEPSU on 23 November 1949. Sardar Sochet Singh argued that 'the Sikhs were not justified in demanding any undue discrimination in their own favour'. He cited figures to show that the Sikhs did not need any protection or privilege. According to him, literacy rate among the Sikhs was the highest at 17.5 per cent. He mainly emphasised that the Sikhs were meritorious and they would be appointed more than their proportion in the population of the country if there were no reservation. He gave certain examples in support of his contention. Agriculture and army being regarded as the two major occupations of the Sikhs, Sochet Singh responded to Hukam Singh's argument by saying that the prevalent position of the Sikhs would continue to persist for some time. He gave the list of prominent Sikh leaders, who did not want that all the Sikhs should be included in the category of backward classes.[6] He said,

> Unfortunately, the trouble with some of our leaders is that they have never throughout their public career had experience of working in any secular institution and they have built their leadership and power on slogans of 'religion or community in danger' and they find it difficult to give up old habits and propaganda or to strike upon new outlook or programme. I can hope that had master Tara Singh ever worked as a Municipal Commissioner in Amritsar and seen in actual practice that Hindu and Sikh Commissioners were equally anxious and keen for sanitation and the health of all citizens living in the municipal town, he could have overcome much of the imaginary fears and suspicions against the majority that are haunting him today. In one breath he declares that Hindus and Sikhs are comrades in life as well as death and in the next that they cannot live under one another's domination.

The Sikh question did not come up for debate again and interestingly with the exception of Khandekar, the matter was taken up only by the Sikh members of the Constituent Assembly and it was clear that the Sikhs were divided on the issue of any further special treatment to them as a minority. The differences were never resolved among the two contesting groups—one representing the Congress and the other representing the Shiromani Akali Dal. It still remains unsettled, though Punjab witnessed one and half decades of terrorist violence that could be aptly regarded as the outcome of the two competing discourses. At this moment, it is important to examine the other religious minorities and the nature of debate in the Constituent Assembly.

III. By Way of Conclusion

The period between 1946 and 1950 is period of great social and political churning, out of which the ecstasy of independence and agony of partition form the two major events and their inseparable relationship is quite obvious. Punjab and Bengal shared common destiny due to partition. Both were among the big states of India and both were ruled by the Muslim League at the time of partition. The only distinguishing feature of Punjab was the presence of a sizeable minority of the Sikhs who were rulers of the state at the time of its annexation by the British. The Sikhs excelled in their glorious martial tradition which was exploited fully by the British. At the same time, as the Sikh historians tell us between the lines, the British decisively and significantly contributed to transform the syncretised religious tradition of the Sikh into monolithic and exclusive tradition. The defined Sikh identity of keeping unshorn hair was strictly adhered to in the Sikh regiments. At the time of partition of the country on religious basis the Sikhs might have nurtured high expectations out of the choice they made to remain with India. As a matter of fact, they did not have any choice, for they had constructed their history and mythology as a struggle against the Muslim rulers, though the idea of Khalistan was floated in the early 1940s. The Sikh leaders, particularly the Akali leaders, expected at that historical moment by way of assurance that their autonomy would be recognised. Still there was another reason for expecting such a deal from the national leaders.

The Sikhs were instrumental in substantiating the power of non-violent Satyagraha as espoused by Gandhi immediately after the end of the First World War. The entire Gurdwara Reform Movement starting from 1920 was fought by Akalis non-violently. It so enraged some of the radicals, such as Arjan Singh Garhgaz, that they organised the Babbar Akali movement which practiced violence for freedom. Interestingly, the Akali leadership remained quite close to Gandhi even after the enactment of the Gurudwara Act in 1925 after which the control over Sikh shrines was handed over to the SGPC. After the end of the Second World War, Gandhi lost his political influence within the Congress, but retained his moral appeal.

There is also another way of looking at the changing position of the Sikhs. The Sikhs are known for their bravery and valour. The discourse of marital race as created by the British in India is the major text of self-perception among the Sikhs. This text has numerous sub-texts of which the relevant may be stated here. The first is the powerful tradition of martyrdom. Fenech (2000: 1) opines that the Sikhs in general identify martyrdom as the 'fundamental feature of the Sikh tradition' and the same feature is also 'noticed' by the non-Sikhs. The word *shahid* is an expression of supreme sacrifice and worthy of worship, as it has happened in the case of Baba Deep Singh. Strongly connected to the tradition of martyrdom is the sub-text of sacrifices made by the Sikhs for the independence of the country.

However, as a part of the construction of the discourse of martial race, the Sikh soldiers in the British army died in larger numbers than those who died for the liberation of the country. Ironically, many of the Sikh martyrs for freedom were ex-soldiers. The number of Sikh soldiers was far more than their proportion in the total population—the fact that establishes their being the pillars of the British Raj.

Gupta (1992), while commenting upon the militancy period in Punjab, has argued that the sub-text of the Sikhs and their relationships with Hindus and the Indian state could be understood how the ethnic imagos and their correlative spaces are constructed. He (Gupta, 1992: 224) writes,

> Analysts are often bemused by the manner in which ethnic combatants arraign themselves and tendentiously portray the situation to justify rival claims and grievances. The ethnic self-images that the communities throw up under these circumstances and the perceptions that they forward seem so clearly farcical, misplaced and unreal that most scholars are quite content to present them as such.

However, Gupta's observation is based on limited fieldwork and he seems to be forgetting the fact that the Sikhs have history to prove their valour and enlarged spaces with not only the list of martyrs but also the fact that their militancy culminated into the establishment of Sikh Raj in the 18th century. Therefore, the text of Sikh valour could be treated as one of the enabling factors in the Sikh's claims for special treatment and it cannot be the sole foundation of such a claim.

It seems that the Sikh leadership, particularly the Akalis, fell into 'historical trap' due to their attempt to carve out a political space in anticipation of the democratic political processes where the size of the religious community mattered. The Sikhs were politically divided with diverse political affiliations and the only way out was to make communal appeal. The politics of the day helped them to remain imprisoned in the trap. Immediately after independence, Urdu as the language of the state was discontinued. The struggle to introduce Punjabi got communalised and as a result, Punjabi written in Gurmukhi script got identified with the Sikhs. The Hindi agitation immediately after Partap Singh Kairon became the Chief Minister when Bhim Sen Sachar resigned in 1956 further contributed to the politics of communities in the state. The Akalis, instead of understanding the Hindi agitation as a politics of power, got trapped into self-actualising prophecy by virtue of which any attempt at contesting certain issues was perceived as anti-Sikh activity. The construction of 'we' and 'they' was founded upon religion. The first 50 years of postcolonial Punjab, the politics of power which began in the absence of Gandhi and the failure of the Congress leaders to treat Sikhs as exceptional from other religious communities, owing to constitutional limitations, witnessed the politics of power manifested through the Punjabi Suba agitation and later on Khalistan militancy turned out to be marked by the Sikh struggle for special treatment. The outcome was tragic.

Notes

1. Detailed discussion on the issue has been given in Chapter 3.
2. See Chapter 3 for details.
3. Kapurthala, Patiala, Nabha and Faridkot states had Sikh rulers.
4. R.K. Sidhwa (1882–1957) was a Parsi belonging to a priest family in Karachi. He was educated up to matriculation. As a result of his social service and determination, he was elected the mayor of Karachi in 1939 despite the lack of support from his own Parsi community (Kewalramani, 1974)
5. The following members had attended the meeting: Sardar Kapoor Singh, Giani Kartar Singh, Sardar Swaran Singh, Sardar Ishar Singh Majhail, Sardar Ujjal Singh, Sardar Singh Mann, Bhai Piara Singh, Sardar Inder Singh, Sardar Gurbachan Singh Bajwa, Sardar Dalip Singh Kang, Sardar Ajit Singh, Sardar Shiv Saran Singh, Sardar Narottam Singh, Sant Narinder Singh, Sardar Hukam Singh, Sardar Tara Singh, Sardar Rattan Singh Moga, Sardar Rattan Singh Logarh, Sardar Gurbachan Singh Ferozepore, Sardar Sajan Singh Mirjandpuri, Sardar Jagjit Singh Mann and Sardar Sardul Singh.
6. The names he mentioned were: Maharaja of Patiala, Sardar Baldev Singh, Jathedar Udham Singh Nagoke, Sardar Partap Singh Kairon and Giani Gurmukh Singh Musafir.

8

Unrevised Perspectives

Third Reading

The present chapter deals with the recurrent themes which have already been examined in previous chapters, but their reappearance does not indicate the continuation of the debate, but an indication that certain matters remained unresolved. The discussion in this final chapter has been divided into two parts, which are relatively independent from each other in terms of the issues involved. The first part is a brief description of the issues which resurfaced again in the third reading of the Draft Constitution. The second part covers the last few days of the Constituent Assembly and the passing of the Constitution after which it was adopted and India became a republic with effect from 26 January 1950.

The Constituent Assembly began functioning on 9 December 1946 and by 18 September 1949 most of its work was complete. The third reading of the Draft Constitution was still two months away, that is, 18 November 1949. No article of the Draft Constitution, whatsoever was its importance, had been passed without sagacious and erudite analysis and examination. Despite the fact that even if certain issues were well settled earlier, the same were taken up in relation to other issues to examine whether there were contradictory clauses or articles in the Constitution. Changes occurred with time among the members and they accepted certain provisions, but still some members continued to steadfastly hold the views concerning their communities and regions. They were committed to making the new India modern along certain lines which should not be the replica of the West. India in their imagination, thoughts and vision should be the one in which diversities were accommodated but not subjugated in the liberal democratic framework with a provision of individual freedom and equality. It is interesting to note that the governance-related articles of the Draft Constitution evoked far less debates than the social issues. Nehru had made it clear in his speeches that there was a need to have broad consensus based on welfare for all. Politics of voting could be a practice for the future.

On 17 September 1949, K.M. Munshi moved the resolution to take necessary steps to translate the Constitution into Hindi before 26 January 1950. The resolution also included the proposal to publish the Constitution in 'other major languages of India'. Munshi informed the House that an Expert Committee of distinguished scholars was constituted on 15 March 1949 for the revision of already translated text in Hindi.[1] The resolution was adopted after some discussion and the President requested members to submit the list of experts so that the translation of the Constitution could be carried on in other Indian languages.

I. Third Reading

The Constituent Assembly met on 17 November 1949 at 10 in the morning in the Constitution Hall for the third reading. Dr B.R. Ambedkar moved the resolution 'That the Constitution as settled by the Assembly be passed'. When H.V. Kamath requested Ambedkar to deliver the speech, he replied that he would speak at the end of the reading. The President informed the House that he had received 71 names of the members who wanted to speak and said that each member would speak for 20 minutes. At the same time, he told the House that he would accommodate if some other members liked to speak. It should be mentioned here that no amendment was moved during the period of the third reading of the Draft Constitution. The members expressed their views and also their full or partial acceptance or rejection of the Constitution. It was clear to all that 26 January 1950 had been fixed for the adoption of the Constitution.

The first speaker was V.I. Munuswamy Pillay from Madras who belonged to the scheduled castes. He expressed his wholehearted support to the Draft Constitution and asserted that Articles 320 and 335 dealing with the reservation for the Scheduled castes in services were worthy of appreciation. Seth Govind Das, the champion of Hindi language, not knowing the implication of his mode of expression said that the way 'Untouchability is a crime' according to the provision of the fundamental rights, cow killing should have been considered to be crime. He found it strange that the name of the country is 'India that is Bharat'. Lakshminarayan Sahu was not happy with the way 'village' had been treated in the Constitution and thought that there was a need to revive cottage industries. He concluded his speech by saying that 'this Constitution is not to our liking' because he thought that the major states would take away most of the funds, and Utkal and Assam would become slaves. K. Hanumanthaiah pointed out certain obvious contradictions in the Constitution. These were: (a) 'A republic with a King above and Rajpramukhs below', (b) a Federal Constitution but almost unitary in essence and (c) it should have been written in our own language, but they had been compelled to write the Constitution in a foreign language.

Professor K.T. Shah might be remembered in the history of the making of the Constitution as a member who moved maximum number of amendments and virtually all were rejected when put to vote. He was a socialist and his amendments carried his ideology, but, at the same time, he was convincing, logical and articulate. He personified and epitomised the quest for socialist society in the face of overt bias towards capitalism and liberal democracy as inseparable elements of modernity. It was his final speech in the Constituent Assembly and he minced no words in expressing what he was thinking at that time. He said,

> Because you are unable to trust in full the people; because you are unable to realise that it is only by working a democracy that democracy will really be established in this country, you have not accepted those suggestions and those amendments of mine which wanted such weapons, such instruments and devices to be introduced in the Constitution, whereby the right action by the will of the people for the benefit of the people and through the representatives of the people could have been established.

> It is not only that you are lacking in a proper faith in the people as a whole. It is perhaps even more true to say that you are lacking in faith in your own leadership. For, if your leadership is really popular; if your leadership is really the open expression of the subconscious feeling, the hopes and aspirations of the people, then you need not doubt at all that the leaders' guidance in crucial moments will be accepted; and the device I have suggested will be fruitful rather mischievous.
>
> I hold, therefore, that this Constitution is not, in the fullness of the sense, a real, working, effective democracy that the people of India had been led to expect they have achieved.

Despite all this criticism, he hoped that it would work to bring real democracy in the country and the people would become real rulers in this country. On 18 November 1949, when M. Ananthasayanam Ayyangar delivered his speech on the Constitution, he made a special mention of Shah and it would be of interest to know what he said:

> Though we have not been able to accept many of the amendments tabled by our Friend, Prof. K.T. Shah, for whose learning, intelligence and capacity I have good deal of admiration, he has confessed to me outside the House when I talked to him that though we were not going to accept his amendments, he tabled them because he wanted to lay his point of view before us. He has accepted the defeats in a spirit of good sportsmanship.

There would still be another entry of Shah in the history of independent India when he fought elections for the post of President of India against Dr Rajendra Prasad. Shah also used an extremely amorphous category of 'people' to construct democracy. The word 'people' was made famous with regard to democracy by Abraham Lincoln's much quoted lines. However, when it is stated that give power to the people, it does not make any clear cut identification of who would have power. At the same time, 'power to the people' catches the imagination of all. In other words, 'people' is an imaginary construct and any attempt to make it operational would end in disaster.

Predictably, the next speaker, R.K. Sidhwa criticised Shah for his comments on the Constitution. Professor N.G. Ranga pointed out that whereas the United States had failed to give the civil rights to Blacks, the Constituent Assembly did that for the scheduled castes. Nazuriddin Ahmad stated that the greatest wonder implicated in the entire process is that the Constituent Assembly has finished two readings of the Constitution. Annie Mascarene from the Travancore state underlined salient issues to put the Constitution in its rightful position. She said,

> This is the first instance when heterogeneous interests in a continent State like India have united themselves to form a homogeneous unit in order to lay down rules and regulations that should lead us or guide us in future to live a national life. Like other nations of the world we have peculiar characteristics. We have differences of caste, community and creed: there is the question of untouchability, the emancipation of the Depressed Classes, provisions for the tribes, for religious and linguistic minorities like Muslims, Sikhs, Christians, their safeguards and protection.

Then she added, 'We are at the beginning of nation-building. We have to survive as a nation'.

There had been continuous streams of opposing views on the validity of the Constitution as such or some of its provisions, showing that there was no consensus on the vision of postcolonial India. Interestingly, the Congress was in a majority and it seemed that its members remained divided on various issues, but voted in accordance with the decision of the party. Such members were aware that their expressed opinions and views would not change the Constitution. It is interesting to note that the members who became prominent political leaders as ministers or chief ministers later on were those who kept quiet on controversial issues by supporting the top leadership through their silence. Interestingly, when Maulana Hasrat Mohani asked the President on 19 November 1949, 'Sir, may I know if there is any chance of any points raised in the speeches of different honourable Members being accepted and introduced onto the Constitution now? If there is no chance, then the whole thing is a farce and I do not find any use, at all of this general discussion'. The President responded, 'I may inform the Maulana that under the rules there is no room for any further amendments at this stage'.

The third reading of the Constitution offered an important opportunity to each member of the Assembly. In other words, the third reading contains multiple discourses hidden into it, and sometimes it becomes difficult to ascertain the real objective underlying the content of the speech of the members. It also became difficult to ascertain whether caste or religion was the dominant factor in India. The crisscrossing of views among members on different issues made it difficult to divide them along party and ideological lines. In such a situation, it may be assumed that if people across religions and castes are banded together to make a united front on question of property rights, then perhaps property issue remained the primary/core element of the Indian society. Let us see how the issues of religion, caste, village, language and property occupied the minds of the members. Obviously, the comments which made the Constitution valid or invalid were not to be taken into serious consideration for examination in the third reading.

Caste and Religion: Knowing well that the third reading was an occasion of congratulating each other for stupendous success in finalising the Constitution by debating each of its articles, some of the members also made critical observations. To start with the good things, M. Ananthasayanam Ayyangar on 18 November 1949 attributed the success in solving the minority problem to the 'integrity of various religious and other minorities'. He was clear that the provision of separate electorate introduced by the British had created divisions between communities. He then added,

> It is now left to the majority community to show that whatever religion an individual may belong to, it is only his talent and spirit of service that will count and not his community and persons belonging to the minority communities will not be discriminated against merely because they belong to particular minority communities.

B.A. Mandloi from CP and Berar, in his speech, changed the content of the discourse on minorities. It is clear that the safeguards for minorities changed radically without any voluntary surrender by them except, of course, the leaders of Christians, Anglo-Indians and Parsis. Mandloi said, 'After the Draft Constitution was presented to this Assembly the safeguards which this Constituent Assembly has provided for the so-called minorities have been voluntarily surrendered by them'. On 19 November 1949, T. Prakasam, in the *Andhra*

Kesari, opined that by abolishing untouchability and bringing to the Harijans equality in all matters of social life was the greatest achievement of the Constitution.

Shibban Lal Saxena turned prophetic in his speech on 19 November 1949, when he said that partition of the country was the greatest tragedy and it was the price of freedom and added, 'That most unnatural division was forced upon the country. I am convinced that so long as this division lasts, neither India nor Pakistan can be at peace'. He further pointed out that the eradication of untouchability was a great step forward towards equality for all and considered untouchability worse than slavery.

Reaction to the resolution to end the provision of reservation for the religious minorities among the members belonging to the 'majority community' was supportive, for they perceived that the provision of separate electorate during British rule was causally connected with the partition of the country. However, the members belonging to the religious minorities were not unanimous on the issue and they showed a degree of ambivalence. Rev. J.J.M. Nichols Roy was clear enough to argue that 'Religion must not be the basis for making difference between one man and another man. We are glad that, this reservation of seats for any community on the basis of religion has been abolished'. However, such a view was not shared by the members of other religious communities, particularly the Sikhs, who began to consistently argue that they had been betrayed because the Congress leaders did not fulfil the promises they gave. The most prominent issue that emerged was connected with the Sikh religious minority, as the Sikh members of the Constituent Assembly spoke about it unambiguously.

Village: The village could be a matter of contention in the making of the Constitution, but it turned out to be crucial for some members due to the influence of Gandhi. It was not expected that the members of the House would spare time after village panchayat was made part of the constitutional provision. However, when the third reading began, the commentary on the significance of village in India was consistently emphasised by many members. The first speaker in this regard was H.V.

Kamath, who gave a suitable attention to the issue of village when he rose to speak on 19 November 1949 as the first speaker of the day. Any mention of village in the House was expected to be the critique of Ambedkar's views on village. Kamath did the expected when he turned to the question of village. He said, 'Dr Ambedkar at first stigmatised the villages as senks [sic.] of superstition and ignorance or something like that, it is good that we embodied in the Directive Principles the salutary provision for village panchayats'. Arun Chandra Guha from West Bengal expressed his displeasure over the little attention paid to villages in the Constitution on 21 November 1949. On 22 November 1949, Shyam Nandan Sahay from Bihar was also not happy with the coverage village got in the Constitution. He said,

> I feel that in the matter of framing the Constitution we have superimposed a Constitution from above and have not made a real effort to start from village life. This matter, as we remember, formed the subject of an important discussion in this House and I must admit that for once and for the first time I thought that Dr Ambedkar was not only in the wrong but very much in the wrong.

Upendranath Barman from West Bengal argued for the immediate formation of village panchayat and the transfer of power to them and opined that 'many of the problems of governing this country will be solved'.

Next day on 23 November 1949, B.P. Jhunjhunwala from Bihar focussed more on the issue of village than any other matter in his speech. He began his comment on the village by criticising the centralisation of power. He said,

> Sir, I do not believe in the theory propounded here that everything should be centralised and that the whole country should be governed from the Centre. But I agree that powers should be given to the Centre so that in times of emergency they can be utilised for the benefit of the people. Sir, the Centre should have only such power as is necessary and cannot be exercised by its component governing parts, for the preservation of the unity and integration of the whole of India. Every other power should be, as much as possible, decentralised and given to the unit of village or groups of villages what to say Province. With that purpose in view, I had given notice of an amendment to the Preamble that after the word 'Republic' the words 'to be worked on the basis of

> autonomous village Units or groups of villages organised on the principle of self-sufficiency as far as practical' be added.

The above view was stated to be in accordance with Gandhian values—an idea of self-sufficient village as unit of governance and self-rule. After suggesting the needed amendment of the Preamble of the Indian Constitution, Jhunjhunwala went on to quote most of the speech on the village delivered by Ambedkar on 4 November 1948. After reading Ambedkar's views on village, he said, 'Nothing can be more uncharitable and unjust to the villagers than what Dr Ambedkar has said'. Same day Deep Narayan Sinha from Bihar emphasised the importance of Indian villages as the custodians of the civilisation, whereas most of the countries of the world are turning to the cities.

O.V. Alagesan from Madras was the last speaker to mention the issue of village on 24 November 1949 at length and after him village did not figure in the speeches of the subsequent speakers. He also tended to respond to those members' views who thought that village had not been adequately covered in the Constitution. He said,

> What was conceived under the village unit system was that the village voters would be called upon to elect the Panchayats and only the members of the Panchayats were to take part in the elections to the various assemblies, Provincial and Central. But now, it is the village voter himself who will be called upon to weigh the issues before the country and elect his representative, and so he will directly participate in the election.

He regarded the adopted method more progressive than the indirect way of electing the state and central leaders.

Village could become the important element in imagining India as nation was one of the notable occurrences in the postcolonial modernity. Ambedkar was obviously right about villages, but most of the people of the country were living in villages and still it is so. Gandhi had made a powerful impact on the minds of a section of the Congress leaders. Village was added to the nationalist imagining as a nation-building process. The debate on village forms the most crucial element in the Gandhian rationality of opposition to the colonial rule. The British came with the package—economic, cultural, social and political. Gandhi created a counter-cultural order as a part of his opposition to what symbolised the colonial rule. In opposition to the urban-industrial world of the capitalism, Gandhi found village and cottage industry with the non-consumerist living as the rightful answer to the Western hegemonic domination.

Property: Chapter 5 covers the debate on the acquisition of property for public purposes and the compensation to be given in such cases. When Nehru moved the resolution on acquisition of property, he initiated the debate on individual right to property and the interest of the community. By community he meant the public good. The resolution to amend the concerned article initiated the discussion of ideological nature creating three groupings, namely the liberal democrats supporting capitalism and social justice, socialists advocating classless society and nationalisation of property, and the landed classes arguing for adequate compensation. When the third reading of the Constitution began, the issue of property did not become the matter of protest or resentment as it had happened in the case of minority issue.

B.G. Kher from Bombay was the first to point out the significance of the decisions taken with regard to the matter related to property and property rights on 18 November 1949. Mandloi hailed the formula the Constituent Assembly worked out to compensate the owners of property which was to be acquired by the state. He said,

> A common formula was evolved, whether it be for abolition of zamindaris or for taking over industrial concerns or for nationalising industry. According to that formula, we find that legislatures have been given plenary powers to make laws for the acquisition of property for public purposes.

The first serious criticism on the concerned article on property came from Begum Aizaz Rasul from United Provinces and it is important to quote here at length as follows:

> But, Sir, I regret to say that article 31 relating to the right of property has been very unfairly and unjustly embodied in the Constitution. Like, builders of cities, the makers of the Constitution frame a Constitution for all times, embodying principles of universal applicability. The Constitution should not favour one party or one group or one province. It is regrettable that

> provisions of article 31 do not pass this test and have been made to facilitate party programme in some provinces. It discriminates against *zamindari* abolition Provinces other than the U.P., Bihar and Madras, and also discriminates between agricultural and industrial property. It takes away the rights of justiciability from agricultural property in these provinces.

Begum Rasul offered no explanation how the discrimination had been built into Article 31, but her comment was an indication that there was a lack of consensus on the issue of property. Sita Ram S. Jajoo from Madhya Bharat speaking on the same day pointed out that there was lacuna in the constitutional provision with regard to property rights. He said, 'It is provided in this Constitution that the *zamindaris* will be abolished only in provinces where bills to that effect are introduced before the 26th January, 1950. This abolition should come into force throughout India on a Uniform basis'. He emphasised that after the adoption of the Constitution on 26 January 1950, not a single zamindar should remain in India.

On 22 November 1949, the most memorable intervention was that of Jadubans Sahay from Bihar. Sahay began with the argument that there was a distinction between political freedom and economic democracy. For 30 years, Indians, under the leadership of Gandhi,[2] struggled for political freedom but did not challenge the economic structure. In the face of both industrial and agricultural crisis being faced, no attempt had been made to solve them. Sahay cautioned the members and underlined that the communist threat was looming large on India through its borders, particularly from China. He said, 'Communism cannot be crushed by bullets, neither by our military nor police. It has to be tackled in a different way. The root cause has to be diagnosed. The disease lies in the discontent of the oppressed and hungry millions of the country'. He identified the paradox involved in the way the Constitution had been framed as a kind of compromise formula between two schools of thought. On the one hand, adult franchise had been given to all rich and poor and on the other hand, the existing economic structure was being maintained. He added,

> I would have been glad if we had incorporated in the Constitution at least the hope of a classless society for the people of this

> country. It is not a socialistic thing, it is not born out of the philosophy of Marx. They were the very words said by Mahatma Gandhi.

No further commentary of significance on Article 31 was made by the members, though some comments were made with regard to the property issue.

Language: Gokulbhai Daulatram Bhatt got the chance to speak in the third reading on 18 November 1949 and told the House that he was not present when there was a debate on language and he was advised by some of his colleagues not to raise the issue afterwards. He said,

> if Gujarati, Marathi and such other languages can all be considered regional languages there is no reason why Rajasthani which is similar to them and is spoken by one and a half crore of people could not be considered as a regional language.

M. Ananthasayanam Ayyangar in his speech on 18 November 1949 highlighted the controversies on the issue of language and said that after meeting outside the house three to four times, the matter had been finally resolved within the given time frame. B.G. Kher from Bombay who spoke after Ayyangar accepted the fact that the issue of national language had been settled after lot of debate and 'bitter controversies' and was hopeful that the national language would evolve well in future and adoption of Devanagari script was a wise decision. Mandloi said, 'The Constituent Assembly has laid the foundation of one common language and script for the entire country and it has been achieved with the unanimous consent of all members hailing from different provinces and speaking different languages'.

Dr Raghu Vira did not participate in the debates the way some members such as Shah and Mohani had done. He spoke once and that too for the purpose of asserting that Hindi instead of Hindustani should be the national language in opposition to the powerful and influential speech of Abul Kalam Azad. He was an important member of the House with the added responsibility of creating a glossary of administrative terms in Hindi. On 19 November 1949, he spoke for the second and perhaps the last time in the Constituent Assembly.[3] His uninterrupted speech was a discourse on linguistic nationalism with overtones of communalism. He began with a comment on the fact that there was no reference to the ancient culture of India in the Constitution. He said,

> The Englishmen imposed their language on us in place of our language. In order that our language be restored its due place and the Constitution be framed in it we felt necessary that all things which the English people had deliberately destroyed in order to consolidate their rule here should be restored, so that our country may recover its soul again. But I say with regret that word 'Dharma' does not find any mention in this Constitution. When I raised this point with a friend here he replied that the Constitution was a law and it could contain only those matters which could be subjects of interpretation in law courts. But, Sir, my submission is that this country is not eager to have new laws alone, it wants earnestly to rise to higher planes than that of laws.

Raghu Vira was disheartened with the fact that there was no reference to Dharma, but elated that one of the Indian languages has been adopted as the official language. Here also he expressed his unhappiness that Hindi would become operative only after 15 years. He underlined 'the deep inter-relationship between language and politics' and opined, 'The decision with regard to nationalities in Europe is always on the basis of language'. The following observations of Vira make an interesting reading:

> Besides I find that real masters of this country still continue to be the Bureaucrats who should as a matter of policy be its servants only. Nor have we made any effort to eliminate litigation from this country. I am afraid that in the next fifteen years the roots of English influence in this country would have become twice as strong as the English people were able to make in their rule extending over a period of hundred and fifty years. The effect of all this is that the reins of power would remain in the hands of English knowing classes. I am however hoping that after elections on the basis of adult franchise many people who do not know English would be returned to the Parliament and they would certainly dethrone English from its ruling position. I am convinced that boycott of English is absolutely necessary for the progress of the country.

Raghu Vira's ideas could be christened as linguistic-nationalist. Knowing that he had got his education in the

West and Hindi was not his mother tongue, his hostility towards English language and arguments for having language of one's own make an interesting case. After he broke away from the Congress, he joined the Jan Sangh and subsequently became its president. However, his efforts did not popularise Hindi. He gave difficult vocabulary and many jokes were made on his brand of Hindi called Raghuviri Hindi.

H.J. Khandekar on 21 November 1949 made it clear that if Hindi was to become the national language, then it should be such that every Indian could understand it. His comment created commotion in the House. Similarly, on the same day, Jaspat Roy Kapoor evoked Gandhi to make his point that 'We have adopted Hindi as the national language, a language which is to be composed of all the languages and which has to take shape from all the different languages of the country'.

In the face of near all quiet from the members belonging to South India on the language question, S.V. Krishnamoorthy Rao's following informative comment might have been a welcome relief for the diehard supporters of Hindi:

> I may bring to the notice of this Assembly that we are already implementing the Resolution that was adopted in the Assembly. I am glad to inform the House that the Government of Mysore has passed an order making Hindi compulsory in all High Schools in the State.

On 23 November 1949, Gurmukh Singh Musafir insisted that the Constitution should be written in Hindi. How wrong were some of members' views on English could be discerned from R.V. Dhulekar's speech, who assured the diehard supporters of Hindi that like the British 'the English language will also walk away from India within one or two years'. The same day, Balwant Sinha Mehta lamented that 'Rajasthani has not found a place in the schedule of regional languages'. Ironically, during the debate on language question there was silence on the issue of regional languages except few comments. His feelings were endorsed by Manikya Lal Verma on 24 November 1949 and he illustrated with examples of the Rajasthani language which, according to him, was full of heroism.

The matter of linguistic organisation of the states was raised by T.J.M. Wilson: 'The several languages and cultures would have been guaranteed and made more effective if it had been buttressed by a provision for such independent States and their distribution on a cultural and linguistic basis'.

Finally, two members from South India spoke on the language issue and they changed the content of discussion by pointing towards what should happen after the issue had been settled. They were A. Thanu Pillai from Travancore State and L. Krishnaswami Bharathi from Madras. Pillay took the language question to a little different footing. He said,

> In regard to the formation of provinces on a linguistic basis, my view is—it may be taken for what it is worth—that language is made too much of in the formation of provinces. No doubt, language has a part to play in administration but it is not everything. There are other equally vital and important considerations to be taken into account in forming new provinces, for instance in regard to the proposal by some that Cochin and Travancore along Malabar should be formed as Kerala Province.

After stating the aspiration of the regional political leaders, Pillay went on to elaborate the crucial importance of working out the strategy to implement the national language. The decision to reorganise states along linguistic lines had been taken by the Congress much early. Interestingly, the issue never surfaced powerfully during the debate on the official/national language of the Indian Union. The moment the language issue was settled, the regional aspirations began to emerge with a strong politics of language. The politicisation of language created immense difficulties in achieving the desired agenda of discontinuing English after 15 years. Bharathi was the first speaker when the House reassembled after lunch on 24 November 1949. Bharathi spoke strongly in favour of Hindi and argued that the states could have their own languages but to work as a nation they must use Hindi. He said, 'There is not going to be question of imposition'. However, by invoking Gandhi he said that there could be a middle way between over-Sanskritised and over-Persianised Hindi—the Hindi which had emerged from the masses. He pointed out that there was a possible and probable contradiction between the regional and the national languages. He said,

> My own impression is that whenever it is a State language it may work to the detriment though it may not be the intention, of the mother tongue. When English was the State language, it worked to the great detriment of the other languages of India, and in other aspects also it was injurious to the mother tongue .... The idea of the creation of linguistic provinces is to foster the mother tongue of the provinces .... The administration must be carried on in the language of the people so that there may be identity of interest and feeling between the Government and governed.

Bharathi tried to argue that both the national language and the regional languages were important, and the linguistic reorganisation of the states was an important step to satisfy the aspirations of the people without compromising the national interest in building the nation.

Subsequent developments in the promotion of Hindi as the national language offered us no evidence that there was a widespread consensus on Hindi. Even the debates on the national language showed that the members were divided within the Congress on the introduction of Hindi. Ironically, if English as an official language was only 200 years old, then Persian/Urdu was older than it. Nobody pointed out that if the Constituent Assembly could reject Persianised Hindustani in favour of Hindi and keep English for 15 years, how was is possible to eliminate Hindustani which was closer to the masses than Sanskritised Hindi? English is still there and there is no sign to predict that it would disappear, particularly in the light of the present globalised world where English is the lingua franca of business, trade and intellectual exchange.

II. Last Days of the Constituent Assembly

The third reading of the Constitution began on 17 November 1949 and concluded on 26 November with the speech of the President of the Constituent Assembly. After this, the House was convened on 24 January 1950 to sign the Constitution. The task that was initiated on 9 December 1946 was accomplished three years later. There are three interesting aspects of what the members said in the House. The first dimension is the commentary on Ambedkar—the chief architect of the Constitution. The second is the speech of Ambedkar in response to the speeches of members in the third reading. The third dimension is the speech of the President and final signing of the Constitution.

The episteme underlying the commentary on Ambedkar could be characterised as unchanged perspective on social structure in such a way that even the modernity is connected with the logic of the tradition. On 21 November 1949, H.J. Khandekar was the first speaker to touch upon the issue with the argument that as a Dalit he was aware of the conditions of the untouchables. He said,

> This country was being governed for ages together by the law of Manu and you know, Sir, what are the effects of this law on this country. Varnas were created, castes within castes formed and even one caste could not see the face of other caste. The untouchables according to the law of Manu were to go and settle outside a village or a town and that too in the east ... If I may do so, Sir, I call this Constitution the Mahar law because Dr Ambedkar is Mahar.

The above quote was the first comment made on Ambedkar by comparing him with Manu—the law giver of the ancient Indian society. Khandekar condemned Manu and praised Ambedkar. On the same day, S.M. Ghose responded to Khandekar's comments and his comments symbolised the Hindu conception of social reality. He said,

> I have heard in this Assembly something about Manu which I consider is not a proper understanding of what Manu stands for or what Manu really means. Speaking about Dr Ambedkar an honourable member was pleased to say that he was not a Manu but a Mahar giving us law. But there is no knowing whether Manu belonged to the Brahmin or the Mahar caste. But Manu represents a conception of Indian people—an ideal of law given for humanity. In that sense Dr Ambedkar was rightly called the Manu of the present age. It is not that anybody who is in charge of making law really makes anything, but he simplifies and codifies the law seen by *rishidrishti*, i.e., seen by intuition. In that sense, whether a man comes from Mahar community or Brahmin community or any other community, if he has that intuition, if he could see and codify things not only for his community, not as his community views things, but for the whole of humanity, he will be rightly called Manu.

The reference to Manu had occurred earlier, but giving Ambedkar the title of Manu was something that occurred for the first time. The novelty of the argument was the construction of Manu as a generic concept according to which the person who codifies law gets the status of Manu. As the third reading was coming to closure, adulations began to pour on Ambedkar and reference to Manu became a natural corollary. On 24 November 1949, K.M. Jedhe was the next to mention Ambedkar and Manu in a critical way. Jedhe pointed out that many members were congratulating Ambedkar and were calling him Manu. He opined that Ambedkar might have been appalled by this title, for he hated Manu for creating Varnas. He said, 'I remember that he has publicly burnt Manu Smrithi in the huge meeting of untouchables at Mohad in 1929'.

However, nothing prevented Hargovind Pant from United Provinces from philosophising how Ambedkar could be deservedly called Manu. He began his speech by saying that 'I have come here to support the motion of Pandit Ambedkar'. He pointed out that he was using the epithet 'Pandit', for he was a great scholar. He then clarified why some members were giving Ambedkar the title of 'Manu Bhagwan'. It is worthwhile to quote him as 'We are passing through the twenty eight cycle of *Vaivashawat*, the Seventh Manu. To bring in a new Manu in this chain may perhaps create a difficulty. Therefore I think that the title of *Up-manu* and not the Manu can be conferred on him'.

One may strangely feel it awkward to hear that the person who was against Manu and *Manusmriti* and regarded the same as responsible for caste system is being given such an 'honour'. As a metaphor, it may be treated as an acknowledgement to the contribution of a scholar who singlehandedly drafted the Constitution and defended its various articles in the debates. It seemed that he had no parallel in the history of India, for unlike Greek city states where one encounters Solon and many other lawgivers, there has been no history of writing the Constitution in India. Thus, only Manu was left in the ancient Indian tradition.

III. Ambedkar's Final Speech

We may now move to the second dimension, that is, the speech of Ambedkar, which he delivered while moving the resolution to pass the Constitution on 25 November 1949. In his speech, he ignored many comments and criticisms and focussed his views on the issues that would/could confront independent India. In this regard, he emphasised that the enemy of India might not necessarily be an outsider but from within. He said that most of the times in the past, India had lost its independence due to 'the infidelity and treachery of some of her own people'. He pointed out the treachery of King Dahar at the time of the invasion of Muhammad-Bin-Qasim and of Jaichand who had invited Muhammed Gohri to attack India. He added,

> When Shivaji was fighting for the liberation of Hindus, the other Maratha noblemen and Rajput Kings were fighting the battle on the side of Moghul Emperors. When the British were trying to destroy the Sikh Rulers, Gulab Singh, their principal commander sat silent and did not help to save the Sikh kingdom. In 1857, when a large part of India had declared a war of independence against the British, the Sikhs stood and watched the event as silent spectators.

He cautioned that people of India must determinedly guard against such a threat.

Ambedkar did not only caution against using violent methods, but also the methods of disobedience, non-cooperation and Satyagraha. He said,

> When there was no way left for constitutional methods of achieving economic and social objectives, there was a great deal of justification for unconstitutional methods. But where constitutional methods are open, there can be no justification for these unconstitutional methods.

He called the unconstitutional methods as 'grammar of anarchy'. Finally, he pointed that 'our political democracy is social democracy' with one man one value. He made clear that the Indian leaders should begin with the understanding that there had been total absence of social equality as well as economic equality. Indian social inequality is graded inequality. He concluded his speech with the following words,

> If we wish to preserve the Constitution in which we have sought to enshrine the principle of Government of the people, for the people and by the people, let us resolve not be tardy in the recognition of the evils that lie across our path and which induce

people to prefer Government of the people to Government by the People, nor to be weak in our initiative to remove them. That is the only way to serve the country. I know of no better.

The most interesting part of Ambedkar's speech was his evoking of history to show how the Indians were not united to save it from foreign invaders. He did not try to respond to various criticisms by way of justifying the Draft Constitution.

On 26 November 1949, the Constituent Assembly met for the final time in that year and B. Das from Orissa pointed out that the House had not yet taken the decision with regard to the national anthem. The President informed that the matter would be decided in January next year. Algu Rai Shastri from United Provinces wanted to know 'when and in which form the Hindi translation of the Constitution would appear'. The President responded by informing that the decision had been taken to continue the official business in English for the next 15 years. The business of the Constituent Assembly had almost concluded and in the end, the President delivered his speech before moving the resolution to pass the Draft Constitution. His was the formal speech touching upon most of the issues of importance. He stressed the fact about the existence of many communities in the country some of which required special treatment. He pointed out that communalism had remained the major challenge and treated it as the 'knottiest problem'. He expressed his satisfaction that the country had been able to 'get rid of separate electorates which had poisoned our political life for so many years'. Interestingly, he also informed the House that the cost of drafting the Constitution was ₹ 63,96,729 and it was 'not too high'. The President gave special attention to the language question. He said,

> One of the problems which the Constituent Assembly took considerable time in solving relates to the language for official purposes of the country. There is a natural desire that we should have our own language, and in spite of the difficulties on account of the multiplicity of languages prevalent in the country we have been able to adopt Hindi as our official language.

He told the members of the House that he wanted to fix some qualifications of the legislatures, which could not be done. Secondly, he felt that the 'first Constitution of free Bharat' should have been in an Indian language. In the end, he thanked all who were involved in the drafting of the Constitution and he had certain good words to say about Ambedkar:

> We could never make a decision which was or could be ever so right as and when we put him on the Drafting Committee and made him its Chairman. He has not only justified his selection but has added lustre to the work which he has done.

After concluding his speech, the President 'put the motion which was moved by Dr Ambedkar to the vote of the House', and 'the motion was adopted' amidst 'prolonged cheers'.

The Constituent Assembly met for the last time on 24 January 1950 and main agenda was the signing of the Constitution. The President of the Constituent Assembly began the meeting with the statement on the issue of national anthem instead of taking the decision by moving the resolution. He told the House that *Jana Gana Mana* would be the National Anthem of India, whereas the song *Vande Mataram* would have equal status to *Jana Gana Mana*. After this, the President informed that the announcement of the result of the election of the President of India would be made. Dr Rajendra Prasad was elected the President of India. His name was proposed by Nehru and seconded by Patel. Finally, the members signed the Constitution. The landscape of modern India had taken birth.

Notes

1. The Expert Committee consisted of Ghanshayam Singh Gupta (Chairman), Rahul Sankrityayana, Suniti Kumar Chatterjee, M. Satyanarayana, Jayachandra Vidyalanakar and Date.
2. Whenever a mention is made of 30 years of struggle for freedom, it means the leadership of Gandhi. Sahay did not mention Gandhi, but 30 years is enough to know what he was trying to convey.
3. He also spoke on 26 November 1949, when asked by the President of the Constituent Assembly whether he should sign the Constitution in Hindi, but he was snubbed.

Conclusions

It took three years to complete the drafting of the Constitution of India and the members of the Constituent Assembly engaged in debates, discussion and controversies with the sole purpose of creating an ideal picture of modern India for future, as it should reflect through the Constitution. There was ostensibly no such thing like a conflict of interests between two parties with different ideologies, for most of the members were from the Congress Party. And in the absence of the members of the Muslim League, it was the only party that mattered. However, the Congressmen were not a homogeneous lot in terms of ideology and perspectives as a result of which divisions among them resulted into its proliferation into various parties at the time of holding the first general elections in 1951–1952. Representation of princely states and some zamindars further made the Constituent Assembly a heterogeneous entity in terms of interests and ideologies. Moreover, members of the Assembly hailed from different linguistic regions, castes and religions. All these people joined together to create modern India and they did their best to do that without necessarily agreeing to each other.

Challenge before the members was multidimensional issues covering governance, development, democracy, justiciable rights, secularism, equality and so on. One major challenge was in the form of threat to the nation-building process which, in the backdrop of partition of the country on religious basis, turned out to be a serious matter. Much more serious challenge, however, was to build modern India based on universal principles of equality, freedom and justice. Many prominent leaders had got their education from the West and others were largely the products of the modern education system introduced by the British in India. Their notion of modernity entailed capitalist development and liberal democracy based on the institution of private property. To make all this operational, well-developed educational institutional structure, industrialisation, functioning democracy and rationalisation of governance were required. The colonial administration was rational and based on the principle of legality. The need was to change certain basic principles of governance by retaining the core elements of colonial system of administration. In the words of Anderson (2012: 105), 'The stability of the Indian democracy came in the first instance from the conditions of the country's independence. There was no overthrow of the Raj, but a transfer of power by it to Congress as its successor. The colonial bureaucracy and army were left intact, minus the colonizers'. The postcolonial governance required both legality and legitimacy visibly distinct from its colonial predecessors.

India was predominantly backward, rural and illiterate with tremendous diversity in terms of region, religion, culture, caste and language. Bringing together such a diverse population under one umbrella required consensus based on serious debates on all such issues. Therefore, the postcolonial modernity began with the writing of the Constitution which simultaneously was a process of creating a consensus for building a nation. Nation-building was a process of creating consensus among diverse elements of the whole with the twin and paradoxical objectives of attaining certain degree of homogeneity as well as recognising diversity by creating inter-group understanding. Therefore, making of modern India was a complex and difficult task and the first goal in this endeavour was achieved through serious debates and controversies. It is difficult to establish that all elements of the totality would remain satisfied and get integrated, though the Constitution of India has remained the most important achievement as the foundation of modern India. It is therefore important to bring out the salient features of Indian modernity as reflected in the Constitution.

Since the Constitution of India was finalised after thorough reading and debate on each article, the diverse views of the members of the Constituent Assembly with regard to the imagining of postcolonial India presented in debates made it clear that there could not be single axis along which the Indian modernity could be understood and imagined. There was a visible division among members on the question of whether the independent India would be developing along capitalist lines or socialist lines. As a corollary to this, the members, largely belonging to the Congress Party, were divided on the issue whether the future India would support private property or classless society. The concern for the poor and backward sections of the society made the Constituent Assembly debates socially relevant and diverse views of the members helped in thinking of modern India from multiple perspectives. However, the final decision rested with the leaders who exercised tremendous influence on the outcome of debates. In this regard, Nehru was one of the most important actors in the situation. Universal principles of equality, justice and freedom were upheld by the members of the Assembly. Gandhian perspective made village as the unit of modernity, whereas the Western modernist perspective represented by Ambedkar regarded village as the site of darkness and backwardness. There has been a general understanding that industrialisation and urbanisation are essential ingredients of modernity or the onset of modernisation. As a matter of fact, sociological perspective regards industry and city as the foundation of modernity.

Sociological perspective is best exemplified by Tonnies' (1955: 28) distinction between two kinds of society, 'Whereas previously the whole life was nurtured and arose from the profoundness of the people (*volk*), the capitalistic society through a long process spreads itself over the totality of this people, indeed over the whole mankind'. The birth of sociology as the distinct discipline took place with the coming of industrialisation and urbanisation. A large-scale movement of people affected by powerful influence of industrialisation created settlements known as cities, qualitatively different from the earlier cites, and became societies by destroying village communities.

Village signified what was traditional India and the architects of postcolonial India wanted it to be modern without losing its distinct civilisational identity. Gandhi's correspondence with Nehru, as mentioned in the second chapter, showed tension between the holders of village as the key to modern India and those who viewed urbanised and industrialised India as modern. The first is based on the premise of singular notion of modernity, whereas the other argued for an alternative modernity. The final decision of the Constituent Assembly recognising democratically elected village level panchayats as the citadel of modern India could be regarded as the distinct character of Indian modernity. How could Indian modernity compromise with the Western notions, particularly in the face of distinct history and culture of India? It was wrong on the part of Ambedkar, in the eyes of many Gandhians, to treat village shabbily when Gandhi had extolled the virtues of village life. The Constituent Assembly decided to go for village panchayats duly elected by the people of the village instead of supporting the traditional village panchayats where age and caste played the important role. In a way, the resolution to have village panchayats was a tacit acceptance of the fact that India was essentially rural. Two-third of India's population lives in villages at present, though villages have undergone tremendous changes in many parts of the country. We have views that Indian villages are disappearing, but such a contention is very difficult to uphold. It is not necessary that with industrialisation and urbanisation villages would absolutely become extinct. Therefore, village panchayats on the liberal democratic framework were a new element in the imagining of modern India.

The tension between the individual and the collective as the unit of citizenship could be observed in the debates of the Constituent Assembly. The collective tended to be identified with communities being constituted on various axes, such as village, caste and religion. In his speech delivered on 4 November 1948 while moving the resolution to pass the Draft

Constitution, Dr B.R. Ambedkar specifically underlined the fact that the individual was the unit of citizenship the implications of which were tremendous. For example, individual got the voting rights, fundamental rights were meant for the citizen, though special provisions were made for certain communities, individual was the unit of those benefits as well as the economic. Interestingly, Ambedkar made individual and village as the binary opposites and articulated his views on village as the mother of all ailments of the Indian society. His strong views on Indian village evoked sharp criticism from the Gandhians. The liberal democratic framework provided for individual liberty and freedom to be the cornerstone of modernity, but Western modernity faced opposition from the Gandhian philosophy where village was treated differently.

Handling diversity emerged as the most challenging task for the Constituent Assembly whose members represented the same diversity. Multiple axes of diversity made the job of the Assembly still more difficult. Caste, religion and language were three major axes that required proper debate and consensus. The limited democracy the British had introduced in India had the practice of separate electorate for the Muslims. When the Constituent Assembly began its meetings before independence, it took up the issue of reservation for minorities. Various minorities identified were Muslims, Christians, Sikhs, Anglo-Indians, Parsis and the depressed classes (untouchable castes). After India got independence and a new sovereign state of Pakistan took birth due to the partition of country, the Constituent Assembly dropped religious minorities from the provision of any reservation of seats. Led by Patel, the view expressed was that the provision of separate electorate in India was mainly responsible for the partition of the country. Therefore, the religious minorities would be excluded from the benefits of all kinds of preferential treatment. It was an important moment in the making of postcolonial India, in the sense that the Congress led by Patel and Nehru found the real factor behind the partition of the country ipso facto exonerating all other political circumstances in which the participation of Congress leader might have worked as the catalyst. Separate electorate and thus the Muslim League were made responsible for the partition due to which a sizeable Muslim population—the largest religious minority still in India—did not deserve any preferential treatment. The Christian leaders had already stated that their community did not want any such treatment. Sikhs who bore the brunt of partition remained quiet, but the Advisory Committee constituted by the Constituent Assembly recognised certain castes among them at par with the scheduled castes. Thus, the only minorities recognised as eligible for reservation were scheduled castes. In a way, caste-based discrimination was recognised as the main challenge for the independent country. Constitutional provision for certain castes among the Hindus and Sikhs was the major step towards eradicating the birth-based inequalities and exclusion.

At the time of independence, India was essentially rural with agriculture as the mainstay of life. Three kinds of revenue systems existed and, as pointed out in the second chapter by referring to Durkheim's comments, Indian revenue system was essentially archaic in nature. The Ryotwari and Mahalwari systems were already in practice while the British introduced zamindari system in 1793 under Permanent Settlement. The postcolonial state based on the Constitution had to get rid of the intermediary tenures. Politically speaking, the zamindars were the backbone of the British Raj and the new India had to bring all cultivators into direct contact with the state. Therefore, the abolition of the intermediaries was an indispensable act for the government to carry out. It was clear to even the zamindars and princely states whose representatives were part of the Constituent Assembly debates. Instead of confiscation of zamindaris and feudal properties, the leaders of the country chose to acquire these properties. In addition, the land issues were made the state issue where the union government could only formulate guidelines to be followed. Confiscation required no compensation, whereas acquisition was predicated upon the principle of compensation. The Constituent Assembly did not debate the right to property but the acquisition of property in public interest owned by the private individuals. In the process, it recognised the right to property in general, including even the zamindars. In the socialist vision of the country, property could be regarded as the axis along which social equality was constructed. By virtue of its recognition to the right to compensation, the Constituent Assembly laid the foundation of the capitalist development.

Apparently there is no relationship between modernity and language; rather language is connected with culture, tradition and communication. History, however, gives us an altogether different picture. The British introduced English in India in the 19th century and since then English sýmbolised elite culture, modernity and career. The nationalists needed an alternative language to replace English as the national language. Many nationalist leaders including Gandhi had got education from England. Impact of Western liberalism and democracy was obvious on many of them, but language issue was linked with national identity. The propagation of Hindi as the national language had already started. However, there is a reasonable basis to doubt the widespread acceptance of Hindi as the national language even before independence. There were diehard supporters of English as the national language. It was a serious challenge being faced by the Constituent Assembly and as a result, it kept on postponing the decision on the language issue. Finally, the decision was taken to adopt Hindi as the language and the Constituent Assembly resolved to continue with English for some time so that adequate vocabulary could be developed in Hindi to meet the need of administration. As such it was a great decision which gave the fullest expression to the sense of freedom and sovereignty to the country.

Since differences were resolved through democratic process despite long discussions, many members remained unconvinced about the decisions taken in certain issues. For example, language issue should have been resolved through consensus, but members failed to agree on making Hindi as the national and official language. Minorities remain dissatisfied, particularly the Sikhs who thought that the Congress had betrayed them. The uneasy consensus in the finalisation of the Draft Constitution was the major factor in creating dissatisfied communities and groups. However, the foundations of the postcolonial modernity were laid. Guha's (2008: 123) following comments may bring out the essence of this postcolonial modernity.

> Granville Austin has claimed that the framing of the Indian Constitution was 'perhaps the greatest political venture since that originated in Philadelphia in 1787'. The outline of a set of national ideals, and of an institutional mechanism to work towards them, was 'a gigantic step for a people previously committed largely to irrational means of achieving other-worldly goals'. For this, as the title of the last section of Austin's book proclaims, 'the credit goes to Indians'.

But all these Indians were largely trained and educated in Western ways and there was no such thing like Indian irrationality. Western modernity was based on instrumental rationality—achieving the goal by using the most effective means. However, the outcome of the debates was the Constitution, which has remained the source of legitimacy for various actions of the political class. At the core of the Constitution is located the political intervention of the state in the matters 'social'.

References

It is important to mention that all quotations and references from the debates of the Constituent Assembly have been mentioned in terms of the dates instead of page numbers.

Primary Sources

Constituent Assembly Debates (Volumes I–XII). 1999. New Delhi: Lok Sabha Secretariat (Third Reprint).

Secondary Sources

Anderson, Perry. 2012. *The Indian Ideology*. Gurgaon: Three Essays Collective.

Austin, Granville. 1972. *The Indian Constitution: Cornerstone of a Nation*. Delhi: Oxford University Press.

Bayly, C.A. 2004. *The Birth of the Modern World 1780–1914: Global Connections and Comparisons*. New Delhi: Atlantic.

Bhosale, B.V. 2003. *Charmakars in Transition*. Mumbai: Nurali Prakashan.

Chandra, Sudhir. 1992. *The Oppressive Present: Literature and Social Consciousness in Colonial India*. Delhi: Oxford University Press.

——. 1994. 'The Language of Modern Ideas: Reflections on an Ethnological Parable'. *Thesis Eleven*, 39: 39–51.

Chandra, Bipin, Mridula Mukherjee, Aditya Mukherjee. 1999. *India After Independence 1947–2000*, Delhi: Penguin Books.

Dumont, Louis. 2002. 'The "Village Community" from Munro to Maine'. In *The Village in India*, ed. Vandana Madan, 31–50. Delhi: Oxford University Press.

Farley, John E. 1982. *Majority-Minority Relations*. Englewood cliffs, NJ: Prentice-Hall, Inc.

Fenech, Louis E. 2000. *Martyrdom in the Sikh Tradition: Playing the 'Game of Love'*. Delhi: Oxford University Press.

Guha, Ramachandra. 2008. *India after Gandhi*. London: Picador.

Gupta, Dipankar. 1992. 'Ethnic Imagos and Their Correlative Spaces: An Essay on Some Aspects of Sikh Identity and Perception in Contemporary Punjab'. *Contributions to Indian Sociology*, 26(2): 223–244.

Guru, S.D. 1972. 'Bhatt, Gokulbhai (1898–)'. In *Dictionary of National Biography*, Vol. I, ed. S.P. Sen, 179–181. Calcutta: Institute of Historical Studies.

Hamilton, Peter. 1992. 'The Enlightenment and the Birth of Social Sciences'. In *Formations of Modernity*, eds. Stuart Hall and Bram Gieben, 18–63. Cambridge: The Open University.

Hobsbawm, Eric. 1996. *The Age of Extremes: A History of the World, 1914–1991*. New York: Vintage Books.

Horkheimer, Max and Theodor W. Adorno. 2002. *Dialectic of Enlightenment: Philosophical Fragments*. Stanford: Stanford University Press.

Huntington, Samuel P. 1968. *Political Order of Changing Societies*. New Haven: Yale University Press.

Israel, Jonathan I. 2006. *Enlightenment Contested: Philosophy, Modernity, and the Emancipation of Man 1670–1752*. New York: Oxford University Press.

Israel, Milton. 1983. 'Ramananda Chatterjee and the Modern Review: The Image of Nationality in the National Press'. In *National Unity: The South Asian Experience*, ed. Milton Israel, 1–46. New Delhi: Promilla & Co.

Judge, Paramjit S. 2012. *Foundations of Classical Sociological Theory: Functionalism, Conflict and Action*. New Delhi: Pearson.

Judge, Paramjit S. and Gurpreet Bal. 2005. 'Dalits and the Urban Social Space'. *Indian Social Science Review*, 7(2): 98–120.

Kewalramani, P.M. 1974. 'Sidhwa, Rustom K. (1882–1957)'. In *Dictionary of National Biography*, Vol. IV, ed. S.P. Sen, 199–200. Calcutta: Institute of Historical Studies.

Khilnani, Sunil.2004. *The Idea of India*, New Delhi: Penguin Books.

Lapierre, Dominique and Larry Collins. 2011. *Freedom at Midnight*. New Delhi: Vikas. (First published in 1975)

Luke, Timothy W. 1990. *Social Theory and Modernity: Critique, Dissent, and Revolution*. Newbury Park: Sage Publications.

Lyotard, Jean-Francois. 1986. *The Postmodern Condition: A Report on Knowledge*. Manchester: Manchester University Press.

Marx, Karl. 1975. *Capital*, Vol. I. Moscow: Progress Publishers.

Masani, M.R. 1974. 'Ranga, N. Gogineni (1900–)'. In *Dictionary of National Biography*, Vol. III, ed. S.P. Sen, 485–487. Calcutta: Institute of Historical Studies.

Narasimham, V.K. 1974. 'Santhanam, K.'. In *Dictionary of National Biography*, Vol. IV, ed. S.P. Sen, 38–40. Calcutta: Institute of Historical Studies.

Nayar, Kuldip. 2012. *Beyond The Lines: An Autobiography*. Delhi: Roli Books.

Parsad, S.N. 1974. 'Tyagi, Mahavir (1899–)'. In *Dictionary of National Biography*, Vol. IV, ed. S.P. Sen, 367–368. Calcutta: Institute of Historical Studies.

Rao, T. Surya Narayana. 1995. *Andhra Kesari: T. Prakasam*. Delhi: Publication Division, Ministry of Information and Broadcasting, Government of India.

Rodrigues, Valerian. ed. 2002. *The Essential Writings of B.R. Ambedkar*. New Delhi: Oxford University Press.

Sahu, N.K. 1972. 'Das, Sarangadhar (1887–1957)'. In *Dictionary of National Biography*, Vol. IV, ed. S.P. Sen, 360–362. Calcutta: Institute of Historical Studies. Sharma, K.L. 2003. 'The Social Organisation of Urban Space: A Case Study of Chanderi, a Small Town in Central India'. *Contributions to Indian Sociology*, 37(3): 405–427.

Singh, Fauja. 1974. 'Prithvi Singh Azad (Baba) (1892–)'. In *Dictionary of National Biography*, Vol. III, ed. S.P. Sen, 410–411. Calcutta: Institute of Historical Studies.

Singh, Gurmukh. 1996. 'Hukam Singh, Sardar (1895–1983)'. In *Encyclopaedia of Sikhism*, Vol. II, ed. Harbans Singh, 292–294. Patiala: Punjabi University.

Singh, Khushwant. 1999. *A History of the Sikhs, 1839–1988*, Vol. 2. Delhi: Oxford University Press.

Singh, Patwant. 2002. *The Sikhs*. New Delhi: Rupa & Co.

Srivastava, H.S. 1974. 'Saxena, Shiban Lal'. In *Dictionary of National Biography*, Vol. IV, ed. S.P. Sen, 95–96. Calcutta: Institute of Historical Studies.

Subrahmanian, N. 1973. 'Iyengar, N. Gopalaswamy (1882–1953)'. In *Dictionary of National Biography*, Vol. II, ed. S.P. Sen, 198. Calcutta: Institute of Historical Studies.

Tonnies, Ferdinand. 1955. *Community and Association*. (Translated by Charles P. Loomis). London: Routledge & Kegan Paul

Vyas, R.P. 1974. 'Seth, Damodar Swaroop (1889–1966)'. In *Dictionary of National Biography*, Vol. IV, ed. S.P. Sen, 132–133. Calcutta: Institute of Historical Studies.

Weber, Max. 1968. *The Protestant Ethic and the Spirit of Capitalism*. (Translated by Talcott Parsons). London: Unwin University Books.

Weber, Max. 1978. *Economy and Society: An outline of Interpretative Sociology*, Vols. I and II, eds. Guenther Roth and Claus Wittich. Berkeley: University of California Press.

Index

Abdulla, Sheikh 112
administrative language 18
administrative structure 4 *see also* rationality
administrative units 59
advisory committee 28–30, 35, 81–83, 85, 103, 220
  constituent assembly 9–15
affectual action 3
Age of Extremes 8
Ahmad, Naziruddin 39, 88, 131–32, 148–49, 196
Akali activist 173
Akali leader 172–73, 185, 189–90
Ambedkar, B.R. 10, 35, 45, 95, 173, 194, 219
Ambedkar's sentiments 26
  national unity 25
  nationalist perspective 25
  secularism 11, 25, 148, 215
Ambedkar–Gandhi relationship 50
anarchism and communism 118
  see also ideologies
ancient Hindu model 51
Anderson, Perry 216
Andhra Kesri 62
Anglo-Indian community 89, 186
Anglo-Indians, 13, 17, 26, 34, 38, 44, 103, 174, 198, 219
anti-clericalism 6
anti-Gandhi stance 55
Assembly of Kashmir 107
Ayyangar, Ananthasayanam, M. 41–42, 61, 145–46, 156, 157, 160–61, 165, 167, 196, 198, 204
Azad, Maulana 14, 167

Babbar Akali movement 190
Backward Classes 24, 28, 176, 178, 182, 188
backward groups 88

backward groups (*cont'd*)
political reservation 38, 71, 74, 78–79, 81–83, 87–89, 91–93, 97–98, 101, 103, 169, 176
backwardness and ignorance
symbol of 47
Baden-Powell 63
Bangla Congress in 1967 26
Bayly, C.A. 5
Bengal and Punjab
partitioned states of 21
Bharathi, Krishnaswami L. 64–65, 79–80, 207–08
Bharatiya Jana Sangh 25
Bhatt, Gokulbhai Daulatram 58, 69, 204
Bhosale, B.V. 67
binary opposition 2, 6, 16, 48, 65–66
birth-based privileges 118
social stratification 118
book-keeping 3
British creation 79
British Government 10, 23, 47, 178
cabinet mission 10, 71, 177
British hegemony 186
British India 12, 81
British Raj 80, 190, 220
British regime 78

capitalism 2–3, 5–8, 48, 92, 118, 121, 133, 136, 195, 202 *see also* new social and economic system
capitalism and liberal democracy 7, 195
capitalist development 216, 221
capitalistic society 217
caste and religion 93, 125, 198, 218
caste Hindus 35, 98, 178, 182
caste-based criterion 27
caste-based deprivation 8
caste-based inequality and discrimination 9
abolition of 9
caste-centric 67
'categories of property' 129
agricultural property 129, 203
corporations 129
firms for public utility 129
land used by private individuals 129
central
government 4
legislature 102
permanent structure 4
Chandra, Sudhir 48
charismatic authority 3, 171
Christian Dalits 100
Christian members 30, 83, 99–100, 104
citizenship
unit of 16, 57, 65, 67, 218–19
civil rights 196
civilisational identity 218
class-centric 67
classification of the time 2
colonial
bureaucracy 216
capitalism 121
construction 66
India 24, 50
law 132
masters 4–5, 13, 158

colonial (*cont'd*)
predecessors 216
rule 132, 201–02
system 216
colonised natives 2
commercial undertakings 129
common language 143, 146, 149, 157, 165, 169, 204
communal
basis 92, 105
identities 74, 147
relations 26
communist ideology 118, 131
Communist Party of India (CPI) 15, 29, 62
communities
rights of 21, 28, 81
community
principles of 20
conceptual and theoretical articulations 2
conceptual articulations 2
Congress nationalist 59
Congress-dominated assembly 26
Congressmen 9, 30, 36, 55, 61, 130, 215
Constitution Drafting Committee 10
constitutional methods
political democracy 211
social democracy 211
constitutional remedy 27
constitutional rights and duties 7
constitutive rules 1
contemporary India 71
CPI 62–63 *see also* Communist Party of India
cultural
package 5
practices 5
'Cultural and Educational Rights' 31
cultural revolution 8 *see also* literacy and educational levels
culture and civilisation 2

Dalit 35–36, 44, 51, 55, 67, 92–93, 100–01, 209 *see also* untouchable caste
Dalit Christians 92–93, 100 *see also* Christian Dalits
Dalit localities 67
dark ages 2, 48
Das, Sarangadhar 57, 68
Das, Seth Govind 63, 145, 147–48, 152, 195
decentralisation
symbol of 60
decentralisation and economic democracy 64
democratic India 24
depressed Classes 9, 26–28, 35–36, 90, 92, 97, 99–100, 184, 187–88, 197, 219
Deshmukh, P.S. 35, 44, 130
Devanagari and Persian scripts 149
Devanagari script 146, 150–52, 154, 161–62, 204
Hindi language 146–47, 156, 158, 195
developing societies 4
discourse analysis 71
distinct castes 178

Dogras 109
draft Constitution 11, 16, 19, 28, 49–54, 56, 58–59, 61, 63, 65, 72–81, 83, 96, 107, 122, 145, 171–72, 183, 193–95, 198, 212, 219, 221
  constituent assembly debates 10, 16, 21, 105, 176, 217, 220
Drafting Committee 10–11, 16, 42, 45, 49, 50–51, 54, 57, 59, 61, 68, 89, 164, 213
drafting of the Constitution 13–14, 21–23, 25, 50–51, 56, 213, 215

economic
  autonomy 123
  decentralisation 64
  democracy 64, 203
  dimension 161
  empowerment 88
  equality 8, 211
  growth 136
  institution 129
  life 6, 129
  modernity 129
  opportunities 9
  philosophy 12
  planning 7
  problem 86
  reorganisation 4
  rights 126
  structure 203
  system 5, 119
Economic and Political Weekly 15
electoral democracy 81
electoral rights 74
empirical and materialist knowledge 6
empirical reality 92–93
enactment and exercise of force 4
enlightenment
  philosophy 1, 6
  thinkers 5
environment
  cost of 5
epistemic category 47
equality
  rights of 29
equality and justice
  universal principle of 9
ethnic and religious identities 171
European enlightenment 6
European modernity 7, 10, 53
European/Western societies 3
existence
  period of 95

Farley, John E. 72
Federal Constitution 195
first amendment 174
first colonialism 2
First World War 93, 189
Five-Year Plans 1
foreign language 157, 195
founding fathers 1
Fraser and Malinowski 2 *see also* social scientists
freedom
  rights of 120
frugality
  idea of 3
fundamental rights 28–31, 41, 43, 82, 85, 120–21, 123, 131, 138, 176, 195, 219 *see also* 'Cultural and Educational Rights'

Gandhi, Mahatma 24, 26, 35, 53, 57, 60, 62, 136, 151, 169, 204

Gandhi–Ambedkar conflict 55

Gandhian activist 57
- model 27
- perspective 48, 217
- rationality 201

Gandhi-led movement 56

Garhgaz, Arjan Singh 190

Gautam, Mohan Lal 87

general constituency 27

Ghadar movement 186

Ghosh, Surendra Mohan 64

Governor General's speech 33

Greek philosophy 48

Guha, Ramachandra 12, 14, 44, 54–55, 200, 221

Gupta, Ghanshyam Singh 149

Gurdwara Reform Movement 173, 189

Gurudwara Act 190

Gurung, Damber Singh 27, 49

Hamilton, Peter 6

Harijan society 177

'Harijans' 35, 74–76, 86–88, 199 *see also* depressed classes

heterogeneous entity 215

'highly nationalistic tendencies' 81

Hind Swaraj 52, 60

Hindu
- communal groups 13
- community 26, 83, 86, 98
- conception of social reality, 209
  - brahmanism 9
  - brahmin community 209
  - brahminic elites 13
- counterparts 181, 184
- religion 9, 182, 185

'Hindu–Muslim' problem 25

Hindustani 23, 32, 147, 149–52, 155, 157–59, 161, 163, 166, 168–69, 204, 208
- business 151
- national language 18, 63, 138, 144–52, 154–59, 161, 164–66, 168, 204, 206–08, 221
- province 163
- religion and language 31, 148, 151, 219
- Roman script 151, 155, 161
- two scripts: Devanagiri and Persian 149

historic document 187
- meeting 32
- moment 24–25

historical significance 123, 145

Hobsbawm, Eric 8

homogeneous national identity 144

Horkheimer and Adorno 7

human degradation 52

human societies 1

Huntington, Samuel P. 7

Hussain, Tajamul 91

ideological commitments 1, 125

ideologies 8, 18, 47–49, 118–19, 124, 144, 147, 171, 215

imperialist governments 4

independent India 1, 7–8, 24, 47, 49, 52, 71, 123, 196, 211, 217

Independent Sovereign Republic 25

India
  partition of 23, 29, 90, 106, 179

Indian
  citizens 7
  culture 5, 56
  nation 49, 53, 126, 152, 181
  people 8, 23, 209
  politics 126
  revenue system 220
  scholars 47
  society, 1, 9, 19, 22, 48, 66, 87, 135, 198, 209, 219
  subcontinent 5, 154
  territory 17, 37
  union 26, 106, 115, 176, 207
  village 16, 47, 49, 52–54, 56–58, 62, 65–68, 79, 201, 218–19
  village verbatim 57

Indian Christians 13, 38, 44, 89

Indian Constitution 10, 22, 24, 201, 222

Indian Muslim League 83

Indian National Congress 126

industrial and agricultural crisis 203

industrialisation and urbanisation 7, 217–18

inegalitarian society 117

institutions and practices 5

interests and ideologies 48, 215

interpretative analysis 10, 73

interventionist strategy 9

Judge, Paramjit S. 3–4, 67

justiciable rights 215

Kamath, H.V. 53–54, 85, 110–11, 127–28, 194, 200

Karimuddin, Kazi Syed 39, 44, 74–76, 152

karma principle 9 *see also* Hindu religion

Kashmir Government 111

Kashmir issue 105–06, 110, 113

Kaur, Rajkumari Amrit 81

Khaitan, Dabi Prasad 49

Khalistan militancy 191

Kher, B.G. 202, 204

King of Kashmir 17

Kripalani, Acharya J.B. 23

Kriplani, Sucheta 31 *see also* *Vande matram*

Krishnamachari, T.T. 45, 50, 68

Kuka rebellion 186

labour
  dehumanisation of 5
  power 5

land
  legislation 121, 124
  reforms 124

Land Alienation Act, 1901 120

language formula 144, *see also* regional–linguistic identities

large-scale movement 217

Lari, Z.H. 85–87, 93

legal
  authority 3
  framework 6
  practice 173

legal and constitutional reform 6

legality
  principle of 216

legislative
  assemblies 10
  vote 148

legitimate monopoly 4
liberal
  democratic framework 194, 218–19
  democratic state 8
  democrats 131, 202
  tradition 129
linguistic
  basis 149, 207
  diversities 143
  identities 143–44
  organisation 170, 207
  zones 143
linguistic and ethnic identities 19
linguistic-nationalist 205
literacy and educational levels 8
literacy rate 178, 188
literature 2, 4, 6, 20, 113, 115, 153, 166, 168
local elites 4
logical construction 85
logico-meaningful 1
Lok Sabha elections 26
Luke, Timothy W. 7
Lyotard, Jean-Francois 2

macrosocial processes 7
Mahalwari system 119, 220
Mahar caste 209
'Maharaja of Kashmir' 111
Mahatma Gandhi's creation 26
Maine, Henry 63, 69
Maitra, Lakshmi Kanta 85, 107, 151
majority community 29, 32, 74, 78, 81, 84, 86, 88–89, 162, 175, 198–99
Mann, Bhupinder Singh 114, 174, 184
Manu Bhagwan 210
Manusmriti 210
Martial Law Regime 186
martial tradition 189
Maru, Kamagata 186
martyrdom
  tradition of 190
Marx 5, 65, 66, 118, 124, 127, 204
  philosophy of 118, 204
    capitalism 2–3, 5–8, 48, 92, 118, 121, 133, 136, 195, 202
    dehumanisation of labour 5
    labour power 5
Marxism 118
  capitalism 2–3, 5–8, 48, 92, 118, 121, 133, 136, 195, 202
  revolutionary system 119
  theoretical foundation 118
members of the Congress 12, 41, 171
minorities
  reservation for 38, 74–78, 81–82, 88, 92, 104, 172, 219
minority
  communities 34, 38, 76–78, 87–88, 174, 198
  community 34, 39, 74, 77, 89, 162
  community people 74
  issue resurfaces 172–84
  issues of 171
  rights 14, 21, 23, 33–41, 82, 102, 164, 171
miscellaneous rights 120–21
models and strategies 4
modern
  practice 6
  state 3, 9, 118
  world 3–5, 48
modern and modernity 2–9, 48

modern egalitarian 129
modern India 1, 3, 10, 16, 19–22, 42, 49, 78, 139, 144, 159, 180, 184, 213, 215–18, 220
modernity 1, 3, 6–12, 19, 27, 48–49, 65–67, 71, 80, *see also* modern and modernity; state and market (capitalism)
  founding principle of 1
  models of 48
Moghul Emperors 211
Mohammed Ismail Sahib 76
Mohani, Hasrat Maulana 15, 29, 73, 91, 107, 111, 138, 163, 197
monopoly of the state 4
Mookerjee, Syama Prasad 15
Mookherjee, H.C. 58, 81, 88, 93, 98
Munshi, K.M. 14–15, 29–32, 39, 45, 101, 138, 167, 194
Musafir, Gurmukh Singh 42, 44, 78, 114–15, 171–72, 187, 192, 206
Muslim community 36, 89, 100
Muslim League 12–13, 15, 21, 23–25, 29, 37, 40, 45, 81–85, 89, 95, 104, 189, 215, 220
Muslim League members 13, 40, 95, 114
Muslim majority state 96
Muslim representation 97 *see also* political representation
Muslim seats 12
Muslim-centric 77
Muslims
  reservation for 76, 88–89, 91
Nagappa, S. 40–41, 44, 86–88, 121, 130
national anthem 144, 212–13
national integration 8
national language 18, 63, 138, 144–52, 154–59, 161, 164–66, 168, 204, 206–08, 221 *see also* linguistic identities; homogeneous national identity
nationalist leaders 221
nationalist movement 56
nation-building 4, 8–9, 17, 32–33, 53, 71, 80, 103, 143, 150–51, 180–81, 197, 201, 216
nation-building process 103, 181, 201, 216
Nehru, Jawaharlal 14, 23, 44, 90, 101, 117, 122
new social and economic system 5
new symbolic universe 5
Nichols-Roy, J.J.M. 30, 43, 76
non-cooperation 211
non-violent Satyagraha 189
non-zamindari areas 8

occident 3
operationalization 3
orient 3
original inhabitants 86
over-Persianised Hindi 207
over-Sanskritised 207
overt sanctions 9
ownership rights 119, 133

Pal, B.C. 63
pant symbolised 28

paradigmatic shift 65
Parbandhak Committee (SGPC) 104
parliament
act of 87
Parsis 13, 17, 26, 34, 38, 80, 103, 152, 178, 198, 219
partition of the country 15, 21–22, 26, 30, 33, 37, 41, 75, 80–82, 84–85, 148, 152, 171, 189, 199, 216, 219
partitioned states 21, 23, 171
Patel, Vallabhbhai 14, 29, 81–82, 90, 101, 121, 178–79
Patiala and Eastern Punjab States Union (PEPSU) 97
'perfect world' 92
permanent army 4
permanent settlement 48, 119, 132, 134, 220
Pillai, Munuswamy, V.I. 35, 63, 76, 195
political
freedom 86, 203
influence 22, 190
institutions 59
isolation 81
practice 4
representation 36, 80, 96–98
space 85, 191
system 6, 51
political and cultural hegemony 4
politico-ideological conceptual tool 2
Poona Pact in 1932 22, 39, 50 *see also* Mahatma Gandhi's creation
population structure 102, 105
postcolonial India 9–10, 24, 101, 105, 168, 197, 217–19,
postcolonial Indian modernity 1
Constitution 1, 6–7, 9–10, 13
enactments 1
Five-Year Plans 1
modern India 21
modernity 7–8, 27, 47, 48, 52, 71, 80, 201, 216, 221–22
'postcolonial societies' 4
post-Second World War period 4
power
transfer of 24–25, 200, 216
power and administration 4
power equation 72
Praja Sabha 107, 109–10, 112–13
Prakasam, Guha, T. 55 *see also* Andhra Kesri
Prasad, Rajendra 14–15, 23, 28, 32–33, 35, 62, 101, 168, 171, 196, 213
Preamble of the Indian Constitution 201
property
acquisition of 121, 123, 130, 135, 138, 202, 220
property and community 117, 122–39 *see also* property matters; acquisition of property
property matters 122
property-related rights 120
proportional representation 76, 85
Protestant Ethic and the Spirit of Capitalism, The 3
protestant sects 3
Provincial Legislature of East Punjab 102

provincial legislatures 13, 57, 59
  franchise of 13
Punjab
  partition of 102, 113, 179
Punjabi-speaking Territory 114

'Quit Kashmir' 108

Rai Shastri, Algu 78, 154, 212
Rajasthani language 206
Rajput Kings 211
Ranga, N.G. 59, 69, 79, 153–54, 196
Rao, Thirumala M. 86
Rasul, Begum Aizaz 57, 88, 202
rational action 3 *see also* 'wertrational action'
  calculations 1
  foundations 10, 25
rationality 1, 3–4, 7, 12, 22
Rau, Madhava 60, 69
Ray, Renuka 39, 79–80
real democracy 196
real rulers 196
Red Communist Party movement 62
regional languages 146, 148, 153, 204, 206, 208
regional–linguistic identities 144
religious
  affiliation 186
  conversion 30
  discourse 118
  minorities 17, 32, 79, 83, 91, 93, 95–99, 103–05, 164, 171–72, 180–81, 189, 199, 219
religious-spiritual basis 118
renaissance and capitalism 2
renaissance in Europe 48
Republic of India 7, 28, 32
Republics of Athens and Sparta, The 63
reservation of seats for minorities
  provision of 17
resolution 14, 16, 23–28, 33, 41, 61, 75, 82–83, 87–92, 106, 108, 114, 157, 174, 179, 194, 199, 202, 206, 210, 212–13, 218–19
revenue collection
  system of 119–20
revolutionary system 119
right to freedom 185
right to property 9, 117, 119–23, 127, 202, 220
rights of the community 29
rights of the individual 29, 123
Rodrigues, Valerian 66
Round Table Conference 39, 57
Russell, John 85
Russian village Soviets 57
Ryotwari system 119, 120, 134, 136

Saadulla, Syed Muhammad 61, 89
Sachar Committee Report, The 92
sacred text 148
safeguard
  perception of 26
Sahay, Jadubans 129, 203
Sahay, Shyam Nandan 136, 200
Sahib, Mohamed Ismail 76–78, 83–85, 99, 167
Sahib, Pocker B. 82, 89, 114

sanad milkiyat intimrari 132
Santhanam, K. 56, 61–62, 64, 68, 85
Satyagraha 189, 211
Satyanarayana, Moturi 60, 69
Saxena, Shibban Lal 57, 68, 126, 199
scepticism 118
scheduled castes 13, 17, 19, 28, 34–36, 38, 41, 44, 74, 79, 82, 84, 86, 89–91, 93, 98–104, 172–74, 176–78, 182–85, 195–96, 220
'scheduled minority' 79
scheduled tribes 79, 103, 174, 177–78
scientific revolution 7
seats
  reservation of 17, 38–39, 74–78, 82, 84, 86–87, 90–91, 104, 176, 199, 219
second world war 4, 7–8, 52, 71, 190
secular state 79, 88, 104, 148
secularisation 118
secularism and national unity 25 *see also* Ambedkar's sentiments; 'Hindu–Muslim' problem
separate electorates 34, 36–41, 75–78, 81–82, 91, 151, 187, 212
separatist movement 103
Shah, K.T. 14–15, 107–14, 128–29, 186, 190, 195–96, 204
Sharma, K.L. 67
Shiromani Akali Dal, The (SAD) 102, 104, 172, 177, 189
Shiromani Gurdwara 104
Sikh
  backward classes 184
  community 29, 97–98, 100, 102–03, 114, 172–73, 175, 179, 182, 185, 187
  Dalits 101
  identity 171, 189
  issue 18, 42, 97, 102, 171–73, 178, 180, 182, 184
  leadership 191
  members 42, 98, 104, 171–75, 182–83, 188, 199
  religious community 82–83
  religious minority 199
  representatives 98, 176
  rulers 192, 211
  separatist 172
  soldiers 185, 190
  struggle 191
  valour 191
Sikh-specific issue 172
Singh, Chaudhary Ranbir 75, 97
Singh, Giani Kartar 115, 173, 192
Singh, Guptanath 133–34, 178
Singh, Hukam 42, 89–90, 99–100, 114–15, 161, 171, 173–83, 185–88, 192
Singh, Sardar Sochet 188
Sitaramayya, Pattabhi B. 108, 115
social
  formations 5, 136
  groups 27, 118
  life 6, 52, 67, 199
  revolution 8
  scientists 2, 7, 30
  transformation 19
social and cultural affairs 1
social and cultural existence 143
social services 129
  urban lands 129
  zamindari land 129

socialism
  ideologies of 8
socialism and economic planning 7
socialist republic 126
socialist vision 128, 139, 220
socialist-minded Congress leaders 128
sociocultural and linguistic diversity 8
sociocultural diversity 9
socio-economic condition 103
socio-economic systems 119
sociological issues 10–11, 16, 98
sociological nature 21
sociological perspective 217
sociological studies 67, 92
sovereign nation 25, 106
'Special Directives' 147
state and market (capitalism) 5
state policy 22
statesmanship 25
statutory reservation 102
struggle for freedom 213
  Gandhi's political life 62
  leadership of Gandhi 54, 203, 213
study of the Constitution 1
Subramaniam, V. 64
subsume class issue 30
symbolic importance 14, 145

Tandon, Purushottam Das 144, 162
tax 4
  collection of 4
technology and science 7
Telangana movement, The 63
temporal classification 2
temporal nature 2
Thakur, P.R. 26–27, 56, 74, 86–87, 130
theoretical discourses 48
theoretical foundation 118
theoretical perspectives 125
theoretical position 1
third dimension 209
third reading 11, 19, 172, 184, 193–94, 197–99, 202–04, 208–10
Third World countries 7
tradition and backwardness 47
traditional action 3
traditional authority 3
traditional India 218
transferrable vote 76
tribals and women 13
Tripathi, Kishorimohan 60, 127
two-nation theory 22, 26, 29, 32, 37
Tyagi, Mahavir 79, 93

underprivileged castes 9
United Provinces 57, 78–79, 85–86, 88, 134, 137, 149, 151, 154, 156, 162–64, 202, 210, 212
universal adult suffrage 8
universal principles 1, 9, 216–17
untouchability 10–11, 22, 29, 98, 120, 185, 187, 195, 197, 199
untouchable caste 25, 50, 100, 180, 219 *see also* depressed classes

untouchables 9, 22, 26, 35, 66, 76, 178, 185, 187, 209–10
  caste-based deprivation 8
  depressed classes 9, 26–28, 35–36, 90, 92, 97, 99–100, 184, 187–88, 197, 219
  oppressed communities 9
  socially backward 178
urban character 67
'urban highbrow' 54
urban-industrial world 202

Vaivashawat 210
Vande Mataram 213
Verma, Manikya Lal 206
very backward class 178
village community 51, 65
village panchayat system 57
village panchayats 16, 51, 54–61, 64–65, 199–200, 218
  Directive Principles 200
village Swaraj 64–65
Vira, Raghu 15, 145, 164, 166, 204–05

warring groups 14
Weber, Max 1, 3
weightage reservation 78
'wertrational action' 3
Western capitalism 2
Western educated 4, 47
Western liberalism and democracy 221
Western modernity 8–9, 47, 129, 219, 222
Western perspective 48
Wilson, T.J.M. 207
world culture 7
writing
  history of 210

zamindari system 8, 119–20, 122, 131, 133–38, 220 *see also* system of revenue collection